MELVILLE'S OTHER LIVES

*Peculiar Bodies: Stories and Histories*

CAROLYN DAY, CHRIS MOUNSEY, AND WENDY J. TURNER, EDITORS

# MELVILLE'S OTHER LIVES

Bodies on Trial in *The Piazza Tales*

CHRISTOPHER STEN

UNIVERSITY OF VIRGINIA PRESS
Charlottesville and London

UNIVERSITY OF VIRGINIA PRESS
© 2022 by the Rector and Visitors of the University of Virginia
All rights reserved
Printed in the United States of America on acid-free paper

First published 2022

1 3 5 7 9 8 6 4 2

Library of Congress Cataloging-in-Publication Data
Names: Sten, Christopher, author.
Title: Melville's other lives : bodies on trial in *The Piazza Tales* / Christopher Sten.
Description: Charlottesville : University of Virginia Press, 2022. | Series: Peculiar bodies :
stories and histories | Includes bibliographical references and index.
Identifiers: LCCN 2022008976 (print) | LCCN 2022008977 (ebook) |
ISBN 9780813945439 (hardcover) | ISBN 9780813945446 (paperback) |
ISBN 9780813945453 (ebook)
Subjects: LCSH: Melville, Herman, 1819–1891. Piazza Tales. | Melville, Herman, 1819–1891—
Criticism and interpretation. | Short stories, American—19th century—
History and criticism. | Human body in literature.
Classification: LCC PS2384.P433 S84 2022 (print) | LCC PS2384.P433 (ebook) |
DDC 813/.3—dc23/eng/20220410
LC record available at https://lccn.loc.gov/2022008976
LC ebook record available at https://lccn.loc.gov/2022008977

Cover art: From *The Encantadas Concluded and Bartleby the Scrivener*,
Matt Kish, 2019. (Used by permission of the artist)

*For Jan*

CONTENTS

ACKNOWLEDGMENTS  ix

Introduction  1
1. "The Piazza" and Melville's Sickroom  21
2. "Bartleby, the Scrivener": The Body (and Soul) in Pain  39
3. "Casting a Shadow": Representing Race and Trauma in "Benito Cereno"  62
4. Playing Smart, Playing Dumb: Performance in "The Lightning-Rod Man"  83
5. "The Encantadas, or Enchanted Isles": Bodies as Fragments  99
6. Docile Monsters and Enslavement in "The Bell-Tower"  123
Conclusion  141

NOTES  147
BIBLIOGRAPHY  165
INDEX  173

ACKNOWLEDGMENTS

One of the pleasures of completing a project of long duration and many origins, like this one, is the chance it provides to recognize other critics, colleagues, and friends who have helped to bring it to fruition. First, I want to acknowledge several predecessors, particularly Richard Harter Fogle, R. Bruce Bickley Jr., William B. Dillingham, and Marvin Fisher, who were among the first to see Melville's short fiction as deserving of serious critical attention; their examples encouraged me to think a book devoted to a close examination of *The Piazza Tales* would be possible and worth the effort. More recently, my colleagues in the English Department at George Washington University supplied much of the theoretical work on the body that opened up the subject for me and suggested its centrality to the stories in Melville's collection. Indeed, the work of David T. Mitchell, Maria Frawley, Jonathan Hsy, Marshall Alcorn, Evelyn Schreiber, and Jeffrey Jerome Cohen on body studies and theories of embodiment has been an education in itself for me, to the point where *Melville's Other Lives: Bodies on Trial* became an unusual sort of collaborative effort—without my colleagues being aware of it. I deeply appreciate their (previously unacknowledged) contributions to my education and to this project, and take this occasion to acknowledge my appreciation and indebtedness to them here. Thanks, too, to several other colleagues at George Washington University who contributed in other ways—Ormond Seavey, Robert McRuer, Jennifer James, Alexa Alice Joubin, and Daniel DeWispelare, in particular; and to my doctoral student, Jim Campomar, who often served as my sounding board and provided technical assistance at several junctures.

Several longtime Melville friends and scholars—Robert S. Levine, Samuel Otter, Wyn Kelley, John Bryant, and Brian Yothers—also provided valuable guidance and critical commentary at various stages. Their advice and encouragement have proved more helpful to me, and are more deeply appreciated, than they can know. Still other Melville friends and colleagues, all fellow members of the Melville Society Cultural Project—Robert K. Wallace, Mary K. Bercaw-Edwards, Timothy Marr, Jennifer Baker, and (again) Wyn Kelley—have freely shared their wit and wisdom over many years, and provided the kind of camaraderie and support that challenges and inspires.

Finally, I am grateful for the support of the University of Virginia Press and the Faculty Review Board in particular. Eric Brandt, editor in chief, welcomed and encouraged my project from the first day and was unfailingly helpful at every turn. Ellen Satrom, managing editor, and Helen Chandler, acquisitions assistant, made sure the publication process ran smoothly and efficiently. Morgan Myers, senior project editor, served as expert guide, advocate, and facilator through the final stages of production. And Marilyn Campbell proved to be the most judicious, exacting copyeditor anyone could hope for. Together they helped to make this a better book than I could ever have managed on my own, and for that I am deeply appreciative. Working with them was a distinct pleasure in every way.

An earlier, briefer version of chapter 5, "'The Encantadas, or Enchanted Isles': Bodies as Fragments," appeared under the title, "'Facts Picked Up in the Pacific': Fragmentation, Deformation, and the (Cultural) Uses of Enchantment in 'The Encantadas,'" in *"Whole Oceans Away": Melville and the Pacific*, edited by Jill Barnum, Wyn Kelley, and Christopher Sten (Kent, OH: Kent State University Press, 2007), 213–23.

MELVILLE'S OTHER LIVES

# INTRODUCTION

All the stories in Melville's *The Piazza Tales* (1856) present encounters with outsiders, minorities, outcasts, or "others"—a seamstress, an office drudge, enslaved Africans in transit to the New World, a traveling salesman, island castaways, the poor and oppressed. All of these stories are also set in widely disparate times and places, removed from the familiar worlds of Melville's readers. These include a Berkshire mountain farmhouse where the narrator is recovering from an illness ("The Piazza"); a Wall Street law office where copyists perform routine tasks ("Bartleby, the Scrivener"); a mysterious slave ship drifting near the coast of Chile in 1799 ("Benito Cereno"); a rural mountain cottage beset by traveling salesmen ("The Lightning-Rod Man"); a Galapagos wasteland hundreds of miles from the South American continent ("The Encantadas, or the Enchanted Isles"); and an emerging Italian town where an ambitious architect fashions a quasi-human bell-ringer ("The Bell-Tower"). In choosing tales for this collection, Melville clearly favored stories featuring strange, unusual, or extraordinary characters and distant, out-of-the-way places that would have been unfamiliar to his audience, while also demonstrating his originality and technical prowess as a storyteller in several genres.

In all these stories, Melville concentrates on the trials of the human body, its pain, abuse, and suffering, its struggles and limitations. Some tales concern common bodily trials such as illness or invalidism ("The Piazza"); the tedium of office work ("Bartleby"); the aggravation of door-to-door salesmen ("The Lightning-Rod Man"). Others concern bodily trials that are extraordinary: the traumatic violence of a rebellion on a slave ship and its aftermath ("Benito Cereno"); the hardships of surviving on a wasteland archipelago ("The Encantadas"); the perils of creating a monstrous "man-machine" ("The Bell-Tower"). At the same time, Melville is concerned also with the body's material markers or signs—its cultural meanings as defined by race or origin, class, gender, and age, among other signifiers—and the social and cultural conflicts or dilemmas such markers can give rise to. In this respect his writings look forward to the work of Michel Foucault, Raymond Williams, and other cultural materialists who have shown how cultures and cultural institutions define, control, or oppress bodies because of their skin color, gender, or class, while also recognizing the important function bodies can serve, in literature, to demonstrate (and critique) the exercise of power and privilege by those who hold authority, influence, or superior strength. The current critical focus on the body, along with enhanced critical and scientific understanding of the experience of bodies at particular times and places, provides a productive entry point for reassessing Melville's stories as expressions of the author's social consciousness (and conscience) on such issues as economic disparity, exploitation and power, the slave trade, confidence schemes, colonialism, and advances in industrial technology. As a storyteller, Melville understood clearly how such cultural dynamics operate everywhere, and seized on our collective obsession with the body as subject, symbol, and vehicle to dramatize his tales.

All the stories in *The Piazza Tales* are stories of bodily suffering or potential suffering—of confinement, captivity, entrapment, abuse, or threat of death—and of resistance, rebellion, or subterfuge. However, only rarely are they stories of successful escape or reprieve (the narrator of "The Lightning-Rod Man," in the end, is an exception in this regard, because he is able to seize control of the situation in the end). Still, whether the characters in these stories escape or are changed, whether they fail in their efforts or are pushed to the breaking point, they all are tested and tried, or "tryed out," to use a Melvillean whaling term from "The Try-Works" chapter in *Moby-Dick* (1851), by the challenges presented by their particular circumstances. Though few if any of Melville's characters can be said to triumph or grow into something larger than life, something heroic, all are transformed, occasionally to their betterment but more often to their harm, as in the examples of Bartleby, Benito Cereno, Captain Delano, and the characters in the late sketches of "The Encantadas" (a possible exception being Hunilla, whose true character and circumstances are something of a mystery, as I will attempt to explain in chapter 5). In Melville's opening story, "The Piazza," the narrator is confined to his Berkshire farmhouse by a sickness that forces him to look for an antidote to his condition (and by implication a solution to his ongoing dilemma as a storyteller), one that leads him to imagine a journey into the nearby mountains in search of a "spot of radiance" seen from his piazza, and ultimately to his discovery of a decaying cottage inhabited by a poor seamstress named Marianna.[1] In "Bartleby, the Scrivener," the title character answers an advertisement for a job in a Wall Street law office and is soon engaged in a one-man strike against his employer. In "Benito Cereno," the American captain of a sealer makes a good-faith effort to come to the aid of a drifting slave ship, only to discover it is not what it seems, but something much more horrifying that almost kills him. For, contrary to his expectations, after a bloody rebellion, the enslaved Africans are in charge of the ship and hold captive their former captors. In "The Lightning-Rod Man," too, things are not what they seem, but here, for once, the tale ends unexpectedly in a triumph for the narrator-host, when the itinerant peddler of the title, after recognizing he is being played, runs away from the narrator before their exchange escalates into violence. In "The Encantadas," Melville's sketches about the Galapagos Islands, sailors, castaways, and aspiring entrepreneurs seek a life away from the known world, while others are desperate to be rescued from these same desolate islands that promise little beyond a Hobbesian life said to be "solitary, poor, nasty, brutish, and short." Finally, in "The Bell-Tower," the man-machine that Bannadonna fashions to strike the hour suddenly turns its force upon its creator and mechanically kills him with its hammer, as an enslaved person might turn on his master when least expected—a parallel Melville hints at in one of three epigraphs to this moral fable.

Despite the recurring themes of trial, testing, or trying-out that run through these tales, the stories in *The Piazza Tales* are remarkably varied in subject and type, and feature varied instances of embodiment in each one, despite some occasional overlap. Thus "The Piazza" can be read productively in terms of discourses on sickness and disability, particularly Melville's contemporary Harriet Martineau's *Life in the Sickroom* (1844) and David T. Mitchell and Sharon L. Snyder's *Narrative Prosthesis* (1997), to explain the heightened sensitivity and acuity of the narrator in that tale, while "Bartleby, the Scrivener" is informed by discourses on spiritual and bodily pain, particularly Ralph Waldo Emerson's "The Transcendentalist" (1841) and Elaine Scarry's more recent exploration of the inexpressibility of bodily torture, *The Body in Pain: The Making and Unmaking of the World* (1985). By contrast, "Benito Cereno," which suggests extreme forms of violence that were common to the slave trade and slave rebellions, is illuminated by the discourse on trauma, as described in the writings of Judith Herman, among other specialists in the field, and in Greg Forter's appropriation of trauma theory to narrative structure. In "The Lightning-Rod Man," the subtle, comic exchanges dramatized between the seemingly innocent narrator and the aggressive traveling salesman are informed by performance and social interaction theories of Erving Goffman and the historical example of Benjamin Franklin, the inventor of the lightning rod and an early practitioner of the arts of performance (not to mention hoaxes), a man who slyly bragged about his successes while playing the "humble inquirer" in his *Autobiography* and whose character Melville satirized in his Revolutionary War novel, *Israel Potter* (1854–55), published near the end of his magazine period. Finally, the fragmented setting of "The Encantadas" and the islands' similarly fragmented inhabitants—a strange mix of half-baked renegades, castaways, entrepreneurs, and petty tyrants—are informed by Deborah Harter's seminal *Bodies in Pieces: Fantastic Narrative and the Poetics of the Fragment* (1996), while my reading of "The Bell-Tower," Melville's moral fable about ambition, monsters, and slavery, builds on Jeffrey J. Cohen's *Monster Theory: Reading Culture* (1996) as well as Michel Foucault's notion of "docile bodies," from *Discipline and Punish: The Birth of the Prison* (1975), in an effort to shed light on Melville's rendering of the human drive, evident during the early Renaissance in Europe (and the New World), to put humans as well as machines at the service of the ambitious and the powerful.

While *Melville's Other Lives: Bodies on Trial* is the first book-length study of *The Piazza Tales*, and the first to focus on a variety of approaches to embodiment in these stories, several other extended studies of Melville's treatment of bodily themes have appeared over the past several decades, all of which concentrate mainly on issues of identity. Sharon Cameron's philosophical meditation, *The Corporeal Self: Allegories of the Body in Melville and Hawthorne* (1981), was the first, though she limited her discussion of "identity and disembodiment" to *Moby-Dick*. Peter J. Bellis, in *No Mysteries Out of Ourselves: Identity and Textual Form in the Novels of Herman Melville* (1990), makes a case for several kinds of bodily identity (physical, genealogical, and textual) in the major fiction, while Clark Davis, in *After the Whale: Melville in the Wake of Moby-Dick* (1995), examines a different set of identities altogether, which he labels divided, ascetic, domestic, and failing, in selected fiction and poetry published after *Moby-Dick*. Samuel Otter, in his richly illuminating *Melville's Anatomies* (1999), looks at a variety of anatomical features and related issues—faces and skin (tattooing and flogging), heads and hearts (craniology and sentiment or emotion), in *Typee, White-Jacket, Moby-Dick,* and *Pierre*. And in 2006, David Mitchell and Samuel Otter coedited a special issue of *Leviathan: A Journal of the Melville Society* devoted to Melville's treatment of disability, a subject Mitchell had earlier explored in "'Too Much of a Cripple': Ahab, Dire Bodies, and the Language of Prosthesis in *Moby-Dick*," in the inaugural issue of *Leviathan* (March 1999). Davis is the only one of these who examines any of the stories in *The Piazza Tales* (namely, "Bartleby," "Benito Cereno," and "The Encantadas"). Like the authors of several of these earlier studies (especially Davis and Otter), I adopt a variety of approaches to the subject of embodiment in Melville's writings, in keeping with the varied subject matter of Melville's stories. Indeed, I employ, and rely on, a different type of theory, or combination of theories, consistent with the principal subject matter of each one.[2] Although there are similarities or thematic connections among the tales, as well as theoretical intersections, Melville appears to have chosen these six stories for inclusion in *The Piazza Tales* in part because they differ so from one another—in subject matter, language, point of view, and genre—a fact that has encouraged me to adopt a different theoretical perspective to illuminate each one.

In the introductory "The Piazza," written after the other pieces had been published in *Putnam's Monthly*, Melville constructed a playful autobiographical fantasy—a sometimes lighthearted and ironic meditation on shifting points of view, inspiration, gender, and class—about a time when his narrator (like Melville himself) was disabled and bedridden with a mysterious illness and dreamed of riding out to the home of a beautiful fairy princess he imagines living in the mountains not far from his home. There, to his surprise, he discovers a poor but hardworking seamstress in a desolate hut, one whose suffering he can readily appreciate because of his recent debilitating illness but also because of the stark material contrast of her simple life with his own relatively privileged comfort and affluence, which she views from afar with envy and a romantic, idealizing imagination that is the equal of his own. It is a sometimes humorous, but finally melancholy performance that provides an unexpected shock to the reader as preparation for the many surprises still to come in the collection (a technique Melville had relied on in the second of his early "Fragments from a Writing Desk," published in 1839 before he was twenty years old). This meditation from the sickroom of the opening story's narrator is followed by "Bartley, the Scrivener: A Story of Wall Street," a grimly amusing but finally tragic tale that is widely recognized today as a classic of American fiction and possibly the most widely discussed story by an American writer from the nineteenth century. Beginning as a modest sketch of an enigmatic copyist in a New York law firm, a "forlorn" figure of profound physical and emotional passivity, it soon turns into a revealing portrait of the bachelor lawyer who narrates the story and serves as an indictment of the emptiness and alienation of corporate life in America's financial capital, for Bartleby's employer as well as for the scrivener. This tale, which captures the lawyer's growing empathy for the scrivener as he comes into closer and closer personal contact with him, is followed by Melville's retelling of the aftermath of a horrific historical event, a slave rebellion at sea, in "Benito Cereno," and the bewildered American captain who attempts to come to the distressed slave ship's aid. Early readers had a hard time deciding about the meaning of Melville's tale, about whether to view it as a protest against slavery or as a warning about Africans' savagery, but as readers have come to know more and more about Melville's views in his other writings, particularly *Moby-Dick* (as well as reports from a number of sources about the dehumanizing treatment of slaves, male and female, during Middle Passage and after), it has become clear to most critics that Melville intended to focus in this story, in subtle and indirect ways that would not alienate some of his more sensitive readers, on the physical and emotional trauma experienced by enslaved Africans—and their shipboard captors as well—as in fact happened in the original of this bloody, real-life slave rebellion on board the slave ship *Tryal*. The violent and deeply disturbing "Benito Cereno" is followed by one of the first published examples of a popular American oral tale, the traveling salesman story, in "The Lightning-Rod Man," a stagey piece, in Melville's treatment, with touches of vaudeville, based on a common sales pitch that Melville and his neighbors are reported to have been subjected to in person, many times, when lightning rods first became popular in New England.[3] Here Melville turns the tables to focus on the sly performance of the narrator, the *object* of the salesman's sales pitch (and not, as readers might expect, on the performance of the salesman himself), particularly the body language and linguistic cues of the narrator whom the salesman assumes he can readily outsmart. Following this clever two-person exchange, which in its ambiguous treatment anticipates similar scenes of apparent duplicity in Melville's *The Confidence-Man: His Masquerade* (1857) where it is hard to determine who is deceiving whom, comes Melville's meditation on "The Encantadas, or Enchanted Isles," ten sketches based on stopovers he made at the Galapagos Islands in 1841 and 1842 during his whaling years, and the fallen world of hissing reptiles, diabolical hermits, and castaways who find it hard to eke out even a marginal existence on these godforsaken islands. This is a dark, fragmented world inhabited by grotesques—broken figures desperately trying to hang on to life or exploit their meager environment for whatever material support it can provide, while also, in some cases, trying desperately to escape from the marginal, impoverished existence found there. Finally, "The Bell-Tower," set in a village in Italy slowly awakening from the "Dark Ages," is an allegorical story of an ambitious orphan turned masterbuilder whose creation—a man-machine, remindful of Frankenstein's monster—unexpectedly kills its inventor, as an enslaved person might turn on his master when the opportunity presents itself. Together, these tales provide windows into life on three continents over a period of four centuries, while also giving voice to some remarkable, if also sometimes quite common, trials of human experience: the heightened perception that sometimes comes with illness; the pain and torment of routine work in a capitalist economy; the traumas and dangers of the slave trade; the alarming sales pitches of itinerant peddlers; the anguish and grotesquery of life on a wasteland archipelago; and the dehumanizing consequences of an emerging "post-human" world, when machinery and slavery came onto the world's stage at much the same time—all presented in distinctly different forms or genres, ranging from dream-vision to biography and history, and on through comic skit, travel sketch, and moral fable.

When Melville began writing short fiction, he did not set out to publish a collection of short stories, let alone one that showed such wide-ranging command of the form. In fact, he did not begin to write short stories until sometime after receiving an invitation, late in 1852, from G. P. Putnam & Co., to contribute to its new magazine, *Putnam's Monthly*, which was scheduled to appear in January of the following year. That invitation came at a crucial time for him, however. His previous two novels, *Moby-Dick* and *Pierre*, had been anything but successful and *Pierre* had been roundly, even viciously, condemned in the press. There is ample evidence, in *Pierre* and Melville's letters to Nathaniel Hawthorne during this period, that he was deeply disheartened by the reception of these novels, but there is evidence, too, that, as an author who rarely gave in to a sense of defeat, he had been working again on a new project, known today as "the story of Agatha," which was never published and survives only as a topic in Melville's correspondence. Melville had approached Harper & Brothers about publishing this work, but the editors declined, presumably on the grounds that his professional reputation had been so tarnished by the nasty reception of his latest novels that they were no longer interested. In any case, Melville did publish his first short story, "Cock-A-Doodle-Doo!," anonymously, in December 1853, in *Harper's New Monthly Magazine*, a production of the same company that published *Moby-Dick* and *Pierre*. Melville published several additional stories in *Harper's*, mostly wryly comic, dolorous pieces ("The Happy Failure," "The Fiddler," "Poor Man's Pudding and Rich Man's Crumbs," "The Paradise of Bachelors and the Tartarus of Maids," "Jimmy Rose," and "The 'Gees"), but his relationship with Harper and Brothers ended there. When "Bartleby, the Scrivener" appeared, anonymously, in November and December of 1853, it was in *Putnam's Monthly*, not *Harper's*. In fact, all the stories included in *The Piazza Tales* (with the exception of the introductory "The Piazza") were published originally in *Putnam's Monthly*, all anonymously (or pseudonymously in the case of "The Encantadas," where Melville used a pen name, Salvator R. Tarnmoor, that echoed the name of Salvator Rosa, a chiaroscuro painter who was one of Melville's favorite artists). Because of his tainted reputation following the popular and critical failures of *Moby-Dick* and *Pierre*, Melville had his own reasons for publishing his short stories anonymously (although some readers almost immediately recognized the author), and presumably did not mind doing so as long as they brought in enough income to allow him to keep ownership of his farm.

With the failure of his most recent novels, and Harper's rejection of his "Agatha" project, Melville had almost nowhere else to turn as a writer except to the popular New York magazines. He had borrowed money from his father-in-law, Lemuel Shaw, on at least two occasions, to help with the purchase of his new home, Arrowhead, in the Berkshires, and he had borrowed from the original owner of his house as well to help pay for several additions and alterations, including the piazza referred to in the title of his collection. Such short-form magazine work provided a welcome opportunity to get more of his work into print, and to do so relatively quickly. Moreover, because his publishers were already familiar with his writing and his strong work ethic, they were willing to pay him the handsome sum of four or five dollars per page, so it was possible for him to realize a good return on his investment—or so he must have thought. For the next three years, he went at the challenge of earning income with his customary energy and determination. Indeed, an examination of Melville's receipts reveals that he had set his heart on bringing in at least fifty dollars a month during the period from November 1853 to December 1856, an ambitious goal he was often able to reach, despite the harmful consequences to his health.[4] In fact, the stories in *The Piazza Tales* are only about a third of the sixteen stories he composed during this period, all but one of which were separately published in *Harper's Monthly* or *Putnam's New Monthly Magazine*. But not until George Putnam sold his magazine to Dix &

Edwards did Melville propose to the latter the idea of publishing a separate volume of five stories, with "some sort of prefatory matter." At one point he suggested as a title, "Benito Cereno & Other Sketches," without a preface. However, before long he changed his mind about the title and the "prefatory matter," offering instead an entirely new, unpublished opening sketch, a generous, semi-autobiographical story, "The Piazza," as a title piece, plus a new plan for ordering the stories.[5]

*Harper's New Monthly Magazine* was a good fit for several of Melville's lighter pieces, such as "I and My Chimney," but *Putnam's Monthly* was better for the more unconventional, nuanced stories that eventually found their way into *The Piazza Tales*. *Harper's* was the more established and popular publication, both in terms of the size and taste of its audience; it also reprinted fiction and articles, as well as illustrations, from other magazines, including British ones.[6] However, from its beginning, *Putnam's* tried to distance itself from *Harper's* by being "the voice of American authorship and the magazine for readers of serious as well as entertaining letters." George Palmer Putnam and his managing editor, Charles Frederick Briggs, initially agreed on the importance of a "high-quality" publication that would appeal to the upper socioeconomic strata.[7] Moreover, after the first issue, when Parke Godwin, as political editor, joined Briggs and George William Curtis (who opposed slavery and helped to found the Republican Party) on the editorial team, *Putnam's* became more overtly political, with clear sympathies for the North and the antislavery cause as well as a decided antipathy for the conservative Democrat president, Franklin Pierce. Nonetheless, in the beginning, Briggs insisted that the magazine would attempt to combine the seriousness of a quarterly review and the entertainment value of a popular magazine, in keeping with Putnam's long-held values.[8] Surely Melville recognized *Putnam's Monthly* to be the more serious-minded outlet that its editors wanted it to be; that is where he sent his more searching, nuanced, and experimental pieces from the beginning. So when Melville proposed to Dix & Edwards, in late 1855, the publication of a separate collection of his tales, we know that, for him, the selection process had already largely been completed beforehand. He originally sent his most challenging, experimental, socially conscious stories to *Putnam's Monthly* because *Putnam's* was predisposed to publish such works, including political stories like the oblique antislavery pieces "Benito Cereno" and "The Bell-Tower," and the tragicomic critique of capitalism, "Bartleby, the Scrivener." In short, the stories in *The Piazza Tales* naturally belong together, not because of common subject matter, treatment, or point of view, but because they represented Melville's most intriguing, arresting, and inventive achievements in the short-fiction form, a fact he had already decided upon when he sent them to *Putnam's Monthly*, where he must have sensed they would be a better fit and more enthusiastically received than if he had sent them to the more broadly popular, convention-driven *Harper's*. In short, I believe Melville intended *The Piazza Tales* as an exhibition of his best short stories from his magazine period, an extended showpiece that aimed at much the same discriminating audience he had appealed to originally when he submitted these stories to *Putnam's Monthly*. Naturally, he also hoped to make money on this collection.

As exceptional as the stories in the collection are, however, *The Piazza Tales* did not sell well. In fact, because sales proved weak and Melville had to pay the printing costs to *Putnam's* new owner, Dix & Edwards, he never received any profits from the book.[9] Even so, the reviews were surprisingly favorable—more so than the sorry financial report would suggest. The collection garnered more than forty reviews or brief notices, a large majority of them admiring and enthusiastic, with only a small handful registering dissatisfaction or distaste (or, in a few cases, bewilderment). Few commented even briefly on all the stories in the volume, other than to observe that they were "fresh," "graphic," or "delightful"; and few offered extensive or incisive commentary. Most often reviewers selected one or two favorites, either "Bartleby," "Benito Cereno," or "The Encantadas," for brief remarks, and then simply mentioned the others by title. "Bartleby" was especially recognized for its originality and humor (and likened to the fiction of Poe or Dickens); "Benito Cereno" for its "thrilling" storyline and sense of mystery;[10] and "The Encantadas" for its "gorgeous" poetic language, or what the reviewer for the *Southern Literary Messenger* referred to as the sketches' "wild, weird clime, out of space, out of time."[11] Not coincidentally, perhaps, these are the three stories from the collection that have moved most securely into the American canon. Enthusiastic reviewers often voiced their pleasure at seeing the return of Melville's familiar style, comparing it with his popular earlier works of South Sea Island exploration, *Typee* and *Omoo*, while others voiced their pleasure at the mysterious, spellbinding manner of his storytelling. By contrast, those who were less taken with his stories found them too metaphysical, morbid, and "rhapsodic" or exaggerated in style. "The Piazza," which rarely inspired much commentary at all, was singled out by the reviewer for the *Albion* (New York) as "one of the most graceful specimens of writing we have seen from an American pen"[12] and received even higher praise from a local *Berkshire County Eagle* reviewer who called it "one of the most beautiful pieces of the kind in the English language."[13] While few bothered to comment on "The Bell-Tower," this most uncharacteristic of Melville's stories had its admirers too; more than one reviewer said it was remindful of Poe, while another found it a "fine conception" but "bunglingly worked out,"[14] a view echoed by a curmudgeonly British reviewer, Henry Chorley, who thought it "barely intelligible"[15] (possibly because he failed to recognize it as a parable). "The Lightning-Rod Man" was the least appreciated of all, one reviewer calling it "a very flat recital" and another, Fitz-James O'Brien (in a long essay on "Our Authors and Authorship," published, ironically, in *Putnam's Monthly*, in April 1857, after the magazine had been sold to Dix & Edwards), condemning it for its "grotesque absurdity and incomprehensible verbiage."[16] These commentators—and many readers since, I believe—may have missed its subtle, delicious irony, while failing to recognize who, exactly, is diddling whom in this story that reads like a preliminary study for *The Confidence-Man* (1857), which Melville published just a year after *The Piazza Tales*.

The stories in *The Piazza Tales* are complex and layered with meaning, more so than casual readers expect from magazine fiction. They delight and instruct, like any good stories, but they also raise questions and challenge conventional thinking and assumptions. They begin on one level and then shift ground; questions abound, mysteries pile up, until we cannot be sure what is going on, or what we are seeing. Perspective in these stories changes and shifts, sometimes often and quickly, as in the opening pages of "Benito Cereno," where Captain Delano tries out several hypotheses about the makeup and movements of a ship he sees in the distance, before concluding that "the true character of the vessel was plain—a Spanish merchantman of the first class, carrying negro slaves" (48), a view that seems perfectly accurate for a while but then becomes amended by Delano to a "negro transportation ship" (49), before regarding it as a slave ship again but one about whose true character he is dangerously wrong. Each story begins with a sense of immediacy, inside the mind of a character, or narrator, who serves as witness or reporter, as in "Bartleby," "The Lightning-Rod Man," and "The Encantadas," but readers are likely to start having questions or detect the presence of ironic touches that make them wonder whether things are what they seem, whether the speaker is simple, misguided, self-deluded, or trying to deceive the reader. In the end, each of Melville's stories in the collection suggests a puzzle, poses a question, or delineates an enigmatic character or ambiguous dramatic situation. While Melville typically provides an answer or solution that relieves the reader's suspense on the immediate level of the plot, these stories are unusual in that they leave readers with new questions or challenges to contemplate on their own. As the reviewer in the *New Bedford Mercury* (probably William Ellery Channing Jr.) observed appreciatively, Melville "leaves some space for the reader to try his own ingenuity."[17]

Melville's stories begin in mystery and end in mystery, but the mystery in the end is often a new one. In this respect the stories in *The Piazza Tales* work against the standard conventions of storytelling. They do not end, as Henry James famously observed about popular fiction, with "a distribution at the last of prizes, pensions, husbands, wives, babies, millions, appended paragraphs, and cheerful remarks."[18] Instead they force the reader to dismiss conventional considerations or reactions and consider something new, something startling or unsettling. In this respect it is fair to say Melville strove to be the kind of storyteller he identified Shakespeare and Hawthorne to be, when in his excited, searching essay-review of Hawthorne's *Mosses from an Old Manse* (1846), he claimed that even Shakespeare, "the profoundest of thinkers," could bring himself to do no more than insinuate "the things, which we feel to be so terrifically true, that it were all but madness for any good man, in his own proper character, to utter, or even hint of them." To a thinking person, the reason for this should not be hard to see: untruths and conventional thinking rule almost everywhere, or as Melville explained in a striking passage, "For in this world of lies, Truth is forced to fly like a scared white doe in the woodlands; and only by cunning glimpses will she reveal herself, as in Shakespeare and other masters of the great Art of Telling the Truth,— even though it be covertly, and by snatches."[19] One consequence of this aesthetic theory is that a good deal of what Melville intended to say had to be buried in his texts, in symbolism and irony, in the body language of the central characters and the implied or unintended significance of what they have to say, where it would probably be missed by censorious readers and "the superficial skimmer of pages."[20]

Despite their formal variety, however, there are more than a few common denominators among the stories in *The Piazza Tales*. Melville's central point-of-view characters are invariably male; also educated, middle class, and professional—a writer, a lawyer, a ship captain, a voyager with a high-sounding name of Salvator R. Tarnmoor, a cottage owner (or renter) living in the mountains, an architect who is also a machinist. Some of these figures reflect the world of *Putnam's* readers, but mostly they stretch the reader's experience of the world to include peculiar characters encountered in distant places like the Galapagos Islands; the treacherous waters off the coast of Chile; an ancient village in Italy; or the rural mountains of New England. Travel writing was a popular genre at the time and at *Putnam's Monthly* especially, the more distant or exotic the region, the landscape, and the culture, the better. The 1850s were a time of growing internationalism for Americans—in travel, exploration, adventurism, and trade (including of course the trade in African bodies), and American readers were eager to learn about the wider world. In "Benito Cereno" and "Bartleby," the narrators or centers of consciousness are innocent, provincial, conventionally minded men (Captain Delano in "Benito Cereno" is a racist and an optimist who believes Providence will protect him; the lawyer in "Bartleby" describes himself as a "safe" man and thinks it a virtue), but they provide the reader's entree into the unfamiliar worlds of a Spanish slave ship and a Wall Street law firm. Blinded by their provincialism, their classism, racism, or bigotry, they are more than a vehicle, however; they constitute a large part of the subject, and a large part of the mystery or "problem" that the story poses as well. Other narrators or centers of consciousness, like the Salvator R. Tarnmoor of "The Encantadas" and the nameless narrator of "The Bell-Tower," are more distant, undefined figures or voices who make few explicit judgments but lots of ironic ones. Or they are distant, enigmatic characters like Benito Cereno, or the seemingly bumbling narrator-host of "The Lightning-Rod Man," who wears a mask and never admits to knowing as much about lightning rods (and sales pitches) as the peddler who tries to sell him one. In the case of "The Piazza," the narrator is a humorous, wistful, self-deprecating version of Melville himself but one forced by a painful earache to seek relief in dreams of a fairy princess and repeated readings of *A Midsummer's Night's Dream*. Some narrators or centers of consciousness seem to change and grow, like the lawyer in "Bartleby," while others clearly do not, as is true of the American captain in "Benito Cereno." But in either case, Melville leaves a trail of evidence to suggest how much they have missed, or misunderstood, because of their narrow mindset, their biases and preconceptions, including the fact that their empathy or humanity has been seriously tested without their knowing it.

Early reviewers often praised the tales for their lively, "graphic" descriptions, and "minuteness of detail," and certainly Melville was a gifted writer in this respect, with a poet's eye and ear and a fresh, ironic, often lyrical, if also convoluted style. What most reviewers did not know is that most of his stories originated in Melville's own experience or achieved much of their sense of immediacy from his use of the firsthand reports of others, originally published in newspapers, journals, and travel narratives, as in the case of "Benito Cereno," where much of the story derived from Amasa Delano's *A Narrative of Voyages and Travels, in the Northern and Southern Hemispheres* (1817). "The Encantadas" was based largely on Melville's personal observations of the Galapagos Islands during two stops he made in 1841–42, but these sketches also relied on the firsthand reports of several other early observers, including the "excellent Buccaneer" William Cowley, whose *Voyage Round the Globe* (1699) Melville quoted in Sketch Fourth, as well as Captain David Porter (*Journal of a Cruise Made to the Pacific Ocean* [1815, 1822]) and Captain James Colnett (*A Voyage to the South Atlantic and Round Cape Horn into the Pacific Ocean* [1798]). Melville mentions all of these earlier voyagers in the course of his narrative, but there were others he relied on as well, including James Burney (*A Chronological History of the Discoveries in the South Sea or Pacific Ocean* [1803–17]), Charles Darwin (*The Voyage of the Beagle* [1838]), and Benjamin Morrell (*Narrative of Four Voyages to the South Seas* [1832]), among other, less certain sources.[21] For a very different sort of story, the simple encounter between two nameless figures in "The Lightning-Rod Man," Melville is rumored to have depended on at least one personal encounter with such a salesman, and on local newspaper coverage of unnumbered such encounters experienced by his Berkshire neighbors in the 1850s.[22] But he also appropriated details about the dangers of lightning and the advice for avoiding electrocution he found in the scientific writings of Benjamin Franklin, whom he had made into an important character in his historical novel of the Revolutionary War, *Israel Potter* (1854–55), which he wrote and published late in the same period when he was writing his short fiction. A more limited set of sources apparently formed the basis of much of "Bartleby, the Scrivener," including a contemporary novel by James A. Maitland, titled "The Lawyer's Story," from which Melville probably borrowed the basic idea for his own tale,[23] as well as a sometimes ironic essay of Emerson's, "The Transcendentalist" (1842), with its dual portraits of the Materialist and the Idealist, which seem to inform, and echo, his portrayals of the starkly contrasting characters of the lawyer and the scrivener respectively.[24]

As suggested in these last several examples, Melville's stories often depend for their graphic descriptions and sense of immediacy on the writings of others to suggest a storyline and provide skeletal dimensions for his characters. But they also depend on the writings of other authors to give his stories richness and complexity, and to situate them in a tradition of writing about similar subjects. That is to say his stories are often highly literary or intertextual; they resonate with examples of the Melville's own ambitious reading habits and retentive memory. Throughout "The Encantadas," for example, he introduces each sketch with a quotation from Edmund Spenser's *Faerie Queene*, Francis Beaumont and John Fletcher, or other early modern writings, that help to set the mysterious, otherworldly mood and provide commentary on the several sketches. In "The Bell-Tower," Melville hints at parallels between the early modern era of Bannadonna and his ambitious fellow citizens and the biblical stories of Shadrach and the Tower of Babel, along with brief mentions of several other Old Testament figures (Anak, Haman, Deborah, Sisera, Jael), as well as figures from classical mythology (Titans, Vulcan)[25] and *The Faerie Queene* (Talus). Finally, in "The Piazza," he repeatedly mentions his narrator's eagerly turning to *A Midsummer's Night's Dream* in an effort to "learn all about Titania" (a distraction from his illness, presumably, and possibly also a source of inspiration) and refers in passing to *Hamlet, Macbeth, Paradise Lost,* and *Don Quixote*—a heavy diet of classic literature requiring a good deal of mental effort. Such literary richness and resonance, whether explicitly mentioned or buried, is typical of almost all of his writings. They are signs that, as he boasted in *Moby-Dick,* he had "swam through libraries," and wrote with an extensive library at his fingertips or stored in his memory.[26]

The stories in *The Piazza Tales* also share a dramatic structure, typically one involving two contrasting, sometimes combative personalities who meet for the first time and engage in a protracted process of mutual assessment and discovery. Such a dramatic structure adds considerably to the "trying-out" process the reader, too, must engage in order to figure out what is going on and who is making an effort to manage, manipulate, or test whom, and the possible reasons for their doing so. Without a reliable (omniscient) narrator to inform and guide them, readers of these stories must pay close attention and expect the unexpected if they are to comprehend the action and meaning at the dramatic center of the story. Typically, where there is such dramatic uncertainty, there is also a suggestion that the characters are testing or putting one another "on trial" as well, as they sift through the limited evidence they are able to glean in their attempt to solve the mystery of their counterpart or gain understanding of them, whether they are named Bartleby, Benito Cereno, Marianna, or an anonymous equivalent like the Lightning-Rod Man. In each instance there is a trying-out process, an effort to "read" the body or performance of the other, a process made all the more challenging when the characters in question engage, as they often do, in enigmatic gestures, deceptive role-playing, or disguise. Each story, that is to say, asks the reader to analyze and make sense of what is happening to the characters in question and the personal trials they are experiencing. In "Benito Cereno," there is even an actual trial at the end involving Babo and the other surviving African rebels, complete with transcripts of court testimony (thought to be boring and unnecessary by some early reviewers as well as Melville's publisher), testimony that turns out to be unreliable at several points but still crucial to an understanding of Melville's larger point about the racism, colonialism, and imperialism of official culture in the New World. In "The Bell-Tower," the climax occurs when Bannadonna attempts to put his monstrous mechanical-man, or "slave," through a trial run to demonstrate how precisely it tolls the hours and, in that way, impress a crowd of citizens and city officials with the brilliance and grandeur of his achievement. But even after the creature has struck and killed its creator, we do not know, and cannot determine with certainty, whether this strange figure is man or machine, or some unprecedented and unimaginable combination of the two.

Perhaps not surprisingly, given Melville's critical treatment of themes of race and class in *Typee, Redburn, Moby-Dick,* and elsewhere, the stories in *The Piazza Tales* also include an unmistakable element of social critique, one focusing especially on the plight of the oppressed, the voiceless, or the outcast, while at the same time appealing to the sympathy and understanding of the middle- and upper-class readership that defined *Putnam's Monthly*. Melville sets the stage for such social commentary early on, in the opening sketch, "The Piazza," where the narrator is surprised to discover not a fairy princess on the mountain overlooking his home, but a poor and lowly seamstress who, he discovers, has been looking down from her simple mountain hut onto what she takes to be his gilded "palace" in the distance. In "Bartleby," he exposes the soul-killing routines of the scrivener and his eccentric coworkers, who labor as low-paid copyists "among rich men's bonds and mortgages and title-deeds" (14) inside the deadening walls of a Wall Street law office. In "Benito Cereno" and "The Bell-Tower," he maneuvers through the landmines of race and slavery to comment indirectly but powerfully on the horrors of slavery and the human toll it inevitably takes on enslaved Africans and white slavers, too. Importantly, Melville also created situations that call on the reader to recognize, appreciate, and respond sympathetically to the sufferings of these oppressed and marginalized people—to awaken the "power of sympathy" in them. That is to say, these stories have the potential to open their readers' eyes to the suffering, hardships, and struggles of the marginalized, the oppressed, and the enslaved. Even in the relatively light, sometimes comedic sketches of "The Encantadas," there is a heartbreaking story of Hunilla, tragically widowed and left alone on Norfolk Island, where she is betrayed by the ship captain who promised to return for her, then apparently raped by the crews of passing ships while she waits to be rescued—or so she leads her rescuers to believe. As Melville's narrator says at the start of Sketch Eighth, "however insignificant to most voyagers, to me, through sympathy, that lone island has become a spot made sacred by the strongest trials of humanity" (151). One famous testimonial to this story's success at eliciting the "power of sympathy" was offered by James Russell Lowell, who claimed "the figure of the cross in the ass' neck," upon which Hunilla stares while riding back to her home after being rescued, "brought tears to his eyes."[27] In spite of Melville's masculinist reputation, these stories (with the exception of "The Lightning-Rod Man") show Melville to be working within a reanimated if subdued version of the sentimental tradition, a tradition known historically as the dominant tradition of female authorship in America and abroad. Melville may have been a decidedly masculinist writer, but in *The Piazza Tales,* he shows a marked sympathy for those of his characters who represent minority populations—women, enslaved Africans, and the poor in particular—who suffer the fate of their natural but culturally inscribed bodies in a world ruled or dominated by others—white males, mostly, whose own bodies have privileged and empowered them to rule over other lives.

# 1

## "THE PIAZZA" AND MELVILLE'S SICKROOM

From its first appearance in 1856, "The Piazza" has been regarded as an introduction to *The Piazza Tales* and an autobiographical tale in its own right. More recently, it has been read as an expression of Melville's aesthetic theory, one based on the piazza Melville added to Arrowhead, his new farmhouse near Pittsfield, and echoing similar treatment of architectural themes in "The Old Manse," Hawthorne's introduction to his collection of several of his previously published tales.[1] However, Melville's opening tale does more than embody an aesthetic theory; it also embodies a social and cultural drama about disability, class, and gender in the contrast between the lives and conditions of the two main characters—the nameless narrator, who enjoys a relatively quiet, leisurely life of reading and contemplation while housebound because of his recent sickness and invalidism, and the poor seamstress Marianna, the woman he finds at the end of his journey into the mountains near his home and whose bodily trials are ongoing but hidden from the world. While several earlier critical studies focus on the piazza and its view of Mount Greylock in the Berkshires, they hardly mention the curious fairytale atmosphere of the piece, with its suggestions of magic and the beautiful "fairy queen" the narrator dreams about, or the mysterious illness that prompted the narrator to build his piazza in the first place. The one extended examination of the "fairyland metaphor"—a searching and exacting essay by Helmbrecht Breinig—concludes that it is finally "reduced to absurdity" because "everything [in the tale] depends on the subjective point of view." The realm of the imagination in "The Piazza," Breinig argues, is presented as an illusion, and the truth to be found there and in the realm of fact or "actuality" "can only be negative."[2]

In the discussion that follows, I read the tale differently, as a story of the imagination—illuminated and intensified by the narrator's mysterious illness—engaging with the world as the narrator finds it but informed also by his personal history, which in its broad outlines resembles Melville's own history as a well-traveled sailor turned writer-farmer, now sharing with his readers the story of his discovery of a poor, hardworking woman named Marianna. Marianna's simple life is a stark contrast to his own, an ironic, naturalistic version of the "fairy" land that inspired him to travel into the mountains in the first place. In my reading, the realm of the imagination in this story is not an illusion but the source of a higher truth, one informed and made possible by the narrator's prior experiences as a sailor, one schooled in the ways of other lives in the larger world, and by his recent trials in the sickroom and on the piazza of his Berkshire farmhouse, where he now looks out on the world from a distance.

"The Piazza" is a two-part tale, a kind of diptych like "The Paradise of Bachelors and the Tartarus of Maids," the first part serving as an introduction to the narrator and his move from the city to a farmhouse in the Berkshires near Mount Greylock, the highest point in Massachusetts, and the second part detailing the unlikely experience of his "inland voyage to fairy-land" (4),[3] when he imagines himself venturing up the mountain one day in search of the source of a mysterious light that catches his eye and where he eventually encounters the poor seamstress, Marianna. The first part is framed in realistic terms and bears a strong resemblance to Melville's own life, when he moved from New York City in October 1850 to the farmhouse he called "Arrowhead," where he wrote much of *Moby-Dick* (in full view of Greylock), as well as *Pierre* (dedicated to "Greylock's Most Excellent Majesty"), *Israel Potter*, and many of his short stories, including the stories in *The Piazza Tales*, and where he experienced painful, occasionally incapacitating rheumatism and sciatica off and on for several years. For Melville's narrator, as for Melville himself apparently, Greylock is emblematic of the world beyond his farmhouse, and serves as the inspiration and source of stories about "other lives," such as Marianna's in this opening story. The function of the piazza, in turn, is to provide a place, and the necessary leisure, for viewing and contemplating the mountain that inspires the narrator's storytelling. His illness and invalidism provide the time and occasion he needs for contemplation.

The longer, second part of "The Piazza" is a daydream or fantasy, an imagined voyage undertaken in search of a shadowy "queen of the fairies"—a voyage that calls to mind Taji's romantic, allegorical search for the exotic Yillah in *Mardi* (1849)—but which in this case is explicitly associated with Titania and *A Midsummer's Night's Dream,* in whose story the narrator shows an obsessive interest, and with Dulcinea, the imagined "true love" of the famous fantasist Don Quixote, another of the narrator's favorite literary personalities whom he describes briefly as "that sagest sage that ever lived" (6). The narrator, who by implication and a broad hint at the end of this introductory story is the author of all the tales in the collection, is similar to Melville but clearly an artificial construct or *persona*—more relaxed and cheerful, a dreamer and avid reader but one with a taste for allegories, romances, and tragedies (*The Faerie Queene, Don Quixote,* more plays of Shakespeare—*Hamlet, Macbeth, King Lear*—in addition to *A Midsummer's Night's Dream*); a familiarity with biblical names and figures (Lazarus and Dives, Moses, Lucifer and Michael, Adullam cave); and an interest in history, particularly as it relates to the revolutions of 1848 in Europe, and anything having to do with Charlemagne. Another seemingly important difference is that the narrator seems to live alone and has a good deal more *leisure* time at his disposal—time to contemplate Mount Greylock and read Shakespeare—than Melville himself ever knew during these years of feverish writing and hard physical labor on his farm. Importantly, that sense of leisure seems to be of relatively recent origin and is entirely consistent with several statements about the narrator being sick and bedridden, a fact generally glossed over by critics, and hardly recognized as related to Melville's own illness at the time.

Nowhere in "The Piazza" is there any mention of Melville's wife and family; no reference to his farm chores or chopping wood; and virtually no explicit mention of his work as a writer until the very end of the story. In this fictional version, the author portrays himself as a "devotee of Nature" who loves to watch the seasonal changes in the "picture-galleries" of these limestone hills—"galleries hung, month after month anew, with pictures ever fading into pictures ever fresh." Indeed, he claims "to *feast upon the view*" and take his "time and ease about it," too. For, he explains, "beauty is like piety—you cannot run and read it; tranquility and constancy, *with, now-a-days, an easy chair*, are needed" (my emphasis). In this respect, Melville's narrator is not simply a sick man but a man of his time, a time he views sardonically as an era of "failing faith and feeble knees," when "indolence" rather than "reverence" is in vogue, and devotees of Nature (unlike the "worshipers of a higher Power" in earlier times) require a piazza or a pew to support their pampered bodies (2). Here, too, we can see an important clue to Melville's conception of his self-indulgent times, and equally self-indulgent audience perhaps, along with the hope that this story, and the others in *The Piazza Tales*, will challenge their easygoing optimism with tales of hardship, struggle, suffering, and trial. Nonetheless, the emphasis throughout the opening section of the tale is on the narrator's fascination with the picturesque seasonal beauties of Greylock (which he typically addresses, without explanation, as "Charlemagne"); his need to take it easy and deliberate over the location of a piazza for his house; and, finally, his illness, something he only mentions, or alludes to, several times, despite the fact it disables him to the point of confinement in his house for most of the story. In short, the narrator portrays himself as a quiet convalescent; a passive observer but one with an active, seafaring past; a devoted reader of romances; and a daydreamer with a sardonic wit and a weird fixation on Mount Greylock—a portrait that seems more a comic, lackadaisical version of himself or of one who is simply doing his best to stay cheerful while passing the time until he heals and can get back on his feet.

For those readers already familiar with Melville's life and writings, there are details in the narrator's self-portrait that closely approximate Melville's own biography: references to exotic places such as he had visited or read about earlier in life (Westminster Abbey, Quito, Memnon, San Carlo theatre in Naples, the Kabba in Mecca) as well as references to his experiences as a sailor: the Holy Stones (used for cleaning ship decks) quarried from these same Berkshire mountains; the December wind that brings back memories of his days pacing "the sleety deck, [while] weathering Cape Horn" (3); the "yellow sinnet" hat and "white duck trowsers"—"both relics of my tropic sea-going"—that he claims to wear later on his journey into the mountains (8); and several features of the distant landscape that remind him of the sea—the "ground-swells" that look like waves; the "blown down of dandelions" that look like sea-spray; the "lonesomeness" of the "oceanic" meadows. The combination of these visual details is so powerfully reminiscent of his sailor past that when he first gets a glimpse of a house in the distance, he claims it is "for all the world like spying, on the Barbary coast, an unknown sail" (3-4). That is to say, his identity as an observer with an illness is layered over his earlier identity as a healthy, well-traveled sailor. It is in this latter remembered capacity that he "recalls *my inland voyage* to fairy-land" (my emphasis)—the "voyage" into the mountains that constitutes part two of "The Piazza" (3-4). Although the language is purposely ambiguous, presumably to create excitement and anticipation about something transcendent and otherworldly while suspending disbelief, this line suggests the entire experience occurs as a "daydream" or fantasy, but one informed by the narrator's past life as a sailor and world traveler. Such a reading seems confirmed by his asserting, ironically, that his trip into the mountains was "[a] true voyage; but, take it all in all, interesting as if invented" (4), a line that asserts the superiority of imagined or transcendent truth, and calls to mind Ishmael's somewhat analogous claim, in *Moby-Dick*, about Queequeg's island home of Kokovoko not being "down in any map; true places never are."[4]

Among other biographical parallels, Melville, too, in fact built a piazza on the north side of Arrowhead. A visit to the house today will reveal it is still there (recently refurbished), a more or less permanent fixture of the house. Also, as already indicated, Melville himself experienced a mysterious illness—usually identified as a combination of "rheumatism and sciatica"—off and on during the period of his residence there. But in "The Piazza," the narrator's explanation for his illness as something that starts with an earache, which he says he acquired while lying on the ground gazing at Greylock, is very different from the chronic condition Melville's biographers describe going back several years to early 1852 when his family began to see signs of his strenuous work schedule coupled with what his mother Maria called his "constant in-door confinement," and which Melville himself (in "I and My Chimney") attributed to "the sciatica" from which he claimed to be "sometimes as crippled up as any old apple tree."[5] As for the piazza, little is known about why Melville added this construction to his new farmhouse, except for the fact that it was part of a larger plan of upgrading and renovation that, as he explained to his father-in-law Lemuel Shaw, included "building the new kitchen, wood-house, piazza, making alterations, painting—and, in short, all those improvements made upon these premises during the first year of occupancy."[6] By contrast, in the opening paragraphs of "The Piazza," the narrator offers an elaborately playful explanation—using language reminiscent of Melville's dedication to "Greylock's Most Excellent Majesty" in *Pierre* (1852), when he reveals that "during the first year of my residence" in the new house he made a habit of watching, from "a royal lounge of turf," the rising and setting of the sun over Greylock to the north (2). With tongue in cheek, he describes this velvety green, moss-padded lounge as "very majestical, indeed. So much so, that here, as with the reclining majesty of Denmark in his orchard, a sly ear-ache invaded me" on account of the dampness within "this monastery of mountains." Only after the earache had stolen upon him does he decide, "A piazza must be had" (2). Although he will soon be confined to a sickbed, he continues to want a view of the outdoors, and of Mount Greylock especially. As his contemporary Harriet Martineau had observed a few years earlier in her *Life in the Sickroom* (1844), having a view of the natural world, with its beauty and signs of the season, outside one's sickroom is always important to sick people.[7]

While Melville's narrator presents his earache as the cause of his confinement, the reference to the poisoning of Hamlet's father with the "juice of cursed hebenon" as a parallel to his own situation ("And in the porches of my ears did pour / The leperous distilment; whose effect / Holds such an enmity with blood of man") suggests a more serious consequence of his exposure to raw nature, if not a conspiracy of some kind.[8] The "poisoning" aside, however, he seems equally intent to suggest (tongue in cheek again), in comparing himself to the Danish king, that he is not a struggling farmer but someone who deserves a comfortable, elevated piazza from which to view his favorite mountain.[9] Melville's narrator points to the "dampness" at the base of the mountains where he lives as the cause of his sickness, but it is clear he wishes to suggest it is his bodily contact with the natural landscape that "poisons" him. This poisonous "dampness" in nature is the first instance of a recurring pattern of nasty unhealthiness inherent in the natural world of this story, seen again later in the "millions of strange, cankerous worms" he finds infesting the blossoms of a Chinese creeper he had installed near his new piazza (6). If the world of Arrowhead and Mount Greylock seems an idyllic or "Edenic" place in the early pages of this story, it is an Eden tainted with signs of evil or corruption.

Significantly, Melville here suggests that the ability to see the world as both beautiful and tainted, or "double," stems from his illness, which is to say from an altered, *expanded* point of view. It is only because he had *"become so sensitive through my illness,"* he explains, "that I could not bear to look upon" the Chinese creeper with its "cankerous worms," which "feeding upon those blossoms, so shared their blessed hue, as to make it unblessed evermore—worms, whose germs had doubtless lurked in the very bulb which, so hopefully, I had planted" (6; my emphasis). But it is also the case that only through the new sensitivity brought on by his illness that he is able to see the "strange, cankerous worms" in the first place, or glimpse the "uncertain object" (later described as "the spot in question" or light) that plays at "hide and seek" in the distant mountains and haunts his imagination during the early stages of his convalescence. "Indeed, for a year or more, I knew not there was such a spot, and might, perhaps, have never known, had it not been for a wizard afternoon in autumn—late in autumn—a mad poet's afternoon" when the magical Indian summer atmosphere turned smoky and mysterious. Although he had at length grown "pretty well again," enough so to sit out "in the September morning, upon the piazza," he was still experiencing "this ingrate peevishness of my weary convalescence" when suddenly he caught a glimpse of "the golden mountain-window" in the distance (6). This, it turns out, is the same "One spot of radiance" (4) that had earlier mystified him but now inspires him to think: "Fairies there . . . once more; the queen of fairies at her fairy-window; at any rate some glad mountain-girl; it will do me good, it will cure this weariness, to look on her" (6). And so, weary though he is, he vows to go looking for her—whether fairy or plain mountain-girl—though in fact he has seen no one.

The crucial link in the convoluted paragraph containing these reflections of the narrator is the one between illness and sensitivity, invalidism and seeing, an uncanny connection, but one given credence in *Life in the Sickroom,* where Martineau testifies to the "intense and growing self-consciousness" that resulted from her own confinement, and then explores the impact of "heightened sensitivity" on her understanding of the world at large.[10] For Martineau, as for Melville in "The Piazza," invalidism is a condition of reduced physical activity, to be sure, but it can lead to a state of heightened mental activity and acuity. Martineau explains this phenomenon by arguing that when the body is confined to a sickroom, the invalid is freed of everyday duties and distractions, while being provided valuable "leisure for reading and contemplation of various sides of questions." Because of the extraordinary opportunities for "reflection" that result from confinement, "we [invalids] must, almost necessarily, see further than we used to do, and further than many others do on subjects of interest."[11] This is particularly true, she adds, if the sickroom includes a "window" that opens onto the outside world, inviting the invalid to engage the world intellectually and imaginatively from a distance. The piazza is Melville's equivalent of Martineau's window. It, too, "marks the invalid's access to the wider world," and functions symbolically as well, as Maria Frawley has argued in an illuminating essay on *Life in the Sickroom,* "to signify the meditative and visionary powers of invalidism." Indeed, for both authors, there is a kind of "omniscience" that comes with "sick vision," to use Frawley's terms,[12] an "omniscience" not unlike that experienced by any accomplished artist who steels herself to "constant in-door confinement," as Melville had done throughout much of his career—to the point where his mother believed it was ruining her son's health.[13]

What that enhanced vision looks like, how it becomes embodied in narrative, is the subject of the second part of "The Piazza," where the narrator appears to carry out his plan to seek out the "queen of fairies" through an *imagined voyage* to Mount Greylock. Although he claims to launch his "yawl" (i.e., horse) and "push away for fairy-land—for rainbow's end, in fairy-land" (6), the narrator is still in a state of "weary convalescence" in which he dreams or daydreams his voyage into the mountains and his encounter with, not the queen of the fairies or even a "glad mountain-girl," but a "lonely girl, sewing at a lonely window" (8) and suffering the bodily trials of "sitting, sitting, restless sitting" while performing "dull woman's work" (12). The entire presentation of the narrator's journey to the "spot of radiance" on the mountain is carefully contrived to seem like an actual occurrence (despite the repeated references to "fairies"!), but on closer inspection it takes on the character of a protracted dream or fantasy. Assuming that to be the case, then, that "one spot of radiance" is neither a distant barn nor a recently roofed cottage, but a symbol of the "light" or moment of insight in the creative process that inspires the story of the narrator's journey in the first place. The whole second part of the tale, in other words, should be read as an allegory about changing perspective and artistic production, featuring the contrast between a man of illness, leisure, and intuition—the storyteller—who goes searching for a "fairy queen," and the weary, hardworking woman he finally encounters whose "strange fancies" lead her to believe the narrator's house, far below her, "looks so happy; I can't tell how," only to admit she sometimes thinks, "I do but dream it is there" (9–10). If anything, the narrator and this lonely woman, the artist and his subject, are kindred spirits.

Where, then, does the story of Marianna come from? If not the product of an actual trip into the mountains and a firsthand meeting, but something imagined, is it based in some way upon the narrator's earlier experience of the world? Again, *Life in the Sickroom* is instructive. In a late chapter titled "Power of Ideas in the Sick-Room," Martineau writes of the naturally occurring sympathy that a sick person often feels for people whose condition is "the converse of our own state" and whose suffering, therefore, is not only greater and more pervasive than the invalid's but beyond amelioration, since in all likelihood they lack access to the saving power of "ideas":

> I must allude to a subject which causes inexpressible pain whenever it occurs to sick prisoners. I have said how unavailing is luxury when the body is distressed and the spirit faint. At such times, and at all times, we cannot but be deeply grieved at the conception of the converse of our own state, at the thought of the multitude of poor suffering under privation, without the support and solace of great ideas. It is sad enough to think of them on a winter's night, aching with cold in every limb, and sunk as low as we in nerve and spirits, from their want of sufficient food.[14]

While this description does not perfectly capture Marianna's condition (it lacks the cold of a winter night, for example), it is similar enough to suggest that her character may have its origin in the invalid narrator's sympathetic response to the condition of someone from his prior experience of the world whose suffering is greater than his own.[15] In this case Marianna stands not as an isolated, realistic character, the product of a chance encounter on a mountaintop, but a representative figure—female, poor, isolated, deprived; dedicated to her sewing, yet longing to escape from her particular form of repetitious labor and confinement. Unlike the narrator, she hardly has time to look out her window or experience the invalid's heightened perception because her eyes are so incessantly fixed upon her sewing. But she does confess to occasionally looking down upon the "far off, soft, azure world" below where the narrator lives, and admits, "'Oh, sir,' tears starting in her eyes, 'the first time I looked out of the window, I said 'never, never shall I weary of this'" (9). So we see that her situation is much the same as the narrator's, but in reverse; both are trapped, he by his illness, she by her poverty and sewing. As a consequence, both are fantasists who see an illusion or phantasm in the distance.

As Marianna's example emphasizes, "The Piazza" is a meditation on perspective and the predilections—and changes—that inform one's point of view. On the personal level, it is the story of the change in Melville's own point of view after moving from the city to the country, from New York to the Berkshires, and more particularly his new "painterly" perspective on the mountains as viewed from his newly constructed piazza—a platform "combining the coziness of in-doors with the freedom of out-door"—at his new home of Arrowhead. In setting the scene, one of the first images he invokes is of the many painters who can be seen engaged in their art in the distant hills, particularly when encountered close up by boys during berry time, as distinct from how they are seen from his own more distant point of view: "A very paradise of painters. The circle of the stars cut by the circle of the mountains. At least, so looks it from the house," he says, and then, shifting perspective, he adds, "though, once upon the mountains, no circle of them can you see. Had the site been chosen five rods off, this charmed ring would not have been" (1). Perspective, he keeps insisting, can add to or subtract from a view, and of course radically alter it, as his perspective on the "fairy princess" he imagines in the Berkshire mountains changes dramatically when he finally meets up with her.

An important variable in the narrator's view of Mount Greylock is that at the time of the story he is sick; his body is in pain and requires what Martineau calls "nature's nursing."[16] Thinking of Greylock in terms of "Charlemagne" takes the narrator out of himself and into a world of beauty and romantic history where he can forget about his ailing body, at least for a time. In response to the question, "What is the best kind of view for a sick prisoner's windows to command?" Martineau says it has to be a view of the sea, because "We should have a wide expanse of land or water, for the sake of a sense of liberty, yet more than variety." Martineau expresses a strong personal preference for the sea over the land, not because of its spaciousness or expansiveness, but because of its motion, the perpetual shifting of objects and sightlines that stimulate the imagination and take the sick person out of herself. While she admits that the "ever changing aspects of mountains are good and beautiful," there is "something more life-like in the going forth and return of ships, in the passage of fleets, and in the never-ending variety of a fishery."[17] For Melville's narrator, sick and landlocked as he is, the mountains are simply a happy substitute; indeed, he tends to view the mountains in terms of images of the sea or memories of his time at sea, in keeping with his early life as a sailor.

Seascapes and landscapes, however, are not the only sources of relief from pain for the invalid. Martineau writes, too, of the beguiling power of various kinds of literature, particularly travel writing, for its capacity to take the invalid out of the "prison" of herself, if only temporarily. "Blessings on the writers of voyages and travels," she exclaims. "A school-boy's or a soldier's eagerness after voyages and travels is nothing to that of an invalid. We are insatiable in regard to this kind of book."[18] A similar idea seems central to "The Piazza" as well, where the narrator's reading—not of travel books but of *A Midsummer's Night's Dream* "and all about Titania"—has the effect of lifting him out of his misery and temporarily restoring "the long-lost sensation of health once more," to borrow Martineau's phrase, a phrase she used to describe the effect she experienced on reading "a Journal of Travels to the Polar sea, or over the Passes of the Alps." Melville's narrator's startling admission that he can hardly "spare" time away from "reading the Midsummer Night's Dream, and all about Titania," intimates just how much distress and discomfort he experienced during this period when he "had to keep to [his] chamber" and also how much relief he was able to get from reading Shakespeare's romance and other works, which serve as a substitute for viewing Mount Greylock while he was still so disabled as to need to be confined to his sickroom, a room, we are told, which did not offer a mountain view (5).

Gradually, the narrator embodies his fantasy about "the queen of fairies" with details, at one point imagining, vaguely, a "haunted ring where fairies dance," and then months later, in May, after his fantasy has had time to mature, he imagines the "spot" of light on the mountain to signal the presence of glass from a refurbished cottage or "a roof newly shingled" (5–6), a hunch that turns out to be surprisingly close to what he finds. Moreover, as becomes clear when he finally strikes out to discover what lies at the end of the rainbow—whether in his imagination or not—it is indeed a cottage, rather than "some old barn," with a new roof on one side and, not abandoned, but inhabited by "a lonely girl, sewing at a lonely window" (8). That part of his fantasy remains true. It is certainly not inhabited by a "fairy queen" and, true to his fantasy, neither is it inhabited by a man. Before he can venture out to confirm his growing suspicions about the distant spot, however, the narrator's illness returns—at the very same time the atmosphere in the mountains proves "unfavorable for fairy views"—a development that sorely disappoints him: "the more so," as he explains, "because I had to keep my chamber for some time after." This, then, is the moment when he claims to be so devoted to "reading the Midsummer Night's Dream, and all about Titania" that he could hardly spare the time to "gaze off towards the hills" to learn more about the mysterious "spot of radiance" (5). Especially significant is his obsession with Titania, the so-called "Queen of the Fairies," also known as Mab, the same "Queen Mab" who rules over Stubb's dream in chapter 31 of *Moby-Dick,* and makes "a wise man" of him by revealing the truth of his unconscious self.

It is only "when pretty well again, and sitting out, on a September morning, upon the piazza, and thinking to myself," that Melville's narrator discovers the "strange, cankerous worms" in his Chinese creeper and catches another glimpse of the "golden mountain-window," with the imagined "queen of fairies" in the distance. Concluding for the first time that "it will do me good, it will cure this weariness, to look on her," he vows to venture out in search of her and "rainbow's end, in fairyland" (6). His first step calls attention to the imaginary character of his voyage when he claims, while adopting a mask of childlike innocence, that he did not know how to get to fairyland, "nor could any one inform me," not even the author of *The Faerie Queene* himself, "who had been there—so he wrote me—further than that to reach fairy-land, it must be voyaged to, and with faith" (6), a line that speaks to the willing suspension of disbelief required of all readers at such a moment. In point of fact, then, this aside ought to be read as an admission of the narrator's earnest desire to join the poet of *The Faerie Queene* in his own wish-fulfillment fantasy.

What follows, for the better part of two long pages, is a poetic, dreamlike passage describing the narrator's morning excursion through a sleepy, enchanted landscape where gentle animals appear, as in a fable, to show the way for him. Letting down the bars of a fenced-in pasture, he is rewarded when a ram appears—"a wigged old Aries, long-visaged, and with crumpled horn"—to lead him through "a milky-way of white-weed" and constellations of forget-me-nots, where he is met by "golden flights" of yellow birds he takes to be "pilots" to "the golden window." At first they seem to guide him toward deep woods that lure him on and then to another fence "banning a dark road" that leads up the mountain. Here Aries, "renouncing me for some lost soul," turns and departs: "Forbidding and forbidden ground—to him," the narrator concludes, but forbidden not to the narrator himself, who reveals he is a man of "faith" by venturing on, in keeping with Spenser's injunction.

Before long he comes upon an old sawmill, covered with vines, and other evidence of human activity from some distant past, especially a "hanging orchard," where he and his horse sample an apple that "tasted of the ground," a sign, he realizes, that he has not yet reached fairyland. Surely, though, it is also a sign he has trespassed into a "fallen" realm of new knowledge, for, seeing that the path had come to its end, and "none might go but by himself, and only go by daring," he leaves his horse and pushes ahead "through blackberry brakes that tried to pluck me back" and "up slippery steeps to barren heights." Eventually, foot-sore and weary, he comes to a rugged pass and then an overgrown "zigzag road" that turned among the cliffs, and finally to a break. There he observes a track that branches upward to where the mountaintop slopes away before dropping down the opposite side, and there, "among fantastic rocks" that will be seen to play an imaginary role in Marianna's daily life, he suddenly spies the house he was seeking, "a little, low-storied, grayish cottage, capped, nun-like with a peaked roof" (7–8), one side covered with moss and the other "newly shingled," as he had supposed.

Finally, he notices, all around the base of the house, "shaded streaks of richest sod," in keeping with the view of Oberon, whom he identifies as "grave authority in fairy lore" (another symptom of his infatuation with the imaginary world of Titania), that as "with hearth-stones in fairy-land, the natural rock . . . preserves to the last . . . its fertilizing charm." In this case, the "shaded streaks were richest" in the front of the house, near the entrance, where a "gentle, nurturing heat is radiated" by the comings and goings of whoever resides there. Even before he has seen inside the cottage or knows whether it is inhabited, he concludes: "Fairy land at last, thought I; Una and her lamb dwell here," signaling that the scene, at first blush, conforms almost perfectly with his dream-vision, as suggested by Spenser's allegory. However, when he approaches the threshold to look through the open doorway, his dream suddenly alters, as dreams tend to do. What he sees is a "lonely girl, sewing at a lonely window," who "shyly started" at his presence, "like some Tahiti girl, *secreted for a sacrifice*, first catching sight, through palms, of Captain Cook," a striking comparison that reveals more about the narrator's frame of reference as a former sailor with experience in Polynesia and knowledge of the exploits of Cook than it does about this "pale-cheeked girl" (8–9; my emphasis), with the narrator imagining himself in grandiose terms in the role of Cook, and poised to save her.

While the two of them have a silent exchange, his first thought is that the cottage is the "fairy-mountain house" he had imagined and this woman "the fairy queen, sitting at her fairy window"—whether she conforms to his conception or not. But when he moves to her window and looks down through the same pass he traveled to get there, he "caught sight of a far-off, soft, azure world," and suddenly exclaims to himself, "I hardly knew it, though I came from it" (9). This moment is the pivot on which this story turns, when social vision and perspective come together, namely, when the narrator discovers that a change in point of view alters everything, even for himself—just as he is about to discover that this woman, whom he had imagined as an incarnation of Spenser's Una, is a sad and weary, lowly seamstress instead.[19] As the scales fall from his eyes regarding her real identity once she tells the story of how she and her orphan-brother came to be the "sole inhabitants of the sole house upon the mountain," he asks whether she finds the view of the far-off world he came from to be as "pleasant" as he finds it now from this new vantage point. And when she points to it, mistakenly referring to it as "that marble one," and asks whether he knows who lives there, he is surprised to recognize, in a moment that completes the story's symmetry, that it is "my own abode" she refers to, "glimmering much like this mountain one from the piazza." Though he is thoroughly familiar with his own modest dwelling up close, he soon understands that "The mirage haze [in the distance] made it appear less a farm-house than King Charming's palace," as it does to Marianna (9).

While the mountain girl thinks whoever lives there "must be some happy one," he reveals a new side of himself—a side that worries about money and knows he is not wealthy—when he asks whether she believes "some rich one lives there?" Dismissing the question of wealth ("Rich or not, I never thought"), she cannot explain why she assumes "it must be some happy one": "it looks so happy, I can't tell how; and it is so far away. Sometimes I think I do but dream it is there," and then adds, unconsciously highlighting the importance of atmosphere in any visual assessment of a scene, "You should see it in a sunset" (9–10). Finally, he begins to show he knows better, for he recognizes how the distant view softens and distorts, and how the sunlight casts a spell: "No doubt the sunset gilds it finely," he tells her, employing a trope Melville had earlier employed in "The Gilder" chapter of *Moby-Dick*, "but not more than the sunrise does this house, perhaps," when looked at from afar, as he had often done (10). Knowing only the close-up view of her own house, she cannot fathom how the sun could gild it: "Why should it?" she asks. "This old house is rotting. That makes it so mossy," and then she goes on to complain about the dirty, disagreeable details of the near view that make her life so dreary, monotonous, and unpleasant: the window that won't stay clean, "do what I may"; the sun that "nearly blinds me at my sewing" and sets "the flies and wasps astir"; the leaky roof; the blocked chimney (10). Even when she tries to shade herself from the sun with her apron, she finds the sunlight "fades it." She cannot imagine how it can "gild" her own house because, as the narrator tries to explain to her, at the point when "this roof is gilded most," she is inside, attending to her sewing.

Inside her cottage, like the people imprisoned in Plato's Cave, she can sense things beyond her immediate situation only as shadows, not as objects of substance. Repeatedly the narrator is struck by Marianna's capacity to sense movement outside her cottage even though her eyes remain fastened on her work. Soon, however, it dawns on him that she has been so steady at her work during her months on the mountain as to learn to measure the passing of a day by the shadows of the clouds, rocks, and trees that fall across her line of vision. One shaggy shadow in particular comes and goes with such regularity, and changes position so predictably with the movement of the midday clouds and sun, that the lonely girl regards it as a companion she calls "Tray," and acknowledges its return every afternoon when it enters the cottage and "lies down" by the door. While the narrator's surprise mounts with increasing evidence of her ability to see a doglike silhouette in the features of a fantastic rock outside the cabin, even to "his head, his face"—while all the time, as the narrator exclaims, "your eyes are on your work"—he is suddenly struck by the tragedy and pathos of her life, its emptiness, loneliness, and alienation from the natural world, working as she does in the equivalent of a cave, with only these moving shadows to mark the passage of time. With growing disbelief, he asks: "Have you, then, so long sat at this mountain-window, where but clouds and vapors pass, that, to you shadows are as things, though you speak of them as of phantoms; that, by familiar knowledge, working like a second sight, you can, without looking for them, tell just where they are, though as having mice-like feet, they creep about, and come and go; that, to you, these lifeless shadows are as living friends, who, though out of sight, are not out of mind, even in their faces—is it so?" (11).

In response to the narrator's incredulity, she reveals her situation to be even sadder than he had realized, for she has recently lost the "friendliest" of her "friends," the shadow of a birch, which had been struck by lightning and cut up by her brother for firewood. Without visitors or even songbirds to break the silence around her ("'Birds I seldom hear,' she says, 'boys, never'"), hers is an impoverished world of almost unimaginable emptiness and drudgery (11). In this moment, "The Piazza" turns from romance to realism, and from the narrator's personal story of illness and recovery to the story of Marianna—as much "a bit of wreck in the mid-Atlantic" as Bartleby the Scrivener (32). Even so, she proves more resilient than the scrivener, for Marianna is a survivor, like Hunilla in "The Encantadas" or the nameless women in "The Tartarus of Maids" who silently go about their routines in the icy paper mills of frozen New England. At the same time, "The Piazza" changes from an autobiographical tale to a story of the other—in this case, a poor, working-class woman who struggles to make a living in the lonely silence of the Berkshire mountains. What began as an introduction to *The Piazza Tales* and its author becomes instead a story in its own right, like "Bartleby," but with a distraught writer recovering from a painful illness instead of a self-absorbed lawyer as the narrator, and an impoverished provincial seamstress, rather than a Wall Street copyist, as its principal subject. It is one of Melville's simplest yet most hauntingly sympathetic portrayals of a female character in all his writings, one that helps to strike a balance with the many male characters featured elsewhere in *The Piazza Tales*.

The remainder of "The Piazza" focuses on the narrator's growing sympathy for this woman, who of course is not the "fairy-queen" of his dreams or even a "glad mountain-girl" (6) but a desperately poor and tragic figure, an example not of the "povertiresque" figures Melville satirized in *Pierre* or in "Poor Man's Pudding and Rich Man's Crumbs," who manage to be comfortable with their poverty, but of the real, abject poverty and suffering. In one respect, Marianna is like the narrator—she lives a life of confinement, but hers is a soul-crushing confinement in an isolated, dilapidated cottage where she does nothing "but dull woman's work—sitting, sitting, restless sitting," while only occasionally daydreaming about the "happy" one who lives in the house near the bottom of the mountain. Her portrait is a study in the pathos of the circumscribed life of the poorest of women—living alone, "knowing nothing, hearing nothing . . . never reading, seldom speaking, yet ever wakeful." Beyond the daily drudgery of her constant sewing, the combination of "this weariness and wakefulness together" has taken a toll on Marianna's mind as well, for as she explains to the narrator, "this is what gives me my strange thoughts—for so you call them." Hers is a life of extreme poverty, endless work, and loneliness with no relief except for the shadows that come and go during the day. Even the nights offer her no respite, for they are "Just like the day," she says. "Thinking, thinking—a wheel I cannot stop; pure want of sleep it is that turns it." And when the narrator suggests a possible cure, saying, "I have heard that, for this wakeful weariness, to say one's prayers, and then lay one's head upon a fresh hop pillow," it seems clear he is offering popular nostrums but also intimating his knowledge of their ineffectiveness, particularly for himself, as hinted in the story's final line when he reveals his nights are sleepless, too. When Marianna says she has tried both remedies without effect, he can only ask helplessly, "Is there no other cure, or charm?" thus suggesting his growing empathy and awareness that her hunger for relief is deeper than his own. In fact, while Marianna's suffering seems to be beyond remedy, he at least has the consolations of his piazza, his reading, and his storytelling. In the end, he can repair to his piazza during the daylight hours, when the "illusion" is "so complete," and be entertained and inspired by the rich, "magical," ever-changing scenery of Mount Greylock. At least in the light of day, he can forget the "weary face" of Marianna and dream of Charlemagne, his inspiring mountain. But at night, "when the curtain falls," there are no such illusions to distract him from the knowledge that "truth comes in with darkness"—the "truth" of the suffering and vulnerability of other people, of rural working women in particular, that are so much greater than his own. At night, when he is weary and cannot sleep, he can only pace his piazza, "haunted by Marianna's face, and many as real a story," while he waits for morning and the return of Mount Greylock and the light of day (11–12).

# 2

## "BARTLEBY, THE SCRIVENER"

### The Body (and Soul) in Pain

Midway through "Bartleby, the Scrivener," the lawyer-narrator comes to a pivotal insight about Bartleby when he concludes that the scrivener "was the victim of innate and incurable disorder. I might give alms to his body; but his body did not pain him; it was his soul that suffered, and his soul I could not reach."[1] Frustrated by his inability to command or cajole Bartleby into returning to his job, the lawyer claims to understand the needs of Bartleby's body but admits to his inability to fathom his "soul," particularly the soul of one so distant and uncommunicative as his "incurably forlorn" scrivener (11). In doing so, he defines the terms of the central conflict in the story between the lawyer and his copyist, and points to the basis of their difference, the difference between the body and the soul, and the needs that distinguish one from the other. At the same time, he all but confesses to his own limitations as a man without a soul or whose soul has never been awakened before. Not coincidentally, a decade earlier, Melville's contemporary Ralph Waldo Emerson provided an illuminating gloss on two very similar figures in "The Transcendentalist," his 1842 essay that Melville appears to have known firsthand and relied on in giving definition to the principal characters in his story. Emerson's essay, which contrasts the Materialist and the Transcendentalist or Idealist of that time on a wide range of topics, provides a useful starting point for addressing popular philosophical thinking about issues of embodiment in the middle decades of the nineteenth century, but in relation to "Bartleby," it has the added value of providing important clues to the behavior and thinking of the two main characters in Melville's story.[2]

While Melville probably did not own any of Emerson's essays himself until 1862, when he purchased and began annotating *Essays, First Series* and *Essays, Second Series*,[3] he reported to his friend Evert Duyckinck that he had "glanced at a book" of Emerson's "once in Putnam's store" and then "heard him lecture" in Boston during the winter of 1848–49.[4] But then a more promising connection occurred just a year or so later, in the late summer or early fall of 1850, when Melville visited the Hawthornes' home in Lenox. There, according to the testimony of Sophia Hawthorne, while waiting to see her husband make his appearance, Melville "shut himself into the boudoir & read Mr Emerson's Essays."[5] It seems likely these "Essays" included "The Transcendentalist," since Emerson, the previous September, had sent Hawthorne a presentation copy of *Nature, Addresses, and Lectures* (1849), where the "The Transcendentalist" appeared in America for the first time.[6]

There is no way to establish for sure that Melville had read "The Transcendentalist" before writing his story of Wall Street, but a comparison of the two suggests that he had, and that he had read it with interest and care, using Emerson's Idealist to give definition to his portrayal of the melancholy Bartleby and his Materialist to fill out his portrait of the practical-minded lawyer-narrator. The parallels are remarkable in both broad outline and detail; at several significant junctures, even the language is similar: "Unless the action is necessary, unless it is adequate, *I do not wish to* perform it. *I do not wish to* do one thing but once. I do not love routine. Once possessed of the principle, it is equally easy to make four or forty thousand applications of it" (my emphasis).[7] This is Emerson ventriloquizing for the radical Idealist (there is some distance, to be sure, between Emerson and the young misanthrope he is speaking for). "I would prefer not to" is Melville's memorable rendering of the Idealist's refusal to act in compliance with the routine demands of the Materialist's world—in this case, the world of law and finance on Wall Street. Possessed of the principle of copying legal documents, Bartleby does not wish to continue performing the mechanical, deadening work demanded by his employer. It is, as the lawyer himself admits, "a very dull, wearisome, and lethargic affair" (20).[8] Like Emerson's young Transcendentalists, Bartleby, too, is "striking work, and crying out for somewhat worthy to do" (99). On a practical level it may be necessary to engage in the world's work simply to support oneself and put bread on the table, but the world's work is so dull and wearisome it cannot begin to satisfy him; it is not adequate to fill the void of his potential. For him, it is better not to allow his ideal conception of himself to be compromised or contaminated by the demands of the body and the material world, even though it may mean he will physically waste away and die, as in fact he does in the end, curled up by a wall in the city's Tombs. For him, the trials of the body in the material world are similar to the trials experienced by Marianna in "The Piazza," namely, the demands of dull, routine work and "sitting, sitting, restless sitting" (12).

By contrast the lawyer, a bachelor who is comfortably ensconced in the "snug retreat" of his Wall Street law office and doing "a snug business among rich men's bonds and mortgages and title-deeds" (14), cannot sympathize with his scriveners who must engage in routine work nor is he capable of recognizing the higher needs of the soul. Like Emerson's Materialist, he, too, seems to feel "secure in the certainty of sensation, mocks at fine-spun theories, at star-gazers and dreamers, and believes that his life is solid, that he at least takes nothing for granted, but knows where he stands, and what he does" (94)—until, that is, Bartleby enters his law office and initiates an ongoing somatic trial of his patience and good will. Elaborating upon the differences between the Materialist and the Idealist, Emerson goes on to explain:

> As thinkers, mankind have ever divided into two sects, Materialists and Idealists; the first class founding on experience, the second on consciousness; the first class beginning to think from the data of the senses, the second class perceive the senses are not final, and say, the senses give us representations of things, but what are the things themselves, they cannot tell. The materialist insists on facts, on history, on the force of circumstances and the animal wants of man; the idealist on the power of Thought and of Will, on inspiration, on miracle, on individual culture. (93)[9]

It is significant that Melville's lawyer-narrator does not begin immediately by relating Bartleby's story but instead launches into his own story, incidentally depicting himself as a man who defines life in terms of "experience" and thinks from "the data of the senses." His own life, unexciting though it is, at least offers some concrete materials on which to begin. Initially, Melville seems to follow Emerson's caricatures of the Materialist and the Transcendentalist almost to a fault, but he does so to good effect. The fact that both are extreme examples of their respective "types" provides an important clue to the comedy of the story in the early scenes, when Bartleby starts to resist the lawyer's "reasonable" expectations for him to copy or compare legal documents, and the lawyer struggles futilely over what to do about it. The fact that both characters are extremes also provides a clue to Melville's comic genius as a storyteller, building his tale around such unusual examples of their respective types as to constitute distinctive and original characters.

The nature of the lawyer's avocations, he tells us, had brought him into "more than ordinary contact with what would seem an interesting and somewhat singular set of men, of whom as yet nothing that I know of has ever been written." As he goes on to explain, he has "known very many of them, professionally and privately, and if I pleased, could relate divers histories"—the kind, he observes, "at which good-natured gentlemen might smile, and sentimental souls might weep." But now that he has lived through the experiences he is about to relate and been moved by Bartleby's example, he realizes these "divers histories" of ordinary scriveners would hold little interest either for him as biographer or for the discerning readers he imagines himself to be writing for—readers who would want to learn something new and be moved beyond a superficial feeling of amusement or sentimentality.[10] Given the opportunity to tell even a fragmented tale of the most unusual example of a Wall Street copyist in his experience, he explains, "I waive the biographies of all other scriveners for a few passages in the life of Bartleby, who was a scrivener the strangest I ever saw or heard of" (13).

In fact, the story of Bartleby is little other than the record of his own experience and frustration with Bartleby, for he knows virtually nothing beyond his limited interactions with him, and is able to glean little more from the scrivener himself. "I believe that no materials exist for a full and satisfactory biography of this man," he admits. "What my own astonished eyes saw of Bartleby, *that* is all I know of him, except, indeed, one vague report" (13), a report he saves until the very end about the scrivener having once worked in the Dead Letter Office in Washington, a report he seems to believe might help to explain the scrivener's mysterious emotional state, if nothing more. So unusual, so beyond the norm is Bartleby, in terms of his behavior and what can be known about him, that, in comparison with other scriveners in the lawyer's experience, he is a true deviant—so much so as to be impossible to explain or pin down. It is his deviancy from the norm that makes him such a challenge to write about but also a subject worth the attempt. It is what begins to try not just the lawyer's patience and routine bodily expectations, but his soul. What is more, if Bartleby had simply fit the norm, there would be no compelling reason to write about him—and little or no reason for anyone to want to read about him either. It is in the nature of narrative that readers want to hear about the extraordinary case, not the ordinary one.[11]

By implication, the narrator, too, is a deviant example of his professional type, an exception to the rule of ambitious lawyers who live for the drama of the courtroom. In his case, however, we are provided a good deal more information about his material presence in the world than we are in the case of Bartleby. Unwittingly characterizing himself as a Materialist, one who has devoted his professional life almost exclusively to the accumulation of wealth and financial security, the lawyer is proud to state that the late John Jacob Astor—widely known as the richest man in America (and "the most hated man in New York"[12])—had pronounced "my first grand point to be prudence; my next, method," and then adds, "I do not speak it in vanity, but simply record the fact, that I was not unemployed in my profession by the late John Jacob Astor; a name which, I admit, I love to repeat; for it hath a rounded and orbicular sound to it, and rings like unto bullion." In addition to the lawyer's cautious self-interestedness, what is revealed here is his adulation of Astor's wealth and power, what Emerson called the Materialist's preoccupation with "the animal wants of man"—financial security, material comfort, and ease. In this regard, too, he is an extreme, a caricature of a certain kind of money-hungry lawyer, not exactly a Scrooge figure but still a caricature. His limited, practical-minded scale of values is further evidenced by his confession that he is "a man who, from his youth upwards, has been filled with a profound conviction that the easiest way of life is the best" and that, as a result,

"All who know me, consider me an eminently *safe* man." In a profession known "proverbially" for its nervous energy and "turbulence," he claims proudly that "nothing of that sort have I ever suffered to invade my peace." Indeed, he is so self-contained as to "seldom" lose his "temper" or "indulge in dangerous indignation at wrongs and outrages." Even when he feels wronged, as he does when the sinecure of his "good old office" of a Master in Chancery is unexpectedly terminated and he loses "a life-lease of the profits" from the position, he lacks the energy and righteous indignation to fight back or do anything to restore his former sinecure (14). Clearly he is a man who values his equanimity and will go to great lengths to prevent it from being challenged, tested, or tried—until, that is, Bartleby enters his "safe" world.

Though we know next to nothing about the lawyer's earlier life, he seems almost entirely a product of Wall Street society; indeed, aside from attending church on occasion and traveling between his workplace and home, he appears to have no identity or personal life beyond his office. He knows his own business interests and office routine but little else. As a consequence, he naturally expects the scrivener to do his job and conform to the role prescribed for him by the nature of his vocation and the institutional culture of Wall Street.[13] Perplexed by Bartleby's refusal to copy or compare documents, or eventually to perform any tasks at all, the lawyer admits that it was "exceeding difficult to bear in mind all the time those strange peculiarities, privileges, and unheard of exemptions, forming the tacit stipulations on Bartleby's part under which he remained in my office" (26). The lawyer is like the Materialist "grave seniors" described by Emerson who insist that everyone show respect to "this institution and that usage; to an obsolete history; to some vocation, or college, or etiquette, or beneficiary, or charity." And if anyone questions or fails to respect these institutions or usages, these "old guardians . . . have but one mood on the subject, namely, that Antony is very perverse" (103). Men like the lawyer want stability, predictability, not surprises or disturbances, not challenges to their authority or to their faith in order and system.

It is more difficult to draw out similarities between Melville's portrayal of Bartleby and Emerson's portrayal of the Transcendentalist because, being virtually speechless and impassive, the scrivener provides little from which to intuit his thinking or state of mind. Yet it is precisely in this trait that he matches the Transcendentalist most closely. "If you do not need to hear my thought," Emerson says, speaking for the Transcendentalist, "because you can read it in my face and behavior, then I will tell it you from sunrise to sunset. If you cannot divine it, you would not understand what I say. I will not molest myself for you. *I do not wish to* be profaned" (99; my emphasis). Bartleby suggests a similar line of reasoning throughout the narrative but especially at the point when, having refused to verify copies, he finally loses patience with the lawyer's demands to explain himself: "'Do you not see the reason for yourself,' he indifferently replied"—a rhetorical (if also accusatory) question that elicits no response from his dumbfounded employer (32). For Bartleby, the bodily trial seems to be whether he can passively resist the lawyer's expectations to the point where the lawyer will see for himself why the scrivener acts as he does and make adjustments in his expectations accordingly. Bartleby's own bodily test is simply to do nothing but wait and hope the lawyer will change his behavior on his own without prompting.

Bartleby, of course, is not absolutely passive. He does act and speak, if only to resist or deny. "At first," the lawyer reports with a sense of wonderment, "Bartleby did an extraordinary quantity of writing," as though he was "long famishing for something to copy." But then, he notes with some alarm, he was anything but "cheerfully industrious" about it. Instead, "he wrote on silently, palely, mechanically" (like the "pallid girls" who mechanically attend to the machines in the paper mill in Melville's "The Tartarus of Maids" [1855]). By the third day, however, he announces to the lawyer that he would "prefer not to" examine a "small paper" with him, thus beginning a pattern of bodily resistance to doing the work he was hired to do (19–20). In this, too, he resembles the Transcendentalists, who, as Emerson says, "complain that everything around them must be denied" and whose "strength and spirits," consequently, "are wasted in rejection" (103). Emerson's essay is further instructive about the pattern of the scrivener's rejections. As he explains, the young Idealist "does not respect labor, or the products of labor, namely property, otherwise than as a manifold symbol." Neither does he respect government; "nor the church; nor charities; nor arts, for themselves," because he "reckons the world an appearance." He refuses to be tried by the demands of such institutions through the simple act of refusing to acknowledge their validity or their implicit claims on him. "His thought,—that is the Universe" (94–95). Although we cannot know whether Bartleby's logic is precisely the same, his eventual refusal to copy anything makes it evident that he, too, does not "respect labor." Like the young Transcendentalists, he is "striking work," and seems to be "crying out for somewhat worthy to do!" (98), a statement that seems a likely explanation for what might be on Bartleby's mind when he decides to stop copying. Neither does Bartleby respect "the products of labor"—not even when they would benefit himself, as when he declines the wages the lawyer offers to him or even a twenty-dollar gift. Furthermore, Bartleby's failure to respect the lawyer's title to the law office when he takes up residence there is cause for considerable indignation on the part of his employer, suggesting still another basis for their conflicting values or convictions, one based on property rights and contract agreements: "What earthly right have you to stay here?" the lawyer demands, when he finds the scrivener occupying his offices outside work hours a second time. "Do you pay any rent? Do you pay my taxes? Or is this property yours?" (35). Here the lawyer's rhetoric takes on a new edge, testifying to the fact that he feels himself to be so emotionally tested on the matter of property rights that he is for once aroused to push back against Bartleby's maddeningly presumptuous behavior. More than anything, the lawyer is wedded to the materialist principles of property ownership and capital exchange, principles on which the operations of America's commercial culture depend. But clearly they have no meaning for Bartleby, who remains unfazed by the lawyer's rare attempt to push back and test the scrivener's mysterious independence.

Of course the lawyer has no clue about Bartleby's puzzling mind-set, however defined. To him, he is simply an enigma. And yet, he feels compelled to tell his story, because Bartleby's story is, finally, the inspiration for his own, the story about how the scrivener has tested the lawyer, tried him, turned him around, and *almost* changed his life. Initially, the lawyer is quite indifferent to his new copyist and treats him as he treats his other employees—with a little psychology, a little tolerance, and an occasional show of indifference, as long as he and the others manage to complete their work as needed. He is willing to accommodate all his scriveners' strange preferences and eccentricities, but in return he expects them to perform their assigned tasks. He acknowledges his employees to be human, with needs and idiosyncrasies of their own, but he does not want to get involved in their personal lives and does not bother even to ask about their lives outside the office. He is simply not interested, unless it relates to his business. He worries that Turkey, the first of his copyists, wore clothes that were "apt to look oily, and smell of eating-houses," not because there is anything wrong with that, but because he fears his odious appearance will be "a reproach" to the lawyer himself among his clients, and he shows frustration with the shady, presumably extralegal dealings of Nippers, his other long-time copyist, but is willing to put up with these, too, because he "was a very useful man to me; wrote a neat, swift hand; and, when he chose, was not deficient in a gentlemanly sort of deportment" (17). He keeps his eye on business, and makes decisions based on the bottom line, not on whether he cares for them or feels any responsibility for them as fellow humans. Surprisingly, he will put up with their deficiencies even though he cannot manage to get more than half a day's work out of either of them. Turkey regularly drinks enough beer or wine at lunch to cause him to be careless and make mistakes in the afternoon, while Nippers suffers from indigestion after breakfast, prompting him to spend the morning adjusting his chair and desk in a constant state of irritability. Making a virtue of necessity, but also revealing how far he will go to avoid confrontation, the lawyer consoles himself with the convenient excuse that "I never had to do with their eccentricities at one time. Their fits relieved each other like guards. When Nippers' was on, Turkey's was off; and *vice versa*" (18). As a consequence, he makes no effort to replace either of them or attempt to change their dysfunctional, on-again, off-again behavior.

What is evident from the examples of Turkey and Nippers, yet all but missed by the accommodating lawyer, is just how miserable all of his scriveners are and what bodily trials their routine work poses for each of them. But their examples go a long way toward explaining for the reader the mystery of what ails Bartleby and why he stops performing his job. Pushed to the extremes demanded in a Wall Street law office, copying eventually begins to feel like a physical trial, even a form of torture, for these men—tolerable perhaps for a while but at some point, it becomes impossible to tolerate any longer. It is not that the work itself is torturous but the repetitive, protracted nature of it, with the result that eventually the copyist's fingers and hand, even a whole arm, can grow numb from constantly exercising the same muscles; and when his back has to remain in a single, fixed position, seated or standing, for hours at a time, it can become physically painful, even excruciatingly so. It is not a coincidence that a standard form of torture, in military or political interrogations, is to require the victim to sit or stand in a fixed position and remain perfectly motionless under the threat of torture or until instructed to do otherwise. As Elaine Scarry has written, in *The Body in Pain: The Making and Unmaking of the World* (1985), "Standing rigidly for eleven hours can produce as violent muscle and spine pain as can injury from elaborate equipment and apparatus, though any of us outside this situation, used to adjusting our body positions every few moments before even mild discomfort is felt, may not immediately recognize this."[14] Under even less demanding conditions than those described by Scarry, the comic reactions and adjustments of the lawyer's copyists to their forced immobility and the rigid requirements of their office routine cease to be comic and become grotesque.[15]

Without explicitly saying so, Melville suggests the reason "Turkey's money went chiefly for red ink" at lunchtime is that he cannot stand to do his job for more than a few hours at a time without seeking some kind of relief (17). He medicates himself at his midday meal in an effort to tolerate his work as a copyist but always ends up making a mess of it in the afternoon. More tellingly, the example of Nippers suggests the body will naturally resist this kind of work because it cannot maintain a comfortable position for long. The naive lawyer believes it is "indigestion" that is responsible for Nippers's "nervous testiness and grinning irritability" in the morning, "causing the teeth to audibly grind together over mistakes committed in copying," not to mention the hissed "maledictions" over his "continual discontent with the height of the table where he worked," to the point where he "would sometimes impatiently . . . seize the whole desk, and move it, and jerk it, with a grim, grinding motion on the floor, as if the table were a perverse voluntary agent, intent on thwarting and vexing him" (16–18). Indeed, the many symptoms of Nippers's bodily trials and resistance to his work, so elaborately detailed in this scene, suggest that Melville himself, as a writer who spent long hours confined to his writing desk every day, may have felt firsthand some of the same painful effects from constant writing and copying, and the body's reflexive resistance to such an unnatural regimen:

> Though of a very ingenious mechanical turn, Nippers could never get this table to suit him. He put chips under it, blocks of various sorts, bits of pasteboard, and at last went so far as to attempt an exquisite adjustment by final pieces of folded blotting-paper. But no intervention would answer. If, for the sake of easing his back, he brought the table lid at a sharp angle well up towards his chin, and wrote there like a man using the steep roof of a Dutch house for his desk:—then he declared that it stopped the circulation in his arms. If now he lowered the table to his waistbands, and stooped over it in writing, then there was a sore aching in his back. In short, the truth of the matter was, Nippers knew not what he wanted. Or, if he wanted anything, it was to be rid of a scrivener's table altogether. (16–17)

Adding to the physical and emotional discomfort of the lawyer's employees is the confining, prisonlike atmosphere of his Wall Street office, with its folding screens and closeup views of a wall inside "a spacious skylight shaft" at one end—so "tame," the lawyer admits in one of his characteristic understatements, as to be "deficient in what landscape painters call 'life'—" and on the other end of his chambers, outside the windows but surrounded by much taller buildings, "an unobstructed view of a lofty brick wall, black by age and everlasting shade," creating the effect of inhabiting "a huge square cistern" (14). A narrowly confined environment like this, with no direct sunlight and windows opening onto blank walls, can hardly be said to extend the body or its pleasures out into the world, as lively modern offices are designed to do, but instead to frustrate and shut down the senses and any feeling of engagement with the wider world.[16] The "walls" in Melville's story seem designed to harness the energies of the body in the service of labor and to restrict or limit consciousness to the immediate environment rather than allow it to expand—in order to keep it focused on the tasks at hand and prevent it from being distracted or stimulated by the world outside, as Marianna, the seamstress in "The Piazza," learns to do through sheer effort of will in her mountain cottage while diligently sewing day after day. These walls constitute a form of imprisonment, and eventually contribute to bodily suffering as well in that they constrict the sources of pleasure to the vanishing point for all three copyists (though they do find small pleasure or relief in the ginger-nuts and Spitzenberg cakes supplied by the office boy, Ginger Nut)—especially for Bartleby, who not only works there but eventually resides there as well. It is the exact opposite of the piazza setting in Melville's opening story, "The Piazza," where the narrator can sometimes forget the pain of his debilitating earache by casting his eye and imagination out of doors and into the mountains around Greylock.

The lawyer, however, remains largely insensitive to the needs of his employees and the harmful conditions in which they must perform their tasks. While he can imagine that "to some sanguine temperaments," the job of comparing legal documents "would be altogether intolerable," he has always found his employees to be more or less compliant, so he naturally expects Bartleby to behave in much the same way (20). Consequently, when Bartleby suddenly declines his request to check copies, saying simply, "I prefer not to," he cannot believe his ears. At first, he attempts to "reason" with him by appealing to "common usage" and his presumed understanding of what is expected in a professionally run business office. "Every copyist is bound to help examine his copy. Is it not so?" he asks rhetorically, expecting the only response he can imagine (22).[17] The radical disconnect between the two is the source of much of the comedy in the story, but, in the end, it is also the source of its tragedy. Because Bartleby refuses to open up, the lawyer is left to try to make sense of his enigmatic employee and puzzle out, on his own, what he is feeling or thinking. While the lawyer is struck by the fact that Bartleby evinces not the least "uneasiness, anger, impatience or impertinence" in rejecting his request to examine even a brief paper with him (a sign the scrivener is passing his own bodily test of maintaining equanimity while refusing to engage with the lawyer's test to perform like a good employee), the lawyer experiences a momentary full stop when he senses the absence of "any thing ordinarily human about him"—an uncanny feeling that serves to explain why he does not "violently dismiss him from the premises," as he claims he would otherwise expect himself to do. Pressed to meet a deadline on the work at hand, the lawyer tries to put Bartleby's strange behavior out of his mind and calls on Nippers to complete the job instead. But the next time he calls on him and is rebuffed again, he feels "not only strangely disarmed" but, "in a wonderful manner, touched and disconcerted" by him, too (21). The scrivener's passive testing of his employer, at this point, is starting to have an effect. The admission that he is "touched" by the scrivener is important—from all we know, it may be the first time this "rather elderly" bachelor has ever felt something like sympathy for a fellow human (13). But his reaction is no more important than the fact that he is "disconcerted" by him, for the latter feeling signals his awakening to a mystery beyond himself and the possibility that all of his strictly materialist thinking, up to this point in his life, has been built on faulty premises and false principles. For a moment, he begins "to stagger in his own plainest faith" and "vaguely to surmise that, wonderful as it may be, all the justice and all the reason is on the other side." Still, he quickly resists that thought and instead looks "for some reinforcement of his own faltering mind" among his other employees, something they are more than eager to supply, since they are jealous of Bartleby's special privileges and upset about the resulting increase in their own workload (22).

For a while the lawyer continues to go back and forth, sometimes forgetting and asking the scrivener to perform his usual tasks, sometimes letting him alone, and sometimes—"goaded on to encounter him in new opposition"—perversely imagining new tests or trials that might elicit "some angry spark" from Bartleby (24). On occasion, too, in an effort to understand the enigmatic scrivener's "late remarkable conduct," he takes the time to observe his behavior more "narrowly," only to learn that "he never went to dinner; indeed that he never went anywhere," and appeared to eat nothing but ginger-nuts. Only at this point does he step outside of himself long enough to recognize how little the scrivener demands of his body and how slight and tenuous his hold on the material world appears to be. Here, then, as he grows more curious about Bartleby's behavior, he moves even further outside of himself and experiences a growing sympathy. At the same time, he also begins to look more closely at his own behavior, and to explore how he might adjust his thinking about Bartleby, or, as he says, "endeavor charitably to construe to his imagination what proves impossible to be solved by his judgment" (23). And so, for a second time, he opens up a little more and responds to the scrivener with a combination of sympathy and pragmatism: "Poor fellow! thought I, he means no mischief; it is plain he intends no insolence; his aspect sufficiently evinces that his eccentricities are involuntary. He is useful to me. I can get along with him. If I turn him away, the chances are he will fall in with some less-indulgent employer, and then he will be rudely treated, and perhaps driven forth miserably to starve" (23).

And then, turning back to look inside himself again, he backslides when he concludes it would be a boon to his own self-interested moral consciousness to allow Bartleby to stay, in spite of his quirks: "Yes," he confesses. "Here I can cheaply purchase a delicious self-approval. To befriend Bartleby; to humor him in his strange willfulness, will cost me little or nothing, while I lay up in my soul what will eventually prove a sweet morsel for my conscience" (23–24). Such a sentiment on the part of the lawyer is hardly distinguishable from pure self-interest at this point, but it does reveal his recognition of the scrivener's suffering and a willingness to accommodate him—even though he is far from understanding or appreciating the reasons for what he refers to as Bartleby's "willfulness."

Several critics in recent years have revisited the longstanding question in Melville criticism concerning the limits of the lawyer's moral sense and the related question of his capacity for sympathy for Bartleby. For David Kuebrich, for example, writing in "Melville's Doctrine of Assumptions: The Hidden Ideology of Capitalist Production in 'Bartleby,'" the "central issue in 'Bartleby' is . . . what it is that makes the lawyer unable to understand Bartleby and respond with compassion." For Nancy D. Goldfarb, in "Charity as Purchase: Buying Self-Approval in Melville's 'Bartleby, the Scrivener,'" the narrator uses "the rhetoric of charity" to "subordinate his guilt over Bartleby's sad story" and turn it into "a self-promoting narrative in which he anticipates and deflects potential criticism" of his own behavior.[18] What these discussions all of which tend to be critical of the lawyer—share is a simple, absolutist construction of the lawyer's moral sense, according to which if it is not engaged and functioning according to the highest standard of selflessly charitable behavior, then it must be regarded as being forever tainted by self-interest. There is no acknowledgment of a mixed or messy in-between stage, and little recognition of a moral awakening or growth on the part of the lawyer as he reaches out more and more in an effort to find some way to come to Bartleby's aid. Instead, I think Andrew Delbanco is closer to the truth of the matter when he observes matter-of-factly that the lawyer is "a good man trying to become a better man"[19]—particularly once his moral sense begins to come to life (though we might differ as to just how "good" the lawyer is in the beginning). Critics who condemn the lawyer tend not to recognize that his moral awakening and growing sympathy for Bartleby is a *protracted process* consisting of several stages in the middle scenes of the story, a process that grows by fits and starts but is never quite finished or complete.[20] Nor is there much if any acknowledgment that this protracted process constitutes the bulk of Melville's story. Every time the lawyer takes a step or two forward, he inevitably takes another step back before recovering his forward momentum again. In addition, these critics tend not to recognize that, as the lawyer reaches out more and more earnestly to Bartleby, the scrivener continues to pull away and resist his efforts to help him. Contrary to Sheila Post-Lauria's reading of the story, I believe it is this inverse dynamic between the lawyer and the scrivener that keeps the moral awakening of the lawyer or his coming into sympathy for Bartleby from being sentimental. What Melville does in this story is to turn the conventional notion of the "power of sympathy" on its head and concentrate instead on the limits of that power. As far as Bartleby himself is concerned, the lawyer's sympathetic efforts to help him are a failure; Bartleby refuses to allow them to have any effect on him. For all practical purposes, those intentions are a failure for Bartleby, and that failure keeps the story from becoming sentimental. It is also what makes the story tragic, for Bartleby and for the lawyer as well. Slowly, slowly, the lawyer comes to feel the stirrings of human sympathy for this strange young man—and beyond that a growing longing to know more about what ails him. When he finally runs out of alternative solutions and invites him to come home with him, he is faced with the recognition that he must care for him even if he cannot alleviate his suffering. By taking this step, he is at least trying to extend himself for Bartleby's benefit. His later, limited efforts to come to his aid after the scrivener has been imprisoned in the Tombs reveal that he continues to try to do what he can to reduce his suffering, but given that Bartleby has pretty much given up at this point and withdraws even further from his former employer, the lawyer's opportunities to help him have been reduced almost to the vanishing point.

It is hard to feel another person's pain. It is also hard to express one's own pain—hard because pain is "inexpressible," to use Scarry's term; it cannot be put into words. Setting aside, for the moment, the question of whether Bartleby (or the lawyer) experiences "physical pain" as opposed to emotional or psychological pain (there is growing evidence supporting the conclusion that they are closely related if not indistinguishable),[21] the problem at the center of Melville's story is that pain cannot be shared. The lawyer can see that the scrivener is suffering, but Bartleby cannot put his pain into words. All he can say when asked to do or say something is to voice his preferences or say what he prefers not to do. Scarry explains:

> [W]hen one speaks about 'one's own physical pain' and about 'another person's physical pain,' one might almost appear to be speaking about two wholly distinct orders of events. For the person whose pain it is, it is 'effortlessly' grasped . . . while for the person outside the sufferer's body, what is 'effortless' is not grasping it. . . . So, for the person in pain, so incontestably and unnegotiably present is it that 'having pain' may come to be thought of as the most vibrant example of what it is to 'have certainty,' while for the other person it is so elusive that 'hearing about pain' may exist as the primary model of what it is 'to have doubt.' Thus pain comes unsharably into our midst as at once that which cannot be denied and that which cannot be confirmed.[22]

No wonder the scrivener proves to be such an enigma. In Melville's version of this dynamic (a dynamic that Scarry argues is absolute and universal), Bartleby is the one who experiences pain and acts out of absolute certainty, while the lawyer is the one who senses or "hears about pain," but finds it so incomprehensible when voiced by this strange other as not to know what it is. Only at the end, when he learns that the landlord has arranged to have Bartleby "removed to the Tombs as a vagrant," does the lawyer's own pain, his growing sense of his own ineffectuality as he tries but fails to help Bartleby, become evident. By that time, his guilty suffering prompts him not only to agree to appear at the Halls of Justice to "make a suitable statement of the facts" in the case, as his landlord has requested, but to "beg" for an interview with the scrivener, to try to mitigate his circumstances somehow, and reach out in human sympathy. However, by the time of their final encounter, all the lawyer can do is to pay the grub-man at the Tombs to provide Bartleby with "the best dinner you can get" and urge him to be "as polite to him as possible" (43). Even these modest efforts at assistance and reconciliation are to no avail, however, because Bartleby has withdrawn so far as to be dead to his employer's entreaties, and eventually to the world.

The reason pain is "unsharable," Scarry postulates, is that it so thoroughly and effectively resists "objectification in language." Indeed, pain's *"resistance to language ... is essential to what it is. ...* Physical pain—unlike any other state of consciousness—has no referential content. It is not of or for anything" (5; my emphasis).[23] When Bartleby utters his iconic line, "I would prefer not to," in response to any number of requests and inquiries of the lawyer's, he is not being evasive or "smart" but revealing the limits of language, its inability to capture a painful feeling or longing that has no name—an existential longing or, to return to Emerson, an unfulfilled Idealist's longing for something more in life, something better than what the world is capable of offering its young.

Confronted with the mystery of his employee's pain, the lawyer is inspired to put into words his experience of the man. However, to do so, he must invent a linguistic structure that can capture an "area of experience normally so inaccessible to language," a linguistic structure known as a story or a biography, but one that, given the deviancy of the scrivener's example and the profound inaccessibility of his inner life, turns out to be more the lawyer's story than it is Bartleby's. Certainly the lawyer's story is the more revealing of the two. Scarry argues that "the human attempt to reverse the de-objectifying work of pain by forcing pain itself into avenues of objectification is a project laden with practical and ethical consequence." This, she argues, can be seen to be the case in the work of medical doctors, lawyers, and activist artists (as well as organizations like

Amnesty International that deal with extreme forms of politically inspired torture), people "who are not themselves in pain" but who take it upon themselves to testify or "speak on behalf of those who are," as the lawyer attempts to testify on behalf of his employee when he sits down to write the scrivener's biography. The lawyer's story of Bartleby might be said, similarly, to attempt to "record the passage of pain into speech" and therefore "enter into a realm of shared discourse that is wider, more social" than the lawyer is accustomed to do in his everyday business relations or in his life generally.[24] However, his task is more challenging and profound than to represent Bartleby's personality or "biography"; his unstated task is to "advocate" for him, not in a court of law but in the public forum of belles lettres, and represent his employee's unexpressed and inexpressible pain to an audience of readers who have never encountered such a thing before.

Why would the lawyer want to do so? Scarry provides one suggestion when she posits that, in the practice of lawyers and doctors and other health-care professionals, there is a strong correlation "between expressing pain and eliminating pain."[25] Perhaps there is something similar to be gained in this case, the expression of a pain that might lead to its elimination (or diminution) for others, if not for Bartleby. Bartleby, of course, dies—apparently of natural causes brought on by an extreme form of disappointment, apathy, or will-lessness that is the result of his pain—even before the lawyer sees fit to write his story. Nothing the lawyer does can change that or help his former employee in any way. Is it possible he sees himself as performing a social service, revealing to his readers the mindlessly mechanical work of Wall Street scriveners and the dreadful conditions under which they must perform their jobs—thus increasing the sympathy and awareness of his readers about their plight? Perhaps that is one motive (and, if so, it would be a further sign that Bartleby's presumed unhappiness and lack of enthusiasm for his job has finally gotten under the lawyer's skin or affected him personally), but I do not see much evidence to support such a reading. On the other hand, this may be one of Melville's motives in writing the story, as has been suggested by Louise K. Barnett, in "Bartleby as Alienated Worker" (1974), and several later commentators,[26] but it is hard to see this as the lawyer's principal motive in attempting to tell Bartleby's story.

Instead, what seems more evident is that his motive in telling Bartleby's story is to make a confession—first of all, a confession of his having ultimately failed Bartleby, despite his efforts to reach out to him in the scrivener's last days, both before he entered the Tombs and afterward, but also a confession of his having barely escaped—and only in his later years at that—the limited, "dead-end" life of an aging materialist, by finally opening up to another person and showing some concern for him in his time of need, above and beyond whatever the lawyer's own selfish, personal guilt might have prompted him to do. In the end, the lawyer has succeeded only slightly in making Bartleby visible or sensible to us. But seemingly without trying, he has been more successful at making *himself* visible—himself and a different sort of pain defined by his growing awareness of his longing to do something for his employee, *to connect in human sympathy*—even as Bartleby withdraws more and more, to the point where he becomes *almost* but not quite a "dead letter" for the lawyer—a man who, in effect if not by intention, came to him on an "errand of life" but ended up "speed[ing] to death" instead (45). Put simply, the lawyer's story is a quiet confession of a modest personal triumph but also of deep and lasting regret. It is a confession, an admission of the discovery of his own previously unrecognized and unacknowledged human pain, by a man whose life, before Bartleby, had been an emotional void.

The lawyer's transformation into a man of sympathetic feeling is a slow and protracted process, with several stops along the way—a process that is still in the early stages when he goes to visit Bartleby at the Tombs for the last time and discovers him curled up against a wall in a fetal position that suggests a return to the womb. The fact that Melville devotes much of the second half of the story to detailing the slow evolution in the lawyer's sympathy and care for Bartleby seems a strong indication of how important it was for him to dramatize this change in the lawyer. At the same time Melville seems determined to underplay the potential sentimentality of the situation by having the scrivener share responsibility for the failure of the lawyer's efforts to reach out to him by continuing to resist those efforts and pull away more and more despite the lawyer's efforts.[27] After the early comic scenes of his burning "to be rebelled against" and his hollow promise to exact "some terrible retribution" for the scrivener's recalcitrance, the lawyer starts to accommodate Bartleby's eccentricities more and more and adjust his own behavior, also comically, rather than insist on his compliance with heretofore "perfectly reasonable" requests to perform the duties expected of scriveners, or threaten to throw him out on the street (24–25). When he becomes upset with Bartleby's passive resistance, he puts off a confrontation and retreats to his home where he can enjoy his dinner alone. And with Bartleby's every repulse of his requests, he admits to being less and less likely to repeat the "inadvertence." When one Sunday morning, on his way to Trinity Church (for the rather worldly purpose of hearing "a celebrated preacher"), he happens to discover Bartleby in his offices keeping "bachelor hall," he is shocked to find him there, and chagrined to think he permitted "his hired clerk to dictate to him, and order him away from his own premises," until the scrivener had time to dress properly to receive visitors (26–27).

This moment, however, also constitutes an important turning point in the emotional development of the lawyer when he suddenly senses "what miserable friendlessness and loneliness are here revealed! His poverty is great," he thinks to himself; "but his solitude, how horrible. Think of it. Of a Sunday, Wall Street is deserted as Petra; and every night of every day it is an emptiness. . . . And here Bartleby makes his home." Only then does he confess, "For the first time in my life a feeling of over-powering stinging melancholy seized me. Before, I had never experienced aught but a not unpleasing sadness. The bond of a common humanity now drew me irresistibly to gloom. A fraternal melancholy! For both I and Bartleby were sons of Adam" (27–28), a discovery that resembles the discovery Melville's narrator makes in "The Piazza," when he comes upon the poor seamstress Marianna in her mountain cottage. When the lawyer finds his melancholy feeling turn to fear and his pity to repulsion, however, he has reached the point of thinking Bartleby is beyond help, "the victim of innate and incurable disorder," and concludes helplessly, "I might give alms to his body; but his body did not pain him; it was his soul that suffered, and his soul I could not reach" (29).[28]

Spooked by this latest discovery of fear and repulsion in himself, he resolves to get rid of Bartleby by paying him his salary and an extra twenty dollars, and then let him go, while also offering to help defray his expenses "if he desired to return to his native place, wherever that might be," or otherwise assist him at some future time of need (29). Still, Bartleby refuses to leave, and then stops copying altogether. But when the lawyer's professional friends begin to gossip and make "unsolicited and uncharitable remarks" about the silent man who haunts his chambers, the lawyer decides that he himself must be the one to move if he is to salvage his "professional reputation" (37–38). However, when Bartleby refuses to leave the lawyer's former offices, the landlord threatens to make the lawyer responsible for the fact that now other "clients are leaving the offices," too, because of the scrivener's ghostly presence in the building is spooking their clients. Fearful "of being exposed in the papers," the lawyer makes one last effort to convince Bartleby to leave, first by trying to interest him in other kinds of employment and, then, in what seems a bona fide (if still partially self-interested) gesture of good will, by offering to have him come home with him. Nothing comes of either effort, except for Bartleby's simple pronouncement: "No: at present I would prefer not to make any change at all" (39–41). The lawyer, obviously agitated by the scrivener's resistance but feeling helpless, answers nothing, then rushes from the building, and "jumping into the first omnibus was soon removed from pursuit" by the landlord or any of the building's exasperated tenants. Once a feeling of "tranquility returned" to him, he confesses, "I distinctly perceived that I had now done all that I possibly could, both in respect to the demands of the landlord and his tenants, and with regard to my desire and sense of duty, to benefit Bartleby, and shield him from rude persecution," adding that although he tried to be "entirely care-free and quiescent," and his conscience "justified" him in doing so, "it was not so successful as I could have wished." Still highly agitated, he turns over his business temporarily to Nippers and attempts to forget about Bartleby as well as the landlord and his angry tenants by driving around the city and into New Jersey, to the point where, he confesses, "I almost lived in my rockaway for a time" (42).

When he finally returns to his office, the lawyer learns that the landlord has petitioned the police, and "had Bartleby removed to the Tombs as a vagrant," but also that the landlord expected the lawyer to appear there "and make a suitable statement of the facts," a request that has "a conflicting effect" upon him, leaving him at first indignant but then approving of the landlord's decisive action, an action, he concludes weakly, that seems "the only plan" (42). That same day, the lawyer does pretty much as requested: he goes to the Tombs, or Halls of Justice, to provide a character reference for Bartleby and then asks for "as indulgent confinement as possible," until "something less harsh," such as sending him to the poorhouse, might be decided upon. When he tries to talk with Bartleby, the scrivener acknowledges him but, "without looking round," tells him matter-of-factly, "I want nothing to say to you." "Keenly pained at his implied suspicion" of the lawyer's role in bringing him to the Tombs, he tries to absolve himself of any involvement in the decision and at the same time attempts to mollify Bartleby by observing to him that "Nothing reproachful attaches to you by being here," and then adds desperately, "And see, it is not so sad a place as one might think. Look, there is the sky, and here is the grass," a minimalist landscape as lacking in vitality, interest, and inspiration as the lawyer's Wall Street offices. When the scrivener responds coldly, "I know where I am," the lawyer concludes there is nothing more to say or do, so, with a heavy heart, he leaves, but not before engaging with the prison's grub-man to supply the scrivener with "the best dinner you can get" (42–43).

Although this penultimate scene has a whiff of betrayal about it, the suggested parallel with the story of Judas Iscariot and his betrayal of Jesus for thirty pieces of silver breaks down when we see the lawyer return to the Tombs "some few days after" to check on the scrivener once again (44).[29] Clearly the lawyer does not attempt to brush him off or forget about him; he continues to show feeling for him and a painful longing to do something to care for him (still possibly, at least in part, out of guilt). But that he is a man changed, that he carries the melancholy pain of longing for some connection with this "odd," "silent" man is attested to by his need to tell his story, and in doing so to tell the story of his own soul's awakening to the desire to come to this young man's aid, even though the lawyer's efforts came to nothing. Even if Bartleby did not intend to have a transformative effect on the lawyer when he answered his ad for a copyist, the lawyer sees him to be—indeed all but calls him—a kind of "dead letter" who, even though he may not have intended to come to him on an "errand of life," has nonetheless had that effect on him. Clearly, the lawyer takes some sad pleasure in this thought, contrived and self-serving though it may be.

If the lawyer's story ends in a new state of consciousness marked by painful, open-ended longing, Bartleby's story ends in continued resistance masquerading as apathy or anhedonia. What is the cause of the attitude that has led Bartleby to give up on living once he finds himself in the Tombs? It is impossible to know exactly, as with so much else about the scrivener, but his parallels with the young Idealists described by Emerson are compelling, especially where Emerson says, "life and their faculty seem to them gifts too rich to be squandered on such trifles as you propose to them" (100). Like them, "His strength and spirits are wasted in rejection" (103), not because he can take no pleasure in the things of the world but because he finds them inadequate or unequal to his potential or the transcendent sort of satisfying activity he can imagine for himself. He is not sick or disabled, physically or psychologically, but dissatisfied with the options his life and culture have to offer him. What we see, from the moment he first says, "I would prefer not to," is a very demanding young man with outsize appetites but no adequate means to satisfy them in the world as constituted. It is because his appetites, his hungers, are so extraordinary, so otherworldly or transcendental, that, in the end, he is someone who "lives without dining," as the lawyer claims in response to the grub-man. It is also why the scrivener in the end sleeps, as the lawyer says, "With kings and counsellors" (45)—like Emerson's young Transcendentalist "martyrs" (102).[30]

# 3

## "CASTING A SHADOW"

### Representing Race and Trauma in "Benito Cereno"

In an April 1855 letter to the publisher of *Putnam's Monthly*, George W. Curtis, its literary advisor, who had read the manuscript version of "Benito Cereno," observed that "Melville's story is very good," but then added: "It is a great pity he did not work it up as a connected tale instead of putting in the dreary documents at the end.—They should have made part of the substance of the story. It is a little spun out,—but it is very striking & well done."[1] Presumably Curtis did not know Melville had borrowed the storyline, along with the court documents, from a historical source, Amasa Delano's *A Narrative of Voyages and Travels, in the Northern and Southern Hemispheres* (1817), and simply failed to appreciate the rhetorical and emotional effect of including a version of the court documents at the end of Melville's own narrative. But there are good reasons for composing the story as Melville did, rather than in the more straightforward way Curtis would have preferred. On one level, the court documents maintain the historical realism of the narrative structure found in Delano's original. On another level, the court documents, in their support of slavery and the racism and racial superiority of Benito Cereno and his crew, provide a larger cultural and legal counterpoint—an official but ironic one (akin to the "authorized" account of the confrontation between Billy and Claggart reported in the naval chronicle in *Billy Budd, Sailor*)—to Melville's subversive inside story of racial animosity and the horrors and traumas of the slave trade.

Even more importantly, placing the court documents near the end permits the reader to experience the same sort of suspenseful buildup of events that Captain Delano was witness to without understanding the true state of affairs on the *San Dominick,* where the formerly enslaved Africans are in control of the ship. Presumably this is what Melville was referring to when, at the start of the final scene where Cereno and Delano are brought together one last time, he interjected that "the Deposition" is intended to serve "as the key to fit into the lock of the complications which precede it" (114). However, as if to emphasize that more is involved than the need to generate a sense of mystery and suspense, Melville went on to say, rather opaquely, "Hitherto the nature of this narrative, besides rendering the intricacies in the beginning unavoidable, has more or less required that many things, instead of being set down in the order of occurrence, should be retrospectively, or irregularly given," and then adds: "this last is the case with the following passages" relating the final exchange between Cereno and Delano, an exchange Melville composed as an entirely new conclusion to his expanded version of the original story. That exchange then ends with the following comment about the Africans' leader, Babo, after he and his fellow rebels had been subdued by Delano's men and put under arrest: "As for the black—whose brain, not body, had schemed and led the revolt, with the plot—his slight frame, inadequate to that which it held, had at once yielded to the superior muscular strength of his captor, in the boat" (116). For the narrative to convey the shock to Melville's nineteenth-century audience that it seems calculated to provide in the end, it was necessary to withhold not just the fact that the slaves had rebelled and taken charge of the *San Dominick* but that they had devised a clever, sophisticated, exceedingly daring plan to deceive Delano into thinking, for one whole day while he walked the deck of the *San Dominick* and conversed with the Spanish captain, that Cereno and what remained of his crew were in charge. This ship was not the "transatlantic emigrant ship" (54) Delano at first thought it to be but a slave ship engaged in the transport of Africans to the port of Callao on the west coast of South America. Among the "many things" that needed to be "retrospectively, or irregularly given," is the all-important revelation that Babo and the other slaves are demonstrably as intelligent and cunning as their captors, in contradiction to the prevailing racist ideology at the time that held all Blacks to be naturally inferior in intelligence to whites.[2]

We know that Melville altered Delano's original story in several respects. He changed the date of the historical incident of the mutiny from 1804 to 1799, bringing it closer to the time when slaves, under the leadership of Toussaint-Louverture, seized power in Haiti in 1791; and he altered the names of the two ships, from the *Tryal* to the *San Dominick,* further suggesting parallels with the revolution in Haiti, earlier known as Santo Domingo, and from the *Perseverance* to the *Bachelor's Delight,* thus calling attention to the inexperience or innocence of its American captain, Delano.[3] Melville made these changes, apparently, to emphasize that the rebellion on the *San Dominick* was not an isolated incident but one in a series of slave insurrections in the New World, with the implication that there were lessons to be learned from them, not the least of which is that beneath the façade of enslaved Africans' apparent docility and acceptance of their lot there burned a powerful desire and determination to be free.[4] However, in one important respect concerning the structure of his tale, Melville made an even more important departure from his original source. He postponed until the very end of the main action any hint of the slave mutiny that had occurred on the *San Dominick* in the weeks before Delano and his crew encountered it off the coast of Chile. And then he added the final scene containing the dramatic exchange between Delano and Cereno, revealing that Delano has been unaffected or unmoved by the events he witnessed on the *San Dominick* while Cereno has been so profoundly altered, mentally and physically, as to send him, at twenty-nine years of age, to an early grave just months after the Lima court, in a pro forma trial, pronounced "criminal sentences" against the Africans for their takeover of the ship, but reserved hanging, burning, and beheading of the body of their leader, Babo, before fixing his head on a pole in the public plaza as a warning to other enslaved Africans (111). Unlike Melville, the historical Delano revealed to his readers the true situation on the slave ship in the second paragraph of his narrative when he wrote that as he departed the *San Dominick* at the end of the day, "to his [Delano's] great surprise the Spanish captain leaped into the boat, and called out in Spanish, that the Africans on board had rebelled and murdered many of the people; and that he did not then command her."[5]

Melville withheld this information, along with any clear indication of the actual situation on the *San Dominick* and the horrifying details about the murder and mayhem, the drownings and dismemberments that had previously occurred during the rebellion on the "negro transportation-ship" (49), until the deposition portion of the narrative where the details quickly accumulate to generate a "shock of recognition" for the reader not only about the fact that the Africans had violently seized the *San Dominick* and murdered or cast overboard several of its crew but also how they contrived and executed a desperate plan to deceive Delano and his men. This necessarily delayed response or "shock of recognition"[6] mirrors Cereno's own shock at the traumatic events he witnessed firsthand in the violent takeover of his ship and the killing of his boyhood friend Alexandro Aranda, events that brought home to him the horrors of the slave trade and left him so emotionally broken and traumatized, that, just "three months after being dismissed by the court," he went, "borne on the bier," to an early grave (117). Cereno's broken spirit—mentioned once in Delano's account but much emphasized throughout the story in Melville's descriptions of his "agitated," "unstrung" behavior (95, 86)—is possibly the most important of the revelations in the final scene where the two captains meet for the last time, and speaks not only to the evils of slavery and the slave trade but also to Cereno's transformative recognition that the men and women forced into slavery are as human as himself.

While it may be argued there is no concrete evidence to support the idea that Cereno has experienced such a complete transformation in his views of the natural superiority of whites as to think of Africans as equally human with himself, such a profound awakening seems implied in the final scene between Cereno and Captain Delano, where the Spanish captain utters just two words, "the negro," in his otherwise mute response to Delano's question about what has "cast such a shadow" upon him (116). Such a revelation, understated though it is, has much the same traumatic shock value for the reader, coming as it does at the very end of Melville's narrative, with the revelation that the Africans had rebelled and taken control of the *San Dominick*. Indeed, structurally, it comes at the point where it serves as the story's final surprise, or "kicker," not as big a surprise, perhaps, as the revelation that the Africans were in charge of the ship all along but more significant in terms of the larger debate over slavery then heating up in America, in the years before the Civil War. Of course, not all racially prejudiced readers will share Cereno's awakening to the humanity of the Africans, in all their shrewdness, rage, and determination to be free. Some, because of ideology, bias, or othering will remain unaffected and repress or "forget" the emotional impact of what they have read or witnessed, as does Amasa Delano, who in his final meeting with Cereno fails to understand why the Spanish captain cannot forget "the past" and turn over a "new leaf," like "yon bright sun," now that they are safely in Lima, the surviving African rebels have been subdued, and their leader, Babo, has been officially tried and executed, with his head displayed in public as a warning to others (116).

"Benito Cereno" is a story of trauma—one of the most horrifically violent tales of slavery and its attendant traumas to appear in the nineteenth century. It seems hardly an exaggeration to say that practically all of the characters (except Delano) are traumatized by the violence they witness or experience firsthand—Cereno by the slave insurrection, the murder and dismemberment of his friend, Aranda, and the threatening behavior of the razor-wielding Senegalese leader, Babo; the surviving sailors by the insurrection and brutal murder of the sailors' mates, whether by improvised weapons or drowning; and the Africans by their captivity, confinement, and the brutalities of Middle Passage. However, the fact of these various traumas is not revealed to Melville's readers until near the very end, when Cereno leaps into Delano's boat and Delano sees that Babo is trying to kill Cereno, and then more fully elaborated in the court deposition, where much of the mystery of the *San Dominick* is finally explained in detail. Melville's story engages the historical trauma of slavery through a clever use of the conventions of the detective story, with its "double plot," made famous a decade or so earlier by Edgar Allan Poe but dating back at least to the eighteenth century.[7] In the conventional detective tale a crime occurs or is revealed once in the beginning (frequently off stage and before the narrative begins) and is then revisited a second time when the detective or crime-solver steps in to solve or explain the mystery of what happened and reconstructs the crime for all to comprehend and appreciate.[8]

In "Benito Cereno," the "crime" or mysterious event (the Africans' takeover of the ship) occurs once off stage, before the narrative even begins, and then a second time in Cereno's reconstruction during his shaky deposition before the vice-regal court in Lima where the Africans' rebellion and takeover are detailed and explained. As in classic detective fiction, the main action is designed to generate a sense of mystery about the earlier events, but in this case, the mystery extends even to the point of hiding the fact that a "crime," in this case a slave insurrection, has occurred. Thanks to Delano, who serves as our eyes and ears but fails to understand what he is seeing during the time of his Good Samaritan visit to the *San Dominick*, we, too, fail to understand what we are seeing.[9] Cereno's deposition then rehearses what we had witnessed on the *San Dominick* through Delano's consciousness, but it does so in a way that reverses or corrects the false impressions and faulty hypotheses generated along the way by the myopic, racist Delano, and that we, too, have been encouraged to adopt because we see things through his eyes. In this way Melville made sure the reader necessarily experiences what happened on the *San Dominick* a second time but in a totally new light, one that is so jarring and contrary to anyone with racist views as to be shocking, even possibly traumatizing—if, like Benito Cereno (and unlike Delano), they come to recognize that the Africans are as human as themselves.

As with other forms of trauma, it is possible for one to experience something that turns out to be traumatic without realizing it at the time. Then a later experience or discovery triggers the original experience, but this time bringing it back with such power as to make the original trauma forcefully significant for the first time—significant and life-changing. Like Delano in his initial experience of the events on the *San Dominick*, Melville's readers experience not trauma but the aftereffects of an extended traumatic event they experience vicariously but misunderstand on a first reading of the initial narrative. Only with the revelation of the Africans' bloody rebellion and hostage-taking can readers *relive* the "shadow" or aftermath of those events they had earlier witnessed without significant feeling or anything but a sense of occasional puzzlement. In the end, however, with new knowledge in hand, susceptible readers can reexperience those events as having traumatogenic significance.[10] In short, by postponing the explanation of the violent takeover of the slave ship until the end, Melville adopted a narrative strategy calculated to induce in his readers an anxiety or disturbance that is akin to trauma without being equal to it—as a shadow is not quite as substantial as the body that casts it. The story as told from Delano's point of view is loaded with cognitive gaps—details the significance of which Melville withholds—thus creating a cognitive paralysis that builds and builds until finally relieved by the revelations in the court deposition concerning the Africans' violent takeover and Babo's elaborate scheme for disguising the rebellion. Readers are made to witness *the effects of slavery*—the performative cunning of the Africans, the speechless but suspicious activities of the Spanish crew, the "signs of nervous suffering," the attacks and fainting spells of Benito Cereno, before they know what they are seeing (52), or before they can know that these are symptoms of what happens when the roles of slave and slave holder, captive and captor are reversed and the instruments of violence, oppression, and destruction have changed hands.[11]

To be sure, Melville does offer abundant signs or symptoms of the traumas of slavery and Middle Passage, and the history of violence and trauma, in the *San Dominick*'s state of decay and disrepair, and the strange, unaccountable behavior of the Spanish captain and his crew and of the African slaves as well—but without our being able to recognize them as such in the early action of the narrative. Even from a distance, however, before he has stepped onto the *San Dominick*, it is clear to Delano that the ship has suffered extraordinary hardship and, by its strange and uncertain movements, shows evidence of being "a ship in distress." When first sighted, the vessel has the incongruous appearance of "a ship-load of monks" or "Black Friars," the first real hint of a world turned upside down, a view that is confirmed, but with little understanding, when Delano makes his way onto the *San Dominick* and sees the upper deck populated mostly by Africans (47–48). Then, too, there is the mystery of the ship's covered figurehead and evidence of the recent addition of a "rudely painted or chalked" sentence, "*Seguid vuestro jefe* (follow your leader)" on "the forward side of a sort of pedestal below the canvas" (49) with its implication of an ongoing contest about who is in charge of this ship, a sentence that can be read either as an exhortation or as a threat to those still on board to maintain discipline or suffer the consequences. Once on board the *San Dominick*, the American captain is immediately surrounded by "a clamorous throng of whites and blacks," with "the latter outnumbering the former more than could have been expected," and all pouring out "a common tale of suffering," with the negresses expressing themselves vehemently in the form of "wails"—all signs of widespread hysteria on this ship having its causes in the *San Dominick*'s recent history (49, 54). Even if they had not all "narrowly escaped shipwreck" off Cape Horn and then "lain tranced together without wind" for days (as initially claimed), with their provisions low and water "next to none," it is clear the ship and its strange collection of white and Black people had been through an extraordinary, protracted period of deprivation and suffering. The battered ship, whose sails were "in sad repair" and whose "spars, ropes and great part of the bulwarks" appeared "woolly and unkempt," had the look of a ship "launched, from Ezekial's Valley of Dry Bones" (48). Add to this general impression the "conspicuous figures of four elderly grizzled negroes," without chains, "crouched sphynx-like" on alternate sides of the ship, chanting and turning "junk" into oakum as well as half a dozen other Black people sitting cross-legged on the deck (also without chains), scouring rusty hatchets with bricks and rags, and it is evident that Delano has stumbled upon a ship where something so devastating has happened as to result in the appearance of constant misery and misrule, not to mention the overturning of regular naval order and discipline (50). Still ignorant of the true nature of the *San Dominick* but assuming it to be some kind of "transatlantic emigrant ship," Delano makes note to himself of "some prominent breaches, not only of discipline but of decency," all of which he ascribes to "the absence of those subordinate deck-officers" who would normally constitute "the police department of a populous ship" (54).

From the start, we see Cereno acting weirdly, anxiously, the "involuntary victim of mental disorder," as Delano suspects at one point, or an agent of disguise and mysterious "design," as he thinks at another (53). And the fact that we see things through the eyes of the conventionally minded Delano makes it all the harder to interpret Cereno's actions. However, in the very first moments, Melville offers a few clues that should put the reader on guard, particularly in the reference to the "lawlessness and loneliness" of the spot near the southern coast of Chile where the American captain sights the *San Dominick* and the fact that, when Delano gets close enough, he can see the ship's stern piece with its image of violent conquest and colonialism (i.e., "the arms of Castile and Leon, medallioned

[with] ... a dark satyr in a mask, holding his foot on the prostrate neck of a writhing figure, likewise masked")—details Melville added to Delano's original to frame the story while hinting at ongoing violence and political struggle (49).

Other details in the narrative hint at the possibility of violence and struggle, past and possibly also to come. These are subtle, too, but more suggestively sinister, and together constitute recurring motifs in Melville's narrative. Chief among these are the various sharp-edged or pointed instruments (mostly metal) that Captain Delano witnesses being handled and polished, or later, wielded, by surviving crew members or Africans at various times in the story. Besides the rusty hatchets Delano observes being scoured by the six Africans, there are knives, hand-pikes, marlin-spikes, razors, scissors, skinning knives. These instruments, of course, are designed for particular kinds of work—chopping, shaving, cutting, skinning, slicing, securing, and so on—the kinds of tools that were needed on almost any type of ship at the time, and as such they might be regarded as innocuous or nonthreatening, but in the context of a ship carrying Africans who are free to move about the deck (even if they are not yet known to be rebel slaves), they might raise some suspicions of possible threats to an outsider like Delano. Nonetheless, in Melville's hands, they are the perfect instruments for hinting at a threatening atmosphere of violence and mayhem, whether past or to come, and they are there as a warning, to be sure, but also to add to the narrative a steadily growing frisson of apprehension for the reader.

At least one such minor incident of violence occurs early on, when an African boy is seen cutting one of the Spanish boys in the head with a knife. This incident appears in Delano's original narrative, but Melville added at least two others, the most remarkable one being the shaving scene that falls in the middle of the narrative, when the apparent body servant, Babo, uses a straight razor to shave Benito Cereno while the latter answers questions posed by Captain Delano about the *San Dominick*'s suspicious history of gales and calms, deadly scurvy and fevers, and other misfortunes resulting in the ruinous state of the ship and its few remaining crew. On a first time through the story, the reader is likely to react more or less as Captain Delano does, and think it strange or ominous that the Spanish captain would so punctiliously demand to be shaved every day at the same time when everything around him appears to be running to chaos. We too might see in Babo "a headsman, and in the white a man at the block," but we would not know what to do with such a conceit. At the same time, however, we would take in the fact that, "when the steel glanced nigh the throat," again Cereno "faintly shuddered," a detail that is immediately followed by Babo's ominous explanation that "master always shakes when I shave him. And yet master knows I never yet have drawn blood," something Babo nonetheless does almost immediately, exclaiming, "See, master—you shook so—here's Babo's first blood" (85–86), and in that way sends a silent warning to Cereno to stick to the script or he will die.

Again, we cannot know this until all is revealed at the end, but Melville keeps dropping hints of potential violence under the surface, as well as vaguely unnerving indications of the violent history of the *San Dominick*, in subsequent incidents, as when he has Delano observe to himself about Don Benito at one point, "He is like one flayed alive" (93), unwittingly hitting on the very process of stripping away the flesh of Cereno's friend Alexandro Aranda that was clearly the most traumatizing experience of the slave rebellion for Cereno. But again, we cannot understand the significance of this suggestion until the end, when Aranda's bones are uncovered and we put this language and the details of Aranda's death and dismemberment together to form a picture of flesh actually being stripped from its bones in retaliation for Aranda's enslaving the Africans and before attaching those bones to the ship's bow. Only after we have read the deposition at the end can we recognize that throughout the barbering scene, Benito Cereno has been "on trial" for his life, with his seemingly docile body servant, Babo, serving as his judge and executioner—even as any African held in slavery is constantly on trial for his life, with his master constantly in the role of judge and executioner.[12]

These hints aside, readers are limited in what they see by Captain Delano's racist point of view, on the one hand, according to which the Africans are "docile" and of limited intelligence, and, on the other, by the cunning, utterly believable performance of the rebels, in concert with the terrified Cereno, in masking who is in charge of the *San Dominick* once Delano comes on board. On the matter of who is in charge, Melville made a significant change in Cereno's deposition to the court that seems designed to enhance the reader's estimation of Babo's intelligence and cunning (and, by extension, that of the other African rebels as well) when he has Cereno state, in the fictional version of his deposition, that it was Babo, not Cereno, who proposed the clever idea of maintaining their customary roles as a ruse to fool the American captain and "to say and do all that the deponent declares to have said and done" on the day of their meeting (109).[13] This is again confirmed at the end of the two captains' concluding conversation, when the narrator reports that it was "the black [Babo]—whose brain, not body, had schemed and led the revolt, with the plot" (116). In the original deposition found in Delano's narrative, Cereno claims *he* was the one who proposed the idea of the ruse "to appease and quiet" the Africans in advance of Delano's approaching ship and the possibility it might try to come to their aid.[14]

The change Melville made at this point flies in the face of the common assumption among whites at the time that Blacks were inferior to whites, particularly on the grounds that they lacked sophisticated intelligence and reasoning powers. Even before Cereno's deposition, however, Melville calls attention to Babo's unusual intelligence, when he has Babo choose to stand behind "not his master's chair, but Captain Delano's" while the two white men converse, and in that way, as Delano speculates (wrongly), "more readily anticipate his slightest want." Delano is not so suspicious as to see that Babo wanted to be able to communicate silently with Cereno and also prevent him from silently communicating with Delano, but he does recognize that Babo here demonstrates more intelligence than he would have expected of an African, enough to prompt Delano to "whisper" across the table (as if to suggest he senses, for the first time, that perhaps Babo is not to be trusted after all), "This is an uncommonly intelligent fellow of yours, Don Benito" (90). Despite any occasional twinges of doubt we might share with Delano, for the shock of the ending to work, readers must be sucked in, just as Delano is, by the rebels' performances as faithful body servants, dutiful laborers, and compliant breeders, even on a slave ship. Earlier, when Cereno first explains to Delano that he owes "not only my own preservation" to Babo but also any success in "pacifying his more ignorant brethren, when at intervals tempted to murmurings," readers are likely to be taken in by the performance of Cereno as well as that of Babo, who sighs in response, while bowing his face, "Ah, master, don't speak of me; Babo is nothing; what Babo has done was but duty." Marking the fact that he has been successfully tricked by their performances, we are told that in response Delano "could not but bethink him of the beauty of that relationship which could present such a spectacle of fidelity on the one hand and confidence on the other," a scene made all the more convincing and "heightened by the contrast in dress, denoting their relative positions," all in keeping with Delano's racialist assumptions (57).

This scene, where Delano remarks on what a "faithful fellow" Babo is, is a necessary setup for the deeply ironic, symbolic, and, for Cereno, potentially traumatizing barbering scene later, when Babo goes through all the motions of shaving his "master" in front of Delano with a freshly stropped straight razor, and draws a drop of Cereno's blood to remind the Spanish captain what the deadly consequences will be if he were to reveal, in any way, that the slaves had taken control of the ship. We cannot know at the time that these scenes have all the potential of life-and-death performances for both men, though with the knowledge of hindsight, it is possible to recognize that the obsequious servant role of Babo has its parallel in nineteenth-century black minstrelsy. Delano, however, seems unaware of this tradition,[15] and of the fact that the relationships performed in minstrelsy were typically designed to mask what was really going on, but he is at least vaguely aware of the related tradition of commedia dell'arte and the figure of the trickster, when he pauses to acknowledge to himself that Cereno's costume, "with its dark velvet Chili jacket," "white smallclothes and stockings, with silver buckles," "high crowned sombrero," and "slender sword"[16] (like Harlequin's "slapstick" or magic wand), which in Cereno's case proves to be missing from his scabbard, is so "incongruous" as "almost to suggest the image of an invalid courtier tottering about London streets in the time of the plague" (57–58).[17] During the shaving scene when it occurs to Delano that "possibly master and man, for some unknown purpose, were acting out, both in word and deed, nay, to the very tremor of Don Benito's limbs, some juggling play before him," he quickly "banished" the thought as a "whimsy, insensibly suggested, perhaps, by the theatrical aspect of Don Benito in his harlequin ensign." Despite his rare alertness in this moment, he dismisses his suspicion when he cannot figure out what Cereno's playacting might signify (87).

Such convincing performances as the one in the barbering scene, of course, are just one reason readers are unlikely to penetrate the true situation on the *San Dominick* until the penultimate scene when Cereno leaps into Delano's boat and Babo dives after him, dagger in hand. As already indicated, another reason has to do with the fact that Melville so tightly limits the point of view in this story to that of Captain Delano, a point of view informed by several factors, including a genial form of racism according to which Black people are seen in stereotypical fashion as belonging to a natural order akin to animals (a Newfoundland dog in the case of the body servant Babo; a "bull of the Nile" [78] in that of the powerful Atufal; or a doe with her fawn in the example of an African mother and her infant child)—associations that underestimate their intelligence and overestimate their "loyalty" and "docility" (84). The odd behavior of their white master, Cereno, Delano explains away by recourse to a number of factors—youth, class, and national stereotypes ("these Spaniards are all an odd set; the very word Spaniard has a curious, conspirator, Guy-Fawkish twang to it," Delano tells himself), and a loosely applied, frequently invoked medical vocabulary of sickness, insanity, lunacy, and invalidism in viewing the Spanish captain (79). Racism and racial stereotypes, particularly the racial view that Black people are naturally "docile" and of "limited mind," are the major source of Delano's blindness to the true situation on the *San Dominick* (84). But he is also blinded by his repeated efforts to play doctor and understand Cereno's strange behavior by engaging in amateurish medical diagnoses, and applying quasi-medical terms having to do with insanity, terms that do not fit Cereno. Even in the beginning, what Delano sees in Cereno is an "undemonstrative invalid" or "an involuntary victim of mental disorder," marked by "debility, constitutional or induced by hardships, bodily and mental." "His mind appeared unstrung, if not still more seriously affected," as he is seen to engage in a series of anxious behaviors, "suddenly pausing, starting, or staring, biting his lip, biting his finger-nail, flushing, paling," and so on. Whatever the cause, Delano concludes, "this distempered spirit was lodged ... in as distempered a frame . . . now with nervous suffering . . . almost worn to a skeleton" (52–53).

What Delano does not recognize or understand is that Cereno shows the symptoms of one who has experienced "prolonged, repeated trauma," the kind that, as Judith Herman has explained, "occurs only in circumstances of captivity," such as we later learn Cereno has been living under for seventy-three days, following the Africans' takeover of the *San Dominick:* hypervigilance, anxiety, agitation; dissociation or loss of memory; also oscillation between "intense attachment and terrified withdrawal"; and finally, "a tenacious state of depression," such as he falls into at the conclusion of his ordeal, when he lapses into "absolute passivity" and loses his will to live.[18] Most emphatically, we see his nervousness and agitation under Babo's razor in the shaving scene (a scene of the most intense and life-threatening captivity imaginable) when he shakes and shudders, while seated in "a large, misshapen arm-chair" that "seemed some grotesque engine of torment" (82–83). Of course we are not aware of his true situation at the time; all we see is his anxiety, not what prompts it, so we cannot recognize it as a situation designed by Babo, his captor, to terrorize or traumatize him (while also reminding him of what happened to his friend Aranda), with the aim of guaranteeing his compliance with Babo's will; nor can we even know he is being held captive. We are structurally "out of the loop," so his behavior is a mystery. Ostensibly he is not in a life-threatening situation; he is simply being shaved by his body servant. So the best that readers can do, at this point, is to assume he is either mentally unbalanced, as Delano comes to suspect, or concealing some nefarious plan against Delano and his ship, as Delano also suspects at another point.

Only after we have read through the court deposition can we understand what Cereno has lived through, and only then can we even begin to sense how he has been altered by earlier and more recent events on the *San Dominick,* or recognize that what he has lived through is not a single traumatic event but a series of traumas that have come back to haunt him in the present of the story—on top of what he knows to be the constant, immediate threat of violence and death at the hands of Babo. In fact, this is typically what happens when a subject experiences a traumatic event; there is a disruption in the flow of conscious experience and a consequent loss of memory, such as Cereno reports during his deposition near the end where we are told "that in some things his memory is confused, he cannot distinctly recall every event" (110). The subject is displaced out of the symbolic order by the traumatic event, leaving only its aftereffects—numbing or forgetting; recurring nightmares and sweats—or a random event returns the subject to the experience of an earlier horror, as when Delano casually speaks of a hypothetical case where the remains of Cereno's friend, Aranda, might be considered to be still on the ship. Echoing Delano's "On board this ship?" in a state of sudden hysteria and disbelief, Cereno then "with horrified gestures, as directed against some spectre, . . . unconsciously fell into the ready arms of his attendant, who, with a silent appeal toward Captain Delano, seemed beseeching him not again to broach a theme so unspeakably distressing to his master." Though the reader at this point still has no knowledge of the basis of Cereno's sudden breakdown, it is evident in the language Delano uses to describe what he is witnessing that their exchange regarding "the deserted body of a man" has somehow brought back a specter or memory that affects Cereno to such a degree that "the bare suggestion, even, terrifies the Spaniard into this trance" (61). In this moment, the reader sees Cereno's reaction more or less directly, only slightly filtered through Delano's consciousness; what it suggests is that the Spanish captain has been horrified by some previous event, or series of events, and is now reliving the traumatic experience even as the two men talk and Delano innocently speculates about the whereabouts of the remains of Aranda.

Again, we cannot know this at the time, but the reader's suspicions of something truly traumatic are likely to mount near the end of this scene when Cereno explains, in answer to Delano, that "the main company of blacks" on the ship "belonged to my late friend, Alexandro Aranda," and with the mention of Aranda's name, Cereno's "air was heart-broken; his knees shook: his servant supported him" (60). Delano takes a big step toward empathizing with Cereno here when, trying to imagine why he is so upset, he recalls the story of the traumatic loss of "my own brother" on an earlier voyage (a story not in the original Delano's *Narrative*). However, it is not simply the loss of his brother at sea that has traumatized

Delano; as he admits to Cereno, the most terrible part of such a loss is the need for the survivor to dispose of the loved one's decomposing body, piece by piece, before its smell becomes unbearable, by throwing it overboard—"that honest eye, that honest hand . . . that warm heart; all, all—like scraps to the dogs—to throw all to the sharks!"[19] "It was then," he explains (after recounting his excruciating memory of the dissection of his brother's body that mirrors what we later learn about the "flaying" of the body of Aranda by his rebel Africans), "I vowed never to have for fellow-voyager a man I loved, unless, unbeknown to him, I had provided every requisite . . . for embalming his mortal part for interment on shore. Were your friend's remains now on board this ship, Don Benito, not thus strangely would the mention of his name affect you" (61). Without realizing it, Delano here reminds Cereno of the very thing Cereno has most desperately needed to repress, namely, that the bones of his friend *are* still on the ship—covered with canvas and affixed to the bow, where they serve as a horrifying reminder to Cereno and his crew that they are all constantly on trial and must do exactly as instructed by the rebellious slaves, or he and his men will indeed "Follow your leader" to a hideous death. By unintentionally touching this nerve, Delano brings back to Cereno the memory of what had happened to Cereno's best friend, thus traumatizing him once again: "with horrified gestures, as directed against some spectre, . . . [Cereno] unconsciously fell into the ready arms of his attendant" (61). That "spectre"—traumatic memory—suddenly returns, only to make him swoon.

Cereno and his crew are not the only ones who have been traumatized by events on the *San Dominick*. Today there is widespread recognition of the traumatic character of life under slavery and other forms of captivity, a recognition that trauma marked the life of an enslaved person at virtually every stage—from capture and imprisonment in Africa and the rupture of being taken from home, through the deprivation and suffering of Middle Passage, and life on the plantations of the New World under the threat of the scourge, rape, torture, and other forms of violence and forced servitude.[20] At least on the surface, it appears that the Africans being conveyed on the *San Dominick* from Senegal to the west coast of South America were not treated unusually harshly. Considered "tractable" by their owner, Aranda, "none wore fetters" and all were permitted to sleep on deck.[21] (Perhaps, as Greg Grandin points out in his detailed reconstruction of the earlier stages of their journey, they may have been simply exhausted by their treatment and travails, and thus only appeared to Alexandro to be docile.[22]) In any case, it is because of Aranda's wish for their lax treatment, and in particular his decision not to chain them as was customary, that the "one-hundred and sixty blacks, of both sexes, mostly belonging to Don Alexandro Aranda," were able to rise up against their oppressors and take over the ship, just seven days out of the port of Valparaiso (104).

There are several suggestions, however, that the Africans had been traumatized by the Spaniards in charge of the ship in the days before they revolted, suggestions that cannot be recognized as such until placed in the context of the revelations in the late documentary section, where it is revealed that many crewmembers were bound by the rebellious slaves and thrown into the sea or leaped to their death to avoid dying a more gruesome death. These suggestions may include the "dolorous," vehement cries or "wails" of remembered suffering that greeted Delano when he first boarded the *San Dominick* (52); more certainly they include several seemingly spontaneous instances of rage and "insubordination" of the slaves toward the crew, as when Delano observed a Black boy, "enraged at a word dropped by one of his white companions, [seize] the knife, and ... [strike] the lad over the head, inflicting a gash from which blood flowed" (59). Finally there is the scene where Delano witnesses a violent exchange between two Africans and a sailor that prompts Cereno to be "seized by his cough" (70), perhaps in memory of earlier violence when the enslaved Africans rose in revolt or possibly as a way of pulling Delano's attention away from this violent outburst. Their evident rage is symptomatic, not of the natural ferocity or "animality" often attributed to Africans by early commentators on the story,[23] but of a deeply felt desire or urge to wreak revenge, an urge that is symptomatic of earlier violence and abuse on the ship, including the violence of prolonged captivity.[24]

In the climactic scene, when Don Benito springs from his ship in a desperate effort to escape, the Africans act "as if inflamed" at the sight, while "flourishing hatchets and knives," as Delano suddenly comes to think (mistakenly), "in ferocious piratical revolt." When Babo, dagger in hand, leaps after Cereno as he dives into Delano's boat, Delano wrenches the weapon away and holds him prostrate, heel on neck, only to see Babo rise up with a second dagger aimed "at the heart of his master, his countenance lividly vindictive, expressing the central purpose of his soul" (98–99). While the female Africans do not join in the violence of the final encounter with Delano's sailors, it is reported in the court deposition that at the time of his murder they were not "satisfied at the death of their master, Don Alexandro" but "would have tortured to death, instead of simply killing" that portion of the Spanish crew singled out by Babo, if the male "negroes [had] not restrained them," and that, "in the various acts of murder, they sang songs and danced—not gaily, but solemnly," in an apparent effort to further inflame their male counterparts during the rebellion (112). Although not chained while under the watch of the crew, it seems clear the African women had experienced the kind of abuse that traumatizes—including, presumably, sexual abuse, something known to be common on slave ships during Middle Passage, as reported as early as the late eighteenth century by Olaudah Equiano and more fully documented in Rediker's *The Slave Ship*.[25] Surely horrible suffering of some kind lies behind their attempts to spur on their male counterparts and their fierce desire to bring pain and destruction to their oppressors. Surely, too, the suffering of all the African captives on board the *San Dominick* can be imagined in their collective uprooting and given some means of measurement by their desperate determination to return to Senegal, the home of Babo and several of the other rebels, or elsewhere in Africa. As the sociologist Jeffrey Alexander has argued, trauma is not limited to the experience of individuals; there can be a social or collective dimension to trauma as well, when the experience is shared by a racial, ethnic, or other group, and that group feels threatened with annihilation or has been forcibly removed from their homeland.[26]

Melville's structuring of the narrative, then, is remarkable in that it mirrors our contemporary understanding of trauma as an experience embodied and made manifest in a delayed or after-the-fact second encounter with a version of the original. Typically, trauma is not an experience that is recognized as such in the immediate moment; instead it is only recognized sometime later, when a sound, a sight, or a sensate experience triggers a memory and its return. Similarly, only at the end, after reading the horrifying details of the slave insurrection in Cereno's court deposition, can the reader understand or feel the full force of what Cereno and the other sailors on the *San Dominick* have lived through in retaliation for what the Africans had been forced to live through earlier. Neither Melville nor Delano attempt to embody the Africans' experience of slavery directly, but in Cereno and the Spanish sailors' experience of their enslavement on the *San Dominick* under the direction of the African Babo, readers can gain a visceral appreciation for the horrors of slavery when the tables are turned.

In fact, the reader's "shock of recognition" concerning the trauma experienced by the slaves is only moderately suggested in the court deposition, where the surviving rebels are silenced and the official, racist ideology of the court asserts its power over them. Instead, it comes in a final, third segment Melville added to the original story in the form of a concluding dialogue between the two main characters, where Cereno explains, in response to Delano's question, that the thing that has "cast such a shadow" over him is "the negro." By adding this final scene, Melville shifted the focus from the traumatizing actions of the slaves—killing and dismembering Cereno's best friend and murdering or throwing overboard most of the sailors at the time of the rebellion—to what Aranda and the sailors had done to the slaves to provoke their rage and rebellion. For, finally, it is this recognition that is so traumatizing to Cereno that it leaves him a fatally broken man. Unlike Delano, Cereno experiences a profound shift away from his earlier embrace of the dominant cultural and symbolic order of things, from blindness about the humanity of the Africans to recognition of the humanity they share with him. By adding this final scene, Melville made his most dramatic intervention in Delano's original narrative, altering the latter's sunny, upbeat meaning and intention, its self-congratulatory celebration of the American captain's self-proclaimed goodness, generosity, and faith in Providence in coming to the aid of the Spanish slave ship (as well as Delano's feelings of the injustice of Cereno's failure to acknowledge his aid with a handsome reward), and moving beyond the actual court's view that the "heinous and atrocious actions" of the rebellious slaves required that they be made "an example to others," by being dragged from prison and hung from a public gibbet "until they are dead," with the heads of the leaders ordered to be "cut off after they are dead, and . . . fixed on a pole in the square of the port of Talcahuano" (841). Ironically, in Melville's version of the conclusion, the bodies of all but one of the rebel leaders have been erased. The one exception is Babo, whose body, after being "dragged to the gibbet," is "burned to ashes," and whose head, "that hive of subtlety"—a remarkable trope that emphasizes Babo's intelligence—is put on public display, as a warning to other potentially rebellious slaves not to challenge the whites' superior power and authority (116). Instead, Melville introduced a new thought, a new point of view, one informed by evidence of a new trauma for Cereno—his retro-determined recognition of the "negroes'" common intelligence and humanity with his own, in all their rage at being kidnapped, held captive, uprooted and tortured, separated from their homes, and treated like animals, with no rights or claims to justice, freedom, or equality with their captors, and of his own complicity in the cruel, dehumanizing practices of the slave trade.

By contrast, Delano shows no evidence of being traumatized by what he has witnessed or learned about subsequently from Cereno. For him, the crucial cognitive gaps remain, and the reigning cultural and symbolic order based on white racial superiority remains in place. A prisoner of race prejudice and his limited view of the humanity of the Africans, he is unable to interpret the events for what they are. Even with his new knowledge, he is unmoved, immune to the trauma of what he has witnessed without understanding. When he and Cereno have their final meeting and express their appreciation for saving each other's life, Cereno corrects his new "best friend," saying, "God charmed your life, but you saved mine." And Delano agrees, saying, "Yes, all is owing to Providence, I know." But then, congratulating himself on his own "good nature, compassion, and charity" on the occasion of their encounter, he goes on to observe that the suffering he witnessed on the *San Dominick* that morning was *"more apparent than real"* (my emphasis). Immune to the suffering of others, all he learns from his ordeal is that more "acuteness" on his part as to the real situation on the ship "might have cost me my life" (115), a perversely limited, obtuse conclusion about what he has learned from his encounter with the *San Dominick* that only encourages him to keep his blinders in place and stick to his faith in Providence and white racial superiority. To be sure, Delano lacks real "acuteness," but it is his racial views that keep him from recognizing the suffering of the Africans and of Benito Cereno, too, whose anguish is to him unimaginable, defined as it is by the trauma of his discovery that the customary justifications for slavery and the slave trade are profoundly wrong. When Delano tries to convince Cereno to forget everything and turn over a "new leaf," as the sun and blue sea appear to have done,—Cereno offers an answer that makes a claim to his own humanity when he says, "Because they have no memory, . . . because they are not human." When a dumbfounded Delano persists by asking, "what has cast such a shadow upon you?"—Cereno answers simply, "The negro," a response that quietly acknowledges the humanity of the Africans whom he and Aranda had held captive through Middle Passage, and his own complicity in the whole evil enterprise.

Delano, by contrast, is impervious to memory; he is an example of repression, indifference, or anesthesia of traumatic response—a sign of his persistent racism (and possibly of repressed and unconscious guilt as well). We know from his experience of the loss of his brother that he is *capable* of the empathic feelings that can come with the experience of trauma or traumatic loss, as long as it involves the loss of one of his own family, someone he sees as being like himself. But as we see in his final exchange with Cereno, it is Delano's failure to regard "the negro" in the same terms as he regarded his brother that prevents him from recognizing the trauma he witnessed on the *San Dominick* or learned about in graphic detail when all was explained to him afterward. Like several of the other stories in *The Piazza Tales*—"Bartleby," "The Piazza," and the tale of Hunilla in "The Encantadas"—this one, too, turns on a recognition of the power of human sympathy to change minds and hearts—or *not* to do so, as with the benighted and convention-bound American Captain Delano who fails to see the evils of slavery even when they are enacted before his very eyes, or recognize the Africans to be as human as his brother, or himself.

# 4

## PLAYING SMART, PLAYING DUMB

### Performance in "The Lightning-Rod Man"

"The Lightning-Rod Man" is unique among the stories in Melville's *The Piazza Tales* as a little one-act drama—a comic set piece of brief duration, involving just two characters, that seems conceived for the stage or burlesque theater. More than a traveling salesman story, it is a dramatic composition, spoken from the point of view of one of the principals, a potential customer, that relies on interior monologue and dialogue to provide context or setting, descriptions of action and bodily movements, and details or suggestions about the lightning-rod salesman's personality and that of the narrator himself.[1] It is structured as a dual performance—a game or "dance"—with the title character taking on a conventionalized role of traveling salesman, with his predictable array of knowledge, exaggerated reactions, and inflated claims about his product, and the narrator seemingly performing another conventionalized role as his clueless customer, who at first appears to lack such knowledge and makes a series of ill-advised or risky moves out of ignorance. While their exchange is largely comic, there is an undercurrent of danger to the story, too, because of the spectacular electrical storm taking place in the background, one that has the potential to do bodily harm to the characters and threaten their lives. In the "terrific tempest" of the menacing storm, which the salesman breathlessly refers to as "this time of terror" (119–20), when a lightning rod might be just the thing the narrator needs to prevent serious injury or death, there is a real and urgent need for the him to test the truth-claims of the lightning-rod salesman who promises peace of mind and protection against injury and death.[2] But when the salesman's scare tactics threaten him with a horrid and grisly death from a lightning strike, like that of a horse trapped in a burning barn, he makes it clear his adversary has crossed a line. The salesman's egregious scare tactics trigger a violent reaction in the narrator that causes him to drop his mask and put an end to their mutual charade by turning on the salesman and chasing him out of his house.

Complicating the picture considerably, however, is the fact that, from the beginning, we do not know whether the lightning-rod man is an honest player, since we only see and hear him and are not always privy to his thinking. But given his similarity to several salesman figures in Melville's later novel, *The Confidence-Man: His Masquerade* (1857), it seems reasonable to suspect him, too, like the incarnations of that confidence man, of being a performance artist—reacting in mock horror, for instance, at the narrator's show of ignorance about dangerous behaviors during an electrical storm while claiming to be a well-intentioned broker offering a lifesaving device to his customers. Uncertain as that may be, it becomes clear the *narrator* is *not* being honest in his dealings with the salesman and instead only pretends to be something he is not, namely, a man ignorant about electrical science and lightning rods, and thus an easy mark for the traveling salesman's exaggerated claims about the protective properties of such devices. To borrow the terms of Erving Goffman, he is enacting a persona or playing a role as a greenhorn, an enthusiast of nature and nature's spectacle but not someone who has scientific knowledge, and he continues to play along in that role until he finally turns the tables on the salesman, asserts the upper hand when the salesman engages in scare tactics, and drives him away in a furious explosion of comic violence and threats. Once we recognize the presence in the story of what Goffman calls the "frame," we can understand the purpose of the narrator's actions as a form of play and appreciate them for the comic ritual they are; perhaps then we can better appreciate the story's subtlety, deceptiveness, and sly humor, and recognize it to be a little masterpiece of theatrical duplicity.[3] To be sure, as in other traveling-salesman tales, much of the humor comes from discovering that the typical or expected situation is reversed, and the narrator is "playing" or tricking the lightning-rod man by pretending to be more innocent than he is, while setting him up for rejection and defeat.

On close inspection, the actions of the narrator suggest he is as knowledgeable about nature's electrical phenomena and the purported successes and failures of lightning rods as the lightning-rod man himself—or as knowledgeable as Benjamin Franklin, the original "lightning-rod man," since the salesman's scientific claims derive almost wholly from Franklin's *Letters and Papers on Electricity,* published in 1751–53 in *Works,* which Melville appears to have consulted for this story and for his portrait of Franklin in his Revolutionary War novel, *Israel Potter* (1854–55), which Melville worked on at about the same time he was writing "The Lightning-Rod Man" (1854). Soon the story becomes a nasty duel of wits, one in which the supposed expert and the supposed innocent exchange places, with the "innocent" exposing the salesman as a charlatan and running him off his property.

In social theory terms, Goffman explains that every person who engages in face-to-face encounters "tends to act out what is sometimes called a *line*—that is, a pattern of verbal and nonverbal acts by which he expresses his view of the situation and through this his evaluation of the participants, especially himself."[4] In this case, the narrator initially acts out a line of innocence about the dangers of lightning by positioning himself on his cottage's stone hearth (an electrical conductor) and by the ignorant things he has to say initially. At the same time, he seems to give positive social value to superior knowledge by his ostensible willingness to learn from the lightning-rod man and hear out his sales pitch. To invoke another of Goffman's key terms, he seems willing to maintain the *face* of an ignorant but willing potential customer, while at the same time assuming, or seeming to assume, that the *face* of the lightning-rod salesman, as the purveyor of a potentially lifesaving instrument, carries some positive social value as well. However, what we soon see is that the narrator is *in wrong face* when he begins to challenge the salesman's truth claims about the effectiveness of lightning rods, and in this way exposes the fact that the salesman exaggerates or makes false claims about his product and is simply a flimflam artist who is *in wrong face* as well. When the narrator's real knowledge base suddenly comes to the surface as he challenges the claims of the salesman with his own counterclaims, we can recognize that he had been engaging in deceitful action earlier while adopting a *wrong face* himself, as a prank or test, in order to expose the *wrong face* of the traveling salesman. Using the language of his body and speech, each man performs a series of tests of the vulnerability of the other while at the same time attempting to convince his counterpart that he himself is something he is not. That is to say, each character puts his own body on trial with the other, pretending he is something he is not, even as he puts the body language and words of the other on trial by looking for signs or examples of truth or falsity, scientific knowledge or misinformation about lightning and the efficacy of lightning rods, and any symptoms of trustworthy or suspicious behavior.

In the beginning, the narrator presents himself as cultured and excitable, a "lover of the majestic," as he says in regard to the current storm, and something of a pedant. But it is hard to tell where performance ends and personality begins. He is situated in his own cottage, "standing," as he explains, "on my hearthstone among the Acroceraunian hills"[5] (meaning "thunder-split peaks" and referring, by way of analogy, to coastal mountains in Greece made famous by Ptolemy and known for violent thunderstorms), while looking out admiringly at the "grand irregular thunder" and "scattered bolts" of lightning that "boomed overhead and crashed down among the valleys." While the feeling of awe in his response suggests he may be new to the territory, he appears to be an experienced observer of such natural phenomena, and eager to make comparisons with storms elsewhere, for he remarks that he finds the thunder "far more glorious here than on the plain," while also speculating ("I suppose") that it must be because "the mountains hereabout break and churn up the thunder" so—not because, as people in earlier centuries often thought, the Almighty was angry about the sinful, "impious" behavior of His people (118). In any case, almost immediately, he begins to sound like a curious combination of novice and aficionado concerning such spectacular electrical phenomena—an apparent contradiction that suggests a playful pretentiousness or the studied, made-up quality of an excited but artificial performance.

To repeat, at the start of the scene, the narrator simply mentions—casually and as if in passing—that he is standing on his hearthstone, where anyone might feel safe and comfortable during a storm. However, given that he is soon told this is exactly the *wrong* place to position himself during a storm, we might wonder why he makes a point of specifying where he is standing. Is it an innocuous detail or a contrived example of body language intended to suggest his ignorance to the person knocking at his door, the first hint of a planned deception? When the lightning-rod man rejects the narrator's invitation to join him on the hearth and dry out, he solemnly warns him to "quit the hearth" and accept *his* invitation instead to "stand with me in the middle of the room." When the narrator resists, saying dumbly, "I stand very well here," the lightning-rod peddler cries out, "Are you so horridly ignorant, then, not to know, that by far the most dangerous part of a house during such a terrific tempest as this, is the fire-place?" (119) (Indeed, Franklin, in his *Experiments and Observations on Electricity*, carefully explained that "[a] person apprehensive of danger from lightning, happening during the time of thunder to be in a house not so secured [with a lightning rod], will do well to avoid sitting near the chimney . . . the safest place is in the middle of the room, . . . sitting in one chair and laying the feet up in another."[6]) Given this ironic starting point, then, we might suspect that the narrator, already well-aware of such dangers, has carefully situated himself upon the hearth, knowing that such a "grand" and spectacular storm as this one will likely bring a string of lightning-rod salesmen to his door, so that when he says to himself, "Who is this that chooses a time of thunder for making calls?" we can probably assume he has already anticipated the answer to his question (118). As he later insinuates to the peddler himself, "From the peculiar time of your call upon me, I suppose you purposely select stormy weather for your journeys" (121). He thus carefully positions himself to deal with the first salesman who knocks, in preparation for toying with him when he arrives. To borrow a phrase from Goffman, he is enacting a persona or playing a role "as a means of negotiating [an] established interpersonal situation"[7]—but it is not the role we at first imagine.

Something of the narrator's motivation for such deception (and Melville's, too) is perhaps suggested by Jay Leyda's discovery many years ago that, in the fall of 1853, newspapers in the area around Pittsfield near Melville's home reported that "the Berkshires were enduring an intense lightning-rod sales campaign, with advertisements and warnings and editorials on the subject in all the Berkshire papers."[8] According to Philip Dray, in *Stealing God's Thunder: Benjamin Franklin's Lightning Rod and the Invention of America* (2005), by the 1840s there were at least fifteen lightning-rod factories in America and presumably a commensurate number of salesmen marketing these products directly to individual buyers; by 1870, the number of factories in the United States had doubled, and the number of traveling salesmen promoting the devices may have reached ten thousand. Given the pervasiveness of such peddlers, the general public naturally found the volume of their efforts annoying, to say the least, but it is also the case that many people, particularly people of faith, objected to them on the grounds that promoting the sale of such devices was tempting buyers to try to usurp or countervail God's will.[9] As John Adams had written about the phenomenon in the eighteenth century, there was widespread fear among religious literalists that what were known then as "Franklin rods" were "an impious Attempt to robb the Almighty of his Thunder, to wrest the Bolt of Vengeance out of his Hand."[10]

When the lightning-rod man knocks, with his "doleful undertaker's clatter" (an ominous sign of the caller's urgency and aggression but a description that also suggests the narrator's knowing, dismissive view of him even before he lays eyes on the man), the narrator brightly welcomes him inside, and, observing his visitor to be soaking wet, makes a point of inviting him to "[s]tand here on the hearth before the fire" to dry out and warm up. This may seem like a natural, welcoming reception, but to a skeptical eye, it looks more like a calculated move designed to deceive the salesman into thinking the narrator is clueless about what to do in a storm, all for the purpose of playing the lightning-rod man along (118). Additional examples of his apparent ignorance—all seemingly performed with the intention of misleading the peddler and all ending in a rebuke from the latter—are seen later when he makes a move to close the shutters to keep the rain out and then suggests securing them with a nearby iron bar (121); or when he requests the stranger to touch the bell-pull and call his young servant to bring a wooden bar instead, only to be told by the agitated salesman, "'That bell-wire might blast you. Never touch bell-wire in a thunder-storm, nor ring a bell of any sort" (122). Ironically, all of these missteps are behaviors that Franklin warned against in his writings on lightning and electricity, just as most of the precautions the lightning-rod man suggests he should take instead to "be safe in a time like this" can be found there, too (or in writings of Franklin's well-known successor, Lucius Lyon, whose *Treatise on Lightning Conductors* appeared in 1853, shortly before Melville wrote his story[11]). These precautions include standing in the middle of the house, as *he* (the lightning-rod man) is doing; or standing on a rug (a "non-conductor") in the middle of the house; or, in what is perhaps the most counterintuitive move of all, getting "thoroughly drenched in a thunder-storm," on the theory that "if the lightning strike, it might pass down the wet clothes without touching the body."[12] "It is the safest thing you can do," the lightning-rod man says blandly, to which the narrator responds with a request and a not so innocent pun, "since our being dumb will not help us . . . let me hear your precautions in traveling during thunderstorms," the very activity the lightning-rod man was engaged in before knocking on the narrator's door. To this the salesman responds by mentioning several tall items he avoids on such occasions, before concluding, "But of all things, I avoid tall men" (123).

Surprisingly, then, when the lightning-rod salesman mentions, in response to a request for business references, that "In Criggan last month, I put up three-and-twenty rods on only five buildings," the narrator unaccountably reveals that he is as familiar with the destruction wreaked by recent electrical activity there as the stranger claims to be, even down to the time and day, when he (the narrator) asks, "Was it not at Criggan last week, about midnight on Saturday, that the steeple, the big elm and the Assembly-room cupola were struck?" and then adds insinuatingly, "Any of your rods there?" (120). If the narrator's cottage is in the Berkshires, as seems to be the case,[13] how could he have known about such a thing? How many newspapers would he have had to peruse before learning about lightning strikes in Cornwall?[14] Criggan is an odd choice of a town for Melville to refer to here, but a revealing one, since the only town in the world with such a name, so far as I have been able to determine, is in Cornwall, England, suggesting either that the whole story takes place in England rather than the Berkshires, as otherwise seems evident from later references to "the granite Taconics and Hoosics" in the vicinity (that is, mountains and a river near Melville's Greylock) or that the lightning-rod man's sales territory extends well beyond New England and upstate New York and into the British Isles (123). (Looking at the matter more closely, it seems likely that the stranger, growing suspicious of the narrator's presumed ignorance, throws out this reference to his alleged sales in Criggan to test the limits of the narrator's knowledge of recent lightning strikes and lightning-rod installations.) In any case, the fact that the narrator knows about this incident in another country seems to suggest he is more than interested in such electrical phenomena but *obsessed* about them—so obsessed as to be constantly on the lookout for news stories about the subject.[15] This idea seems borne out by a deadly accident in Canada with which the narrator also happens to be familiar and about which he asks the stranger: "Did you hear about the event at Montreal last year? A servant girl struck at her bed-side with a rosary in her hand; the beads being metal. Does your beat extend into the Canadas?" (120). Instead of being ignorant about lightning, as appears to be the case in the beginning, here it is revealed that the narrator knows quite a lot, including a number of tragic anecdotes, and is eager to know more—unless, of course, they are both making up these incidents and then pretending to go along with the other man's claims by citing examples that are entirely fictitious. To me, the former seems the more reasonable explanation for why each character cites such odd, geographically distant incidents. If that is the case, then both characters are performing as confidence men, and the game is on, with each trying to outsmart, outwit, and expose the other as being *in wrong face*.[16]

By contrast, the lightning-rod man, whom we would expect to be well informed about the science of electricity, is repeatedly put on the defensive by the narrator and feels compelled to keep demonstrating his superior knowledge about the laws of electrical phenomena, even as he attempts to convince his host about the dangers of lightning and the need for protection, as he does when he points out that "the heated air and soot are conductors;—to say nothing of those immense iron fire-dogs" (120). "Not for worlds!" he exclaims, could he bring himself to step on such a hearth with such heavy ironwork during a thunderstorm. Instead he holds his ground "in the exact middle of the cottage," though, having brought a lot of rainwater inside the cottage with him, he is now standing in the middle of a puddle, "his strange walking-stick vertically resting at his side" (118). This device the narrator describes in considerable detail without ever saying exactly what it is or what he thinks it is, referring to it only as "the thing," before "bowing politely" and then launching into a facetious little speech in which he queries his visitor about who he is and whether he is the one responsible for brewing up the current storm, all the while using oddly inflated language reminiscent of the famous prankster Franklin, whom Melville caricatured in *Israel Potter* (the first installment of which was published in *Putnam's Monthly* just a month before "The Lightning-Rod Man" appeared there in August 1854): "'Sir,' said I, bowing politely, 'have I the honor of a visit from that illustrious god, Jupiter Tonans [i.e., Jupiter the Thunderer]? So stood he in the Greek statue of old, grasping the lightning bolt. If you be he, or his viceroy, I have to thank you for this noble storm you have brewed among our mountains. Listen: That was a glorious peal. Ah, to a lover of the majestic, it is a good thing to have the Thunderer himself in one's cottage'" (119).

When the narrator "invitingly" plants a chair on the hearth and encourages his visitor to be seated there, the stranger, hearing another awful crash outside, calls out in warning to his host to "quit the hearth." When the latter resists, he cries out again, "Are you so horridly ignorant, then, as not to know, that by far the most dangerous part of a house during such a terrific tempest as this, is the fire-place?"—a line that speaks directly to a central question in the story about knowledge, knowledge about the science of lightning and electrical conductors in particular, and the dangers to life and limb that can result from ignorance about that science (119).

Hearing this, the narrator, feeling (or pretending to feel) intimidated, admits his ignorance and "involuntarily" steps away from the hearth onto the "first board next to the stone," but then immediately claims to feel so abused and admonished by the arrogant air of the stranger that he steps—"quite involuntarily again" (another suspicious claim)—back onto the hearth while adopting a new bodily pose, namely, the "proudest posture I could command" (119–20). Pride, it seems, is a stronger motivator for the narrator than the natural human desire for safety, thus making him appear not only insecure but reckless and stubborn, though surely this, too, is an act on the narrator's part. Continuing to show more concern for his dignity than his safety, he addresses his visitor once again as "Mr. Jupiter Tonans," and stiffly intones, "I am not accustomed to be commanded in my own house." As their conflict heats up, the stranger, equally offended now, warns the narrator, "Call me not by that pagan name. You are profane in this time of terror" (120), a line that admonishes the narrator but also hints at a broader historical or metaphysical, religious conflict emerging between the two.

However, rather than respond to the charge of being "profane," the narrator changes the subject and asks his visitor to "be so good as to tell me your business" and identify himself (120). To this the stranger responds simply, "I am a dealer in lightning-rods." Before, however, he can explain his "special business," he is interrupted by another huge thunderbolt, which prompts him to turn the tables, go back on the offensive, and ask the narrator—in a way that appears designed to threaten him personally, if not bodily—whether he has "ever been struck—your premises, I mean?" before promising to "make a Gibraltar" of his cottage "by a few waves of this wand" and the sale of one of his lightning rods. The narrator, without answering the question, exposes the stranger's evasiveness when he reminds him that he was about to explain his "special business," observing, "You interrupted yourself." Only then does the salesman say explicitly that the nature of his business is "to travel the country for *orders for lightning-rods*" (my emphasis)—not to sell and install lightning rods, but simply to take "orders," and presumably collect payment, *in advance*, at a price of "only one dollar a foot." Given such sly, carefully constructed language on the part of both interlocutors, it seems evident that Melville was doing a preliminary sketch, in this story, for his tour de force novel *The Confidence-Man* that would soon follow, with its parade of characters engaging in ambiguous sales pitches and showing at best a questionable kind of trust. It is at this point that the salesman, trying to close a deal, claims to "have the best of references," only to fumble in his pockets in a showy effort to supply something concrete before coming up empty-handed, substituting instead the odd, geographically distant claim about the twenty-three lightning rods he had recently installed in Criggan.

Again it seems clear the narrator is acting or *performing* the role of innocent—despite his extensive knowledge about electrical storms—in order to get the better of the lightning-rod man, by exposing him as a charlatan, a man *in wrong face*. At several new turns, he tests the stranger's truth claims, at first pointing out that his rods were evidently useless in Criggan (at which juncture the lightning-rod man shifts the blame to the shoddy execution of the workman who installed the rods there); and then by asking, a bit irrelevantly, whether the salesman had heard about the fate of the poor Catholic servant girl in Canada who was struck dead by lightning while clutching her iron beads, a sad story that has less to do with the efficacy of lightning rods than with the relative dangers of various metals during lightning strikes. Here the salesman puts in a pitch for his copper rods as being far superior to the iron rods typically used by the "fools" in that country, a claim that suggests how adept the narrator is at getting the salesman to condemn his competitors, thus undermining the case for lightning rods in general. Still playing the role of innocent interlocutor, but alert to problematic claims by the salesman, the narrator observes that "this abuse of your own calling in another might make one distrustful with respect to yourself," at which juncture the stranger quickly changes the subject again. Finally, showing real suspicion now, the narrator challenges the lightning-rod man for making house calls at the most coldly calculated time, namely, "When the thunder is storming" (120–21). Some people, in the aggressive sales atmosphere of the time, or so he implies, will take every advantage, make any dubious claim, or do whatever else it may take to secure a sale.

The real crisis in this little drama, however, occurs when the stranger offers up another bit of scientific arcana—a reverse principle, according to which lightning sometimes passes from earth to sky, rather than, as people usually think, from sky to earth. The narrator's ears perk up at this discovery ("Something you just said, instead of alarming me, has strangely inspired confidence")—presumably because it means such a device cannot provide complete protection even during an electrical storm. Nothing can. Also at play here perhaps is some of Franklin's own thinking about this discovery, which he, too, as a deist, found to be a relief. For if, as Dray explains, "some of the force that created lightning originated in the earth, that meant it was coming from a location opposite to where God presumably dwelled, and there was now even less reason to object to man's 'presumption' in trying to defend himself from it."[17] Having learned about the phenomenon of "the returning-stroke," the narrator responds by muttering to himself, "Better and better," before inviting the stranger once again to join him on the hearth to dry out (122), in recognition of the fact that if there are no absolute protections from electrical strikes after all, he might as well make himself comfortable. Here the narrator begins to gain a rhetorical advantage over the salesman, and the lightning-rod man's sales pitch starts to crack and fall apart.

Thinking fast and shifting ground, the narrator goes on the offensive, while all but admitting he has been "playing dumb" until this point, when he challenges the salesman: "'And now, since our being dumb will not help us,' said I, resuming my place, 'let me hear your precautions in travelling during thunderstorms'" (123). Clearly lightning rods are of no use at such times, which for a salesman, traveling from door to door, must be most of the time! How good, after all, can they be, if the rods cannot protect the lightning-rod man himself? In response, the stranger—never at a loss for words—runs off a litany of some of the many things he avoids, such as "pine-trees, high houses, lonely barns" and such, only to end by saying that, more than anything, "I avoid tall men." Acting shocked, and twisting the meaning of the salesman's confession to make it seem the lightning-rod man is advocating misanthropy, the narrator responds (with an exclamation of mock horror that sounds like the Cosmopolitan in *The Confidence-Man*): "Do I dream? Man avoid man? and in danger-time too?" This, however, is the moment when the salesman, after making an effort to clarify his own much narrower, commonsense meaning, finally loses all patience and exclaims, "But, sir, *you have kept me so long answering your questions,* that I have not yet come to business. Will you order one of my rods?" (123; my emphasis). Given the salesman's explosive, frustrated response, we can finally see what the narrator has been up to: by repeatedly asking questions that test the stranger's credibility, he has prevented him from working his sales pitch, until the lightning-rod man grows so frustrated as to lose all patience and immediately play his high card, a grisly, horrifying scare tactic, which he blurts out angrily, "Will you order? Will you buy? . . . Think of being a heap of charred offal, like a haltered horse burnt in his stall;—and all in one flash!" (124).

At this, the narrator goes ballistic, launching into an extended tirade in which he claims to expose the salesman as a "false negotiator" or "pretended envoy extraordinary and minister plenipotentiary to and from Jupiter Tonans," not to mention a latter-day version of Johann Tetzel, the German Dominican preacher who became famous for peddling "indulgences from divine ordinations" (124). At the same time, he coolly claims that he himself, "in thunder as in sunshine," stands "at ease in the hands of my God," though pointedly, his statement is perfectly timed to coincide with the moment when "the scroll of the storm is rolled back; the house is unharmed; and in the blue heavens" he can read "in the rainbow, that the Deity will not, of purpose, make war on man's earth" (124). In other words, it is only when all danger has passed and it is safe for him to make such a claim that the narrator speaks assuredly of his faith. With a blue sky and a rainbow overhead, even an atheist might claim to be living in a secure world. Even so, here the narrator continues to maintain *face,* the face of an innocent man, but now also a man of religious faith, though by his own testimony, his faith appears to be viable for him only when the sky is blue and he has no reason to feel threatened.

Several critics of Melville story, starting with Ben D. Kimpel, writing in *American Literature* in 1944, have regarded Melville's story as a religious allegory or debate between science and religion,[18] the rationalist tradition of Benjamin Franklin versus the evangelical Protestant tradition of Jonathan Edwards, sometimes with the salesman, who asserts emphatically, "*Mine is the only true rod,*" viewed as a peddler of religious dogma in disguise.[19] Most such readings take the concluding exchange between the lightning-rod man and the narrator at face value and argue either that Melville, impatient with the growing influence of science in his own century, satirizes the scientific claims about lightning rods or (working around the religious censors who refused to publish another of his stories, "The Two Temples," written just months earlier) makes fun of uncritical, unexamined religious claims about the efficacy of evangelical Christian faith.[20] More recently, Joshua Matthews has turned attention to the portion of the exchange between the two characters at the end when the lightning-rod man accuses the narrator of being an "Impious wretch" and vows to expose or "publish" his "infidel notions" to the world (124). For Matthews, the explanation for this curious ending to the story lies in eighteenth- and nineteenth-century American discourses on lightning rods, which lead him to conclude that Melville is satirizing "two American types—the rural democrat and the door-to-door salesman," while critiquing "the rhetoric of consumer marketing in commercial periodicals" and at the same time "commenting on political and religious divisions in American culture."[21] While the study of these early discourses is useful in providing historical context for Melville's story, as well as illuminating commentaries on it, what needs to be recognized is that both characters are performing their respective roles in the competing discourses of science and religion, and that the narrator appears to be the more dishonest and deceptive of the two—because he is so clearly playing the role of one who is ignorant about lightning.

In my reading, the narrator is not someone who necessarily believes in what he says about his religious faith but instead adopts his position for the nonce and with the goal of outthinking the salesman, his opponent, to the point of defeating him and sending him on his way without a sale. In fact, it is hard to know what the narrator believes, because he seems to ask questions and take up positions merely to counter, frustrate, delay, or provoke his opponent. But just because he claims it is not always possible to "thoroughly avert the supernal bolt," even for one who may be so gifted as to be able to "strike a bit of green light from a Leyden jar," as Franklin himself was known to do,[22] that does not mean he is an evangelical Christian. When he asserts to the salesman, "In thunder as in sunshine, I stand at ease in the hands of my God" (124), he may be doing nothing more than expressing his fatalism, as someone who believes his end will come when it comes, no matter what measures he may take to prevent it.

It seems certain, however, that the lightning-rod salesman has met his match even as he has finally figured out that the narrator is another "lightning-rod man" like himself—or a rough approximation, someone who knows as much or more about electrical storms and lightning rods than he does. When the stranger "blackens" his face and "foams" at the narrator, calling him an "Impious wretch" with "infidel notions," that sort of language makes sense in the context of the story only if he has concluded that the narrator is really a lightning-rod man in disguise, one who in their final exchange proves himself untrue to his calling, and claims to be a fatalist or man of religious faith rather than a man of science who puts his faith in lightning rods. The *salesman's* threat at the end of the story to *call him out* seems to rest on the assumption that any lightning-rod man who articulates the sort of faith expressed by the narrator is a discredit to his trade and needs to be exposed as a fraud. Whether the narrator does succeed, to any degree, in exposing the salesman seems doubtful, for he ends by confessing that the lightning-rod salesman, though driven from his house, still "dwells in the land," where he continues to "travel in storm-time, and drives a brave trade with the fears of man," in spite of the narrator's efforts to warn his neighbors about him. Their entire interaction is presented as a contest, a game of intelligence or wits, an early instance of "the dozens," wherein the two try to outtalk, outcurse, outthink one another. However, in this case the potential victim turns the tables on his antagonist and drives him from his house, proving, in this instance at least, that he is the superior player.

In the end, however, the narrator remains the slipperier player, too—as sly and manipulating and hard to pin down as the Franklin caricatured in *Israel Potter*. In their final confrontation, after calling each other names or likening one another to animals—a charred horse, in the one case; a wet, shiny worm, in the other—the lightning-rod man, in a fit of pique, rushes at the narrator and aims his "tri-forked thing at my heart." The narrator, equal to the occasion, responds with a frenzy of his own, exclaiming, "I seized it; I snapped it; I dashed it; I trod it; and dragging the dark lightning-king out of my door, flung his elbowed, copper *sceptre* after him" (124; my emphasis). In this comic, climactic moment he incarnates, in an ironic way, the well-known tribute that Benjamin Franklin, in his later years, had earned in recognition of his achievements as the clever scientist who tamed the electrical energy in lightning and the wily diplomat who secured French aid for the American cause in the fight for independence from Britain: *Eripuit caelo fulmen sceptrumque tyrannis* ("He snatched lightning from the skies and the scepter from tyrants").[23] Clearly, the predatory practices of lightning-rod salesmen had reached a fever pitch in the region of Melville's Berkshire mountain home, enough so that he came to think of these salesmen as more than a nuisance and called them names; they were not only "tyrants" but "worms"! What is equally evident is that

Melville continued to be fascinated by Franklin, his eighteenth-century kinsman who seems to have served as both the model for his narrator and the inspiration for his lightning-rod salesman.

In the end, the salesman is the one who is most clearly and emphatically exposed as being *out of face* or *in wrong face* as the result of their encounter. He alone—unmasked and driven out as an imposter—has reason to feel ashamed and inferior because of his confrontation with the narrator. Certainly he is the one who has the most reason to feel his reputation as a legitimate salesman has been seriously challenged as a result of his encounter with the narrator. At least for this moment, he loses his composure and runs away, while the narrator experiences a soul-satisfying triumph for his success in outtalking and outtricking his maddening adversary. His sense of triumph is short-lived, however, as he discovers that "spite of my treatment, and spite of my dissuasive talk of him to my neighbors, the Lightning-rod man still dwells in the land; still travels in storm-time, and drives a brave trade with the fears of man" (124). In the world of aggressive itinerant salesmen, where scare tactics and appeals to the customer's fear of death—a grisly death by entrapment in a building engulfed by fire—are so outlandish as to be infuriating and deserve to be called out, there is always another customer, another victim, and other scare tactics, too, an idea that Melville explored at length in *The Confidence-Man*.

# 5

## "THE ENCANTADAS, OR ENCHANTED ISLES"

### Bodies as Fragments

Readers have long puzzled over the loose, fragmented structure of Melville's "The Encantadas." For Leon Howard, the sketches were a failed attempt to "arrive at some sort of central narrative" while trying to make headway on a larger, never-completed book on "Tortoises or Tortoise-Hunting." Howard was among the first to point out that Melville used a variety of sources to supplement the memory of his own brief experiences during two visits to the Galapagos, in 1841–42, but none of these, and none of his own experiences, "gave him the narrative framework he needed." Melville at this point in his life, Howard said, "lacked invention."[1] William B. Dillingham and others have argued for an underlying unity in these pieces—unity of mood, for instance, in the burned-out atmosphere; or unity of theme, such as the fall of man or the circles of Hell in Dante's *Inferno*.[2] However, no critic has viewed the fragmentation of this collection into separate "Sketches" as purposeful, new, or experimental, even though from the start of his career, with "Fragments from a Writing Desk" (1839), through *Moby-Dick* (1851) and *The Confidence-Man* (1857), Melville had shown a penchant for the fragment and for composing works with experimental designs, as in his diptychs, "The Paradise of Bachelors and the Tartarus of Maids" and "Poor Man's Pudding and Rich Man's Crumbs," among other works. Consistent with his practice at other times in his career, I see Melville's sketches as a series of fragments that are strategically ordered to form a pattern suggesting not so much unity of theme but the construction of a worldview, piece by piece, one with historical and cultural implications for the Galapagos Islands, South America, and the Americas more generally.

In these ten pieces, Melville writes under a pseudonym, Salvator R. Tarnmoor, an ironic, poetic, dark-minded figure whose name is remindful of Salvator Rosa, the Italian painter of desolate landscapes Melville so admired, but suggestive of someone of mixed European heritage and cosmopolitan in character ("Tarnmoor" is a British place name but not a common family name). That pseudonym, especially in the case of the sketches' original publication in *Putnam's Monthly*, where Melville's own name did not appear, was a kind of disguise but also a clue to Melville's use of artifice and enchantment in these stories.[3] As a former sailor, the narrator presents himself as a careful observer who has visited the islands, explored several of them firsthand, and read widely in the records of their history. While intrigued by early whalers' reports about the islands' mysterious movements, he explains away such movements as the product of powerful currents and otherwise presents himself as the kind of observer who sees through the islands' mysteries. To be sure, he can be a dreamer, but his dreams—which in one colorful instance become a "wild nightmare" involving monsters, Brahmins, and "volcanic mazes"—seem always to center on the "spectre-tortoises" that are so naturally identified with the islands. As suggested by the sketches devoted to Rock Rodondo, with its "Pisgah View" of the islands, he is otherwise occupied with observing, orienting, collecting information, assessing, and reporting. Like the three authorities he claims to be the only eyewitnesses "worth mentioning touching the Enchanted Isles:—Cowley, the Buccaneer (1684); Colnett, the whaling-ground explorer (1793); [and] Porter, the post captain (1813)"—he portrays himself as a reliable "eye-witness,"[4] one who depends on his own knowledge, even when it contradicts these authorities. This is a point he makes explicit in an elaborate Note at the end of Sketch Ninth, saying that if any readers doubt the existence of such a crazy, "diabolical" creature as the Hermit Oberlus, they will find confirmation in Porter, but without missing a beat, he then confesses he has "added to Porter's facts accessory ones picked up in the Pacific from reliable sources; and where facts conflict," he adds with a nod and a wink, he "has naturally preferred his own authorities to Porter's," as he does when he "corrects" the name of the island inhabited by Oberlus (169–70). Trust me, he seems to say, I know my subject. In any case, his *practice* suggests that one should trust one's own eyes and sources and not those of others, but also that all eyewitness accounts are subjective and subject to revision or correction, a practice that seems especially appropriate regarding a place like the Encantadas, where the islands reportedly move around, and stories abound about the weird, and in some cases monstrous people and animals who inhabit them.

Finally, the narrator claims to be someone who does not turn away from dark truths or depressing events, though he does admit to having his limits. In the sketch of the Chola widow, Hunilla, where he speaks of the futility of persons in authority banning books deemed "baneful," he does so to underscore his feeling that censorship of any kind is ridiculous when it comes to protecting the sensibilities of others, since real events can be so much "deadlier" or more baneful than the "dreams of doting men." Even as he hints to his readers that something quite terrible happened to Hunilla, something he refuses to name, he asserts with matter-of-fact realism, "Those whom books will hurt will not be proof against events," adding sardonically, "Events, not books, should be forbid" (156), an assertion that more than hints at the narrator's firsthand experience of a wide range of truly "baneful" events. Throughout he appears careful to report only what he knows, or can verify from other sources, even if these matters involve only partial truths or fragments. Still, in Hunilla's case, she is the only one who knows what happened on Norfolk Isle and the most crucial part of her story is implied or communicated silently; the narrator will not say more. More generally, the narrator's task is a tricky one: he must re-create a distant world that is so unusual as to seem "enchanted," and he must do so for an audience made up of readers of *Putnam's Monthly,* who have surely never seen its like anywhere in the world before.

Islands, particularly constellated islands, are necessarily fragments, pieces of a larger whole, and must be portrayed in series if the reader is to imagine and comprehend them, either individually or in the aggregate. For the most part, this is how they are experienced or taken in; so this is how they need to be described. Moreover, for these especially strange and distant "Enchanted Isles," with their limited human history, it is also the case that whatever can be known about them, from personal observation or other travelers, is at best haphazard and fragmented—pieces of history, anecdotes, partial descriptions, "facts" with little context or none at all.[5] Melville had composed a work with a similar fragmented structure several years earlier in *Mardi* (1849), but there the incidents—set in a much larger, worldwide archipelago—are held together by the hero's quest for his lost love, Yillah, and the utopian society he feels must be her hiding place. Here, by contrast, there is no quest; only the narrator's serial treatment of several of the very peculiar Galapagos Isles known to few people since their accidental discovery by the Spanish bishop of Panama, Father Tomas de Berlanga, in 1535.

Deborah Harter, in her study of fantastic fiction titled *Bodies in Pieces: Fantastic Narrative and the Poetics of the Fragment* (1996), makes the useful observation that "all narrative reality is a problem in emergence—a strategic uncovering, in a strategic order, of images that can only ever be partial. Regardless of the genre, the writer must construct a world through the process of description in language, and to describe a thing is already to be obliged to break it into its parts before striving in the telling to reassemble its wholeness." The writer relies on the fragment, building up his subject and its meaning, as Roland Barthes had earlier argued in *S/Z* (1970), piece by piece, block by block.[6] Harter describes two basic modes of representation—realist and fantastic—with consequent differences in treatment. In the one, the realist writer reproduces an image, uncovering it piece by piece, "as we expect to see it," while the fantastic writer "transform[s] that image into something else"—deforms it into something strange, and unexpected, possibly even something monstrous. In realistic renderings, our vision is invited to "settle ultimately on moments of assembly," and we are encouraged to "'see' the images before us as completely as possible, as quickly as possible." By contrast, fantastic narrative "short-circuits description as process. It becomes fascinated with isolated, constitutive moments. It emphasizes the halting stages before the picture is complete."[7] The fantastic, or in this case the enchanted, seizes on detail, stops short at a fragmented picture, though some approximation of the whole may be still suggested to the reader's imagination in a partial, distorted form. For the reader, the test for such fantastic renderings of the world is whether they are credible and bear some resemblance, some recognizable connection to the world the reader knows firsthand.

Does Melville engage in "a strategic uncovering, in a strategic order, of images" in these sketches? In the middle of the nineteenth century, the Galapagos Islands remained one of the least known places on earth. Charles Darwin, who visited there just a few years before Melville did and whose *The Voyage of the Beagle* (1839) Melville almost surely knew, explained why: they are so isolated and remote as to provide a wholly insulated, unique environment for the development of unfamiliar species of plants and animals, separate from but parallel to their cousins in the world outside. At the time when Melville wrote, the Galapagos Islands were the closest thing anyone had ever seen to a separate world, a world within the known world, yet one to which we feel a tie, to borrow a phrase from Henry James. Implicitly, Melville posits the islands as a "test case," a little, unknown world within the larger known world of Latin America and beyond, while reporting back to his American readers about what has happened on these islands since the first records of their discovery in the early sixteenth century, all with the objective of taking his measure of the colonial enterprise, in miniature, and its aftermath in the Western Hemisphere—not as a historian working on a broad canvas but as a landscape and portrait painter doing sketches on a small scale.

Ostensibly the first five sketches explore what is known of the landscape, natural history, and location of the islands, and what can be understood to be the distinctive operations of natural law there. But at another level these initial sketches treat the tools of analysis, or principles, required to engage in the kind of critique Melville himself was undertaking in these stories, from the awakening of the moral sense in the discovery of "difference" and death, and the awakening of the aesthetic imagination in the discovery of disfigurement, deformation, or deviance in Sketches First and Second; then through the discovery of hierarchies of power—first among species, specifically birds and fishes at Rock Rodondo, then among social classes, which the narrator identifies in terms of "thrones, princedoms, powers, dominating one above another in senatorial array" (135)— and the equally important and related discovery of historical succession, first Spanish, then English (another hierarchy of power, defined by nation-building and colonial expansion and contraction) in Sketches Third and Fourth; and finally on to the recognition that all experience is culturally mediated or subjective, and susceptible to the wars of nations—the War of 1812, in this case—in Sketch Fifth. The last five sketches, in turn, explore five cultural models defined by race and gender, class and nation, and five sets of characters representing various levels of alienation or entrapment and their responses to the environmental and cultural challenges of life on individual islands within the Encantadas. All qualify as "bodies on trial" because of the challenges of living and surviving on these dry and desolate islands on the equator, hundreds of miles from the mainland—English buccaneers; a Creole adventurer from Cuba; an enterprising mixed-race Indian woman from Peru and her husband and half-brother; a "wild white creature" and would-be dictator named Oberlus from Europe (162); and an assortment of "runaways, castaways, solitaries" (170) who have sought shelter or refuge on these Pacific outposts of South America. These two worlds, the little one of the islands and the large, continental one beyond, slowly inch closer and closer together over time, and begin, ever so slightly, to merge, in history and in the popular imagination—a process that Melville contributes to in publishing "The Encantadas." Without ever explicitly saying so, Melville seems to ask, What do these several human portraits, slim and fragmented though they are, tell us about the larger, Pacific world we live in, circa 1854? And what do they portend for those of us who are outsiders? If Darwin had made an evolutionary discovery on the Galapagos Islands about the larger world's biological condition, what might Melville's sketches reveal about the condition, politically and culturally, of the larger world of his readers?

The first sketch, "The Isles at Large," presents a droll version of a creation myth ("Take five-and twenty heaps of cinders dumped here and there in an outside city lot . . ."). The islands are a bleak, burned-out extreme—"cinders"—and together constitute the most "desolate" place on earth; unlike anything ever seen before, they seem entirely *other*-worldly, but dark, mysterious, evil, dying or dead—a direful reminder of a forbidding truth about what is possible in extremis—an extended if fragmented memento mori. Or so it seems. For no matter how much the narrator declaims about the "desolateness" and deadliness, the changelessness and "uninhabitableness" of these equatorial islands; no matter how much he is reminded of "abandoned cemeteries of long ago" and of the world at large "after a penal conflagration" (126) or the ashy "Apples of Sodom" and the fallen worlds of Pluto and Tartarus (127–28), what he recalls after the fact, after he has returned home and finds himself under the "mysterious" and persistent influences of nature there, are the haunting images of living creatures, particularly the "dusky shells, and long languid necks" of the Galapagos tortoises (129) that, by their example, give new meaning to theories of the persistence of life and undaunted purpose, even as they and the other animals on the islands gave new meaning, to Darwin, about the agelessness of the natural world and the relentless unfolding of the generations. While the Ferryman who speaks in the excerpt from Spenser's *Faerie Queene* (II.xii) that opens "Sketch First, The Isles at Large," encourages his listener to "shone" [shun] the islands, "For they have oft drawne many a wandring wight / Into most deadly daunger and distressed plight," Melville's narrator, the pseudonymous Salvator R. Tarnmoor, has not so "fastened / His foot thereon" as "never it recure" [recover] nor does he "wandreth ever more uncertain and unsure." More than being tested or tried by his experience on the islands, the narrator has been changed or transformed by it, but not so much that he has simply exchanged one monolithic view for another. Instead, he has been compelled to view the world in binary terms that make for ambiguity, as embodied in the figure of the Galapagos tortoise, with its dark and bright sides.

Sketch Second, "Two Sides to a Tortoise," confirms the discovery of difference, of death, but extends it to the awakening of the aesthetic imagination as well, and the recognition of pleasure and pain, beauty and disfigurement or defect. The epigraph for this sketch (a continuation of the epigraph from II.xii of Spenser's *Faerie Queene*) reads, in part:

> Most ugly shapes and horrible aspects,
> Such as Dame Nature selfe mote feare to see,
> Or shame, that ever should so fowle defects
> From her most cunning hand escaped bee;
> All dreadfull pourtraicts of deformitee.

A second epigraph, however, from this same sketch, contradicts this view, or "turns it over," as one might turn over an ancient black tortoise to see its bright underside:

> Fear naught, then said the palmer, well avized,
> For these same monsters are not these indeed,
> But are into these fearful shapes disguized.

As such, this composite view of Spenser's, as it comes to us through Melville's narrator, Tarnmoor, seems to support Harter's argument that the fantastic cannot be taken in all at once but must be apprehended in fragments or stages to determine its true character.

If Sketch First sees the Galapagos Isles as a desolate wasteland that asks the question, How could anything live there, or how persist, if life is so parched and unpromising as it appears?, then the second, "Two Sides to a Tortoise," answers with the suggestion that there is, perhaps, another view of the matter, that there are two sides to existence—a dark and a bright, just as there are two sides to the "spectre-tortoise"—if one only knew where, and how, to look. In this binary, which is central to Melville's imagery and to his conception of this entire collection, we find an instance of the sense of strangeness or deformity, the "enchantment," that comes with a partial or fragmented view, followed by the tempering of that extreme "deformitee" when another fragment, with a separate frame of reference, is brought into the picture to complement or complete it, for as Spenser's Palmer explains, "these same Monsters are not there in deed, / But are into these fearfull shapes disguized." What began as "enchantment" or "magic" becomes, not humanized, but *naturalized* after a second look and when married to a second dimension, to the point where we can recognize the Galapagos tortoise to be a part of the natural order. Once that happens, through a process of change known as "anamorphism," the giant tortoise is no longer viewed partially, in a distorted or "disguized" form, but in an approximation of it as whole. Add to this new knowledge the tortoises' incredible persistence, their "drudging impulse to straightforwardness in a belittered world," and they begin to be familiarized even more, even humanized—as Ishmael humanizes the fantastic, larger-than-life features of the sperm whale in the cetology chapters of

*Moby-Dick* (132). Here, then, we encounter Melville's first suggestion as to the meaning of "enchantment" in these sketches; rather than something inherent in the islands themselves, enchantment is a sense of things that comes from a partial or fragmented view of them—a first impression in which their real complexity or layered-ness is "disguized" by the distortion of oversimplification. It is the narrator's job to present to his readers the distorted, deformed, "disguized" view of the islands, but it is also his job to remove the disguise and "dis-enchant" us, something he does, with comic effect, in Sketch Second when he shifts from talking about three particular Galapagos tortoises as "antediluvian-looking," "mystic creatures," victims of "a downright diabolical enchanter" yet somehow also identical to those "whereon the Hindoo plants this total sphere" (131–32) to something as mundane and appealing to the senses as a dinner or "merry repast from tortoise steaks and tortoise stews" for the narrator and his shipmates (132–33), a culinary reference that echoes the sumptuous dinners in Melville's "The Paradise of Bachelors." To be sure, in "The Encantadas," Melville was not writing a travelogue or a travel report, as Darwin had done in composing his *Voyage of the Beagle,* but a work of imaginative literature *disguised* as a travel report, one with a richer set of objectives than critics sometimes assume to be the case—a miniature cosmology, a taxonomy, an allegory, and a history all in one.[8]

Melville devotes Sketches Third and Fourth to Rock Rodondo, a "high stone tower" of an island that stands "solitary and alone" (133), the first one providing views of what the rock looks like from afar while the second comments on the view of the surrounding sea from the top of the rock, in much the same way Ishmael looks out on the ocean from the masthead of the *Pequod*.[9] In both cases, the view involves deception or misperception and something like disguise. Though Rock Rodondo is "visible at a distance of thirty miles," it "fully participat[es] in that enchantment which pervades the group," leading to its "invariably" being "mistaken for a sail," especially when first seen from afar, thanks to the streaks of bird-lime from "unnumbered seafowl" that stain the tower from "sea to air" (134).[10] There he pauses to observe the various "outlandish beings" that occupy the several shelves of Rodondo: particularly the penguins, their bodies "grotesquely misshapen; their bills short; their feet seemingly legless;

while the members at their sides are neither fin, wing, nor arm." Neither "fish, flesh, nor fowl," they are the "most ambiguous and least lovely creature yet discovered by man." On the next shelf above, he observes "woebegone regiments" of pelicans, "large strange fowl" with ashy plumage who stand "for hours together without motion," while on the next shelf above them are the gony or gray albatross, "anomalously so called, unsightly, unpoetic bird, unlike its storied kinsman," the "snow-white ghost of Capes Hope and Horn." On higher shelves still, he simply mentions the remaining marine birds who inhabit the tower but, as if to underline the existence of a biological hierarchy of power among them, he notes in general that they are all "serially disposed in order of their magnitude:—gannets, black and speckled haglets, jays, sea-hens, sperm-whale birds, gulls of all varieties:—" and then adds, as if to suggest parallels or analogies with the hierarchy of power among nations, "thrones, princedoms, powers, dominating one above another in senatorial array" (135). Turning briefly, then, to the lifeforms under the water around the tower, the narrator notes that "Rodondo had its full counterpart in the finny hosts which peopled the waters at its base." Without enumerating, he simply asserts that "All were strange; many exceedingly beautiful," before saying flatly, "Nothing was more striking than the complete novelty of many individuals of this multitude. Here hues were seen as yet unpainted, and figures which are unengraved" (136). Like the Wall Street world of "Bartleby, the Scrivener," the world of the Galapagos Islands is populated by oddities or deviants from the norm; this is as true of the birds and fish the narrator observes as it is of the people he will later write about in the last several sketches, all of which initially appear strange or fantastic but quickly challenge readers to normalize or naturalize them to the point where they can begin to be regarded as creatures of the known world.

The second sketch of Rodondo, subtitled "A Pisgah View from the Rock," turns things around and provides an ironic account of what can be seen from the vantage point of this rock, for rather than view a promised land as Moses is said to have done from Mount Pisgah, in Gilead, Melville's narrator admits that, once you look "edgeways, as it were," past the "Burnt District of the Enchanted Isles," "*You see nothing*" (my emphasis), and then, since there is nothing for one to see, he goes on to entreat the reader to "permit me to point out the direction, if not the place of certain interesting objects in the vast sea," including their distance from Quito and the rest of South America to the east, and their relation to the Kingsmill Islands and the islands of Polynesia to the west and southwest, before turning to the Enchanted Islands themselves, in spite of the fact that even these cannot be seen from Rock Rodondo (137)—thus ironically calling attention to the fact that much if not all of this "pointing" and orienting could have been done just as well (and may have been done in fact) from the comfort of the author's writing desk at home as from the top of Rock Rodondo itself. As he admits near the end of his discussion of the islands of Narborough and Albemarle, "Where we still stand, here on Rodondo, we cannot see all the other isles, but," he adds wryly, "it is a good place from which to point out where they lie" (141). Even when he confesses to rely on another eyewitness account to fill in the blanks for him, the published voyages of Cowley, he quotes Cowley as saying he named a particular "fantastic isle" after himself, "Cowley's Enchanted Isle," but still does not know, exactly, what he has seen, "for we having had a sight of it upon several points of the compass, it appeared always in as many different forms, sometimes like a ruined fortification" and at another like "a great city." To which Melville's narrator adds, "No wonder though, that among the Encantadas all sorts of ocular deceptions and mirages should be met" (142). In this Sketch Fourth, too, he lays the groundwork for future discussion of the important historical and geopolitical fact of colonial succession, as seen in the renaming of the islands after English kings, rather than the earlier Spanish ones, once England had become the world's dominant sea power.

After the two Rock Rodondo sketches that orient the reader biologically, in terms of birds and fish and nature's hierarchy of power, and then geographically, in terms of the islands' positions relative to one another and to other islands in the Pacific farther west, then comes Sketch Fifth on Captain David Porter. Here Tarnmoor begins to orient the reader—particularly the American and the British reader—historically, and engages in some political boosterism about America's emergence as an international power in the region as well as some storytelling about its chief connection to the islands, in the War of 1812, when Porter's frigate *Essex* encountered an "enigmatic craft" that flew "American colors in the morning and English in the evening—her sails full of wind in a calm." Eventually the mystery craft got away, and Porter's frigate went on to enjoy "the strangest and most stirring [cruise] to be found in the history of the American navy," capturing the most distant vessels of the Britain's navy and decimating her Pacific whaling industry in the vicinity of the Galapagos Archipelago. Here Tarnmoor also chooses to mention there are "but three eye-witness authorities worth mention touching the Enchanted Isles": "Cowley, the Buccaneer (1684); Colnett, the whaling-ground explorer (1798); Porter, the post captain (1813). Other than these you have but barren, bootless allusions from some few passing voyagers or compilers" (143). Perhaps tellingly, he makes no mention of Darwin, the greatest eyewitness authority of all, even though it is very likely that Melville (but presumably not Tarnmoor) had read Darwin's *The Voyage of the Beagle,* either on his long return from the Pacific on the *United States*, which had a copy on board, or sometime after he purchased the book in 1847.[11]

These various efforts at orientation accomplished, Melville's narrator then moves entirely into the second or anecdotal human history portion of the sketches, all of which treat themes of deformation—deformation of bodies as well as character—amid cultural conflict, struggle, confinement, and exploitation. In keeping with the islands' powers of enchantment, all the characters who come to the Galapagos, even the relatively carefree buccaneers, are radically transformed or deformed, and made monstrous in the process (or so it seems) as their bodies and minds are necessarily forced to undergo trials of strength, resourcefulness, and endurance as a result of the desolate conditions on the islands and their isolation from the known world. The islands have a long history of such transformations, going back to an old superstition among sailors that "all wicked sea-officers . . . are at death . . . transformed into tortoises" who must dwell forever after "upon these hot aridities" in punishment for their cruelties to sailors (128–29). The tyrannous "Dog-King," who attempts to set up a colony on Charles' Isle, becomes as ferocious as his own cavalry of dogs; Oberlus, the "hermit" turned "tyrant" (166) of Hood's Isle who enslaves stray sailors by force or trickery, is changed into a "wild white creature" (162).[12] Even the noble Hunilla is so transformed as to become mad, "entirely lost" in time's "labyrinth" (156), by the endless waiting, uncertainty, and feeling of imprisonment she suffers on Norfolk Isle; and the early buccaneers who left behind an assortment of odd, open-air seats and sofas on Barrington Isle become—if "not unmitigated monsters," then simply monstrous, for they could lounge and take in the sights "like the poet Gray" one day and turn "greatest cutthroats" and perpetrators of "the greatest outrages" the next (145–46).[13] Says the narrator at the end of Sketch Sixth concerning the transformation of the buccaneers from robbers and murderers one day to "meditative philosophers" and poets the next: "Not so improbable. For consider the vacillations of a man" (146). Consistent with the fragmented quality of these sketches, and the artistic drive to create an aura of enchantment, Melville offers at best incomplete explanations for the deformations his characters undergo on the islands. Even in the case of the tragic Hunilla, whom we are led to believe suffered grievously when she witnessed the drowning of her loved ones and is abandoned on the island for months afterward, there are huge gaps in her narrative that Melville's narrator only hints at, vaguely mentioning "two unnamed events which befell" her but refusing to reveal more, on the grounds that he does not want to provide ammunition for the scoffers or misanthropes of the world (157).[14]

Melville develops these themes of deformation and enchantment, of bodies and personalities removed from the usual constraints of law, custom, and example, but free to morph and turn ugly under the pressures of limited resources and opportunities to do evil, all within the context of larger cultural themes of injustice, tyranny, and repression—economic and political; ethnic, racial, gendered, and national—and the struggle for freedom that inevitably attends them. This idea is broadly hinted at in the epigraph for Sketch Sixth, "Barrington Isle and the Buccaneers," where the various trials these piratic figures have suffered earlier in life boil down to the exploitation of "the sons of earth," who have been robbed of their "patrimony" by the wealthy, powerful few but are now getting justice as buccaneers working outside the law (though, clandestinely, inside it as well):[15]

> Let us all servile base subjection scorn,
> And as we be sons of the earth so wide,

> Let us our father's heritage divide,
> And challenge to ourselves our portions dew
> Of all the patrimony, which a few
> Now hold in hugger-mugger in their hand.
> . . . . . . . . . . . . . . . . . . . . . . . . . . . . . . . .
> Lords of the world, and so will wander free,
> Where-so us listeth, uncontroll'd of any.

These lines, from Spenser's *Mother Hubberd's Tale,* apply most directly to Melville's buccaneers, but they are relevant as well to the Dog-King; Hunilla and her husband and brother; the Hermit Oberlus—colonizers or colonized, seekers of rightful "patrimony" all—and perhaps also to the "Runaways, Castaways, [and] Solitaries" who desert at the isles to escape a "tyrannic ship" (170), only to end up trading one set of bodily trials for new ones.

The history of the Western Hemisphere is the history of European colonization in the sixteenth and seventeenth centuries, followed by creolization in the eighteenth century, a process that fostered notions of colonial dignity and a desire for home rule or nationhood that eventuated in the wars of independence in the late eighteenth and nineteenth centuries. According to the historian Felipe Fernandez-Armesto, the Northern Hemisphere emerged from these wars relatively united, but the Southern Hemisphere was not able to overcome the "protracted, internecine, sanguinary" independence struggles and *caudillismo* that prevented the emergence of democracy and economic vitality there.[16] Melville's last five sketches recapitulate much of this history, starting with the wars among colonizing powers, Spain and England, in the chapter on the buccaneers; through the wars of independence and warlordism in the Dog-King sketch; and the chaotic aftermath that included the thirty to fifty years or so leading up to Melville's own time, the period of so-called "progress" and "modernization," following industrial models from Europe, which Melville turns on its head in the grimly satiric portrait of the Hermit Oberlus. Barrington Isle is something of an exception—a deviant even among deviants. While it proves "a harbor of safety, and a bower of ease," for the buccaneers who repair there to count their treasure and "enjoy their free-and-easies," it is "so unlike most of its neighbors," providing water, food, fuel, and "long grasses good for bedding," that "it would hardly seem of kin to them" (144–45). Other islands in the archipelago inhabited by humans are more like prisons or penal colonies controlled by tyrannical figures like the Dog-King or lonely outposts where the inhabitants suffer deprivation and other crushing challenges from which they cannot escape, as in the case of Hunilla.

Sketch Sixth goes back "near two centuries," to a period when the "famous wing of the West Indian buccaneers had been driven out of Cuban waters," only to turn their energies to "ravaging" the "Pacific side of the Spanish colonies." There, "with the regularity and timing of a modern mail, [they] waylaid the royal treasure ships plying between Manilla and Acapulco," and then repaired to Barrington Isle to count their treasure, "say their prayers," and relax in those "symmetric lounges of stone and turf" whose "fine old ruins" so fascinate the narrator (144). Melville's narrator focuses on the English examples of these buccaneers, particularly the "gentlemen" such as "a Dampier, a Wafer, and a Cowley"[17]—and then all but apologizes for their bloody deeds by going back into their painful, impoverished personal histories to explain that their "worst reproach was their desperate fortunes; whom persecution, or adversity, or secret and unavengeable wrongs, had driven from Christian society to seek the melancholy solitude or the guilty adventures of the sea" (145). Presumably he knew there were French, Portuguese, and Dutch buccaneers as well plying these waters, and that all of them were permitted to attack Spanish treasure ships because their governments were jealous of Spain, and fumed over its refusal to open its markets to international trade. But the English buccaneers were unusual in that their efforts were sometimes officially sanctioned, to the point where, when they returned home, they divided their booty with the crown and received royal pardon.[18]

Sketch Seventh, concerning "Charles' Isle and the Dog-King," in turn, reads like a parody of the colonization and *caudillismo* that defined the period immediately following the wars for independence in South America. Melville's narrator claims he acquired the story "long ago" from "a shipmate learned in all the lore of outlandish life" (146). But Rodrigo Lazo writes that Victor Wolfgang von Hagen, in the epilogue to his 1940 edition of "The Encantadas, or Enchanted Isles," revealed that the story is based on the life of General José Villamil, a Creole not from Cuba but Louisiana. As Lazo explains, "Villamil went on to fight with Ecuador in its war for independence and later attempted to establish a colony on Charles' Island." Melville simply substituted "Cuba" for Villamil's true background, "Peru" for "Ecuador," and fictionalized other details of the Dog-King's story. As Lazo further explains, "The dog-king sketch comments not only on colonization in general but also on the more specific dynamic of filibustering" and "the filibustering expeditions to Cuba in the early 1850s," which were being much debated in the United States at the time and "in the pages of *Putnam's*," too, shortly before Melville published his sketches there.[19]

In Melville's version, the Dog-King is a "Creole adventurer from Cuba" who "fought on behalf of Peru" during the time of the revolt of "the Spanish provinces from Old Spain." Rising to "high rank in the patriot army" (147), he was given his pick of the Enchanted Isles in payment for his services by the new government, and chose Charles' Isle, as Villamil had done. In *Imagined Communities* (1991), Benedict Anderson argues that Creole communities—composed of persons of European descent but born in the Americas—developed conceptions of their "nation-ness" well before most of Europe, even if their "nation" was still to be formed. Melville's Creole has no allegiance to the new nation of Peru, but instead seeks his own independent fiefdom—"for ever free from Peru, even as Peru of Spain"—with himself serving as "Supreme Lord of the Island, one of the princes of the powers of the earth" (147). With his canine cavalry to support him, he becomes the "lord and patron" of a sizable settlement of "eighty souls," but things quickly deteriorate because of the lawless character of his pilgrims, who get so out of hand he "was forced at last to proclaim martial law," and even hunt down and shoot some of the rebels (147–48).[20] Later recruits from among discontented sailors prove equally recalcitrant and lawless, and at one point a violent battle ensues, leaving several men and dogs dead and the Creole King forced into exile. The remaining pilgrims then formed not a republic or even a democracy, but a "permanent *Riotocracy*, which gloried in having no law but lawlessness." However, they, too, tried to swell their numbers by enticing deserters from ships that touched their shores, proclaiming the island "the asylum of the oppressed of all navies" and hailing every runaway sailor as "a martyr in the cause of freedom" (149), a crude parody of nation-building farther north.

As much as anything, what is reflected in this brief history is not so much the nation-building that followed the revolutions of 1808–26 in South America, but the fragmentation that came after, a fragmentation seen not just in warlordism but in the breakup of Bolivar's Gran Colombia and the United Provinces of the Rio de la Plata into their earlier constituent states, the first into Venezuela, Colombia, Panama, and Ecuador, and the second into Argentina, Uruguay, Paraguay, and Bolivia.[21] Significantly, Cuba, the home of Melville's Creole in this sketch, showed no hope of gaining independence in the decades before Melville's time. Despite sporadic slave revolts, which were brutally suppressed by the Spanish, Cuba remained a Spanish colony until the end of the nineteenth century and the Spanish-American War. Melville's Dog-King evidently saw no promise to his staying in Cuba, and sought instead to improve his lot in a place where he could be in charge and free from outside interference.

The story of "Norfolk Isle and the Chola Widow," in Sketch Eighth, is the most mundane and domestic of the five concluding sketches portraying characters who "scorn . . . servile . . . subjection" and make an effort to recover some portion of their patrimony. It is also the most poignant, even tragic, of the sketches because bitterly ironic, as the last of the epigraphs for Sketch Sixth, on the subject of the buccaneers, suggests by way of contrast: "How bravely now we live, how jocund, how near the first inheritance, without fears, how free from little troubles!" Here, in miniature, is the universal ideal, the one that the poor and disenfranchised everywhere strive for. Finally, the eighth is the longest of the sketches, the one in which Melville seems to have been most deeply invested, presumably because, as Robert Sattelmeyer and James Barbour have argued, in "The Sources and Genesis of Melville's 'Norfolk Isle and the Chola Widow,'" Melville had been considering writing a similar story of a long-suffering widow's endurance and strength along lines suggested in the "Agatha letters," which Melville wrote to Hawthorne in 1852, when he proposed that his friend might want to take over for him and do something with the real-life story of one Agatha Robertson, a Quaker woman whose husband had deserted her for seventeen years.[22] Although cultural matters enter into the story, particularly in connection with the gender and ethnicity of the title figure, it is a deeply moving and sentimental story marked by fate and chance, bad luck, and human treachery—or so it seems. Hunilla, the Chola or mixed-race Indian woman from Payta, in Peru; her pure-blood Castilian husband; and her Indian brother are enterprising young people, nascent capitalists, who venture to Norfolk Isle to collect tortoise oil, "a fluid which for its purity and delicacy is held in high estimation wherever known" (152–53). Together, they share the prospect of making quick money without much of an investment beyond their own time and effort. Newly married and of a nurturing spirit (they take their "two favorite dogs" with them), Hunilla and her husband enter into a contract with a French whaling captain to take them and the woman's brother to their chosen island and then return for them again after four months. For whatever reason (Melville's narrator can only speculate)—contrary winds? shipwreck and death? betrayal or plain treachery?—the whaleship never returns, and Hunilla's husband and brother, celebrating the successful completion of their tortoise hunting, are killed in a boating accident, while the disbelieving woman watches helplessly from the shore. Her "Romish faith" severely shaken by these losses and the loneliness that follows for weeks and months, we are told she is subjected to two additional forms of "treachery," one when ships pass her by but refuse to stop and the other, which Melville refuses to name on the grounds that "In nature, as in law, it may be libelous to speak some truths," though it is hinted to involve "whaleboats" and so also whalers (155, 157–58). What it was that drove her nearly "mad" is left to the reader's imagination, but we can guess it has to do with her being cruelly treated as a body in pieces, a "fragment" of a woman by these whalers. When we see her for the last time, in the brief sequel, returning to Payta town, "riding upon a small gray ass" and stolidly eyeing "the jointed workings of the beast's armorial cross" formed by its shoulders,[23] she becomes an image of long-suffering, long-enduring women everywhere, abused yet enduring and accorded at least a "silent reverence of respect" by the sailors on the ship that finally rescued her (159), sailors who, without Hunilla's knowledge, or so we are told, added their own contribution to the proceeds from the sale of the tortoise oil that the captain arranged for Hunilla to receive when they reached "the little port" near Payta.

However, as Melville's narrator structures it, Hunilla's story may be a fabrication. Carole Moses, in "Hunilla and Oberlus: Ambiguous Companions," argues that "there are strong internal clues that Hunilla is not what she seems" and encourages readers to look closely at the epigraphs for her story, since they seem to be inconsistent with the narrator's presentation of her story and suggest a more ambiguous tale than the straightforward, sentimental one described here so far. Most tellingly, Sketch Eighth opens with an epigraph from Spenser that describes "a temptress trying to waylay Guyon from his quest in Book II of *The Faerie Queene* by telling him a false story of her wrongs and appealing to his sympathetic nature."[24] With the suggestion of this seemingly parallel situation in mind, the whole story suddenly falls under suspicion; and when we look at the other two epigraphs, from Thomas Chatterton and William Collins respectively, both of which speak of what Moses refers to as the "false death" of a husband or lover who in both cases are "actually very much alive," it seems even more evident that Hunilla's story, as told by Melville's narrator in the guise of a personal memoir (he is the one who sighted her when his ship stopped at Norfolk Isle to replenish its supplies of tortoise meat), may be more complicated, or at least more ambiguous, than even the narrator is aware. Whoever speaks through the three epigraphs for this sketch, whether "Salvator R. Tarnmoor," Melville himself, or an anonymous, implied "author" (who silently includes the three epigraphs with this sketch), implicitly warns readers to think of Hunilla as a temptress, one who perhaps fabricates the story of her experience on Norfolk Isle in a way that seems intended to maximize the sympathies of her rescuers, whoever they are and whenever they may arrive, with the goal of gaining favorable treatment and possibly also a financial windfall, the equivalent of "guilt money," for her suffering, or maybe just for her prowess as an inventor and storyteller. For, as Moses also points out, the previous Sketch Seventh ended with the seemingly innocuous bit of information that it was common practice for sailors who had deserted ships at one island to make their way to neighboring ones "and there [present] themselves to strange captains as shipwrecked seamen," a ruse that "often succeeded" not only in their "getting on board vessels bound to the Spanish coast," but ultimately in their being given "a compassionate purse made up for them on landing there" (150).

In fact, virtually everything we know about Hunilla comes directly from herself to the narrator, who is the first to spy her on the island, and from exchanges he overhears between Hunilla and the captain of the ship that finally rescues her. There is little or no evidence to corroborate Hunilla's story besides the chest, which could be hers or it could be one that washed up on the beach like the remnants of "a vessel's wreck" (156) or the piece of "cane" she found on the beach one day which served as her calendar; and the containers of tortoise oil that the captain and crew take on board on the day Hunilla and two of her little dogs are rescued, but which might have been there on Norfolk Isle since long before she arrived. Her story of a husband and a brother who died in a boating accident? This may be true, but it is hard to know for certain. She might have been carried to Norfolk Isle and abandoned there by a wicked or jealous husband. Her husband, "he of husbands the most faithful during life," may not have been so faithful after all and been killed by her brother or even by Hunilla herself (158). The gravesite, which the narrator sees her hanging over in the distance at one point shortly after he arrives, could be her husband's; but it could also be her brother's; or it could be a sham, planted there to give credence to her story of his death. Why would Melville have introduced this sketch with the second and third epigraphs, about the "false death" of a husband or lover who in both cases was "actually very much alive," if Hunilla's husband and brother did in fact die in that boating accident, as Hunilla claimed?[25] Even if her personal story is true, and her brother and husband had drowned, the story she tells appears to be constructed or refashioned in such a way as to increase the sympathies of her rescuers by portraying her suffering of body and mind as so extreme as to be unimaginable and thus increase the chances of a handsome financial payoff for her, such as the one she receive from the sailors who rescue her. If something like this accounts for the shape of Hunilla's story, then the seemingly tragic woman is a much more deceptive and "enchanting" figure than she seems, and, like the other characters in these last several sketches, something of a monster—a woman deformed and disguised as something she is not. What is more, then "Salvator R. Tarnmoor" is something he is not as well, for upon close examination, he, too, seems to have done what he can to enhance his readers' sympathies for Hunilla's plight, by sentimentalizing the presentation even more than she has, in the idealized description of the scene of her husband's and brother's deaths, where, as the narrator says, "The real woe of this event passed before her sight as some sham tragedy on the stage," artificially outlined by the branches of a thicket that "formed an oval frame, through which the bluely boundless sea rolled like a painted one. And there, the invisible painter painted to her view the wave-tossed and disjointed raft," before it "all subsided into smooth-flowing creamy waters. . . . Death in a silent picture" (154). The dishonesty of the presentation seems especially apparent here, permitting Melville to offer his audience the kind of sentimental story they might naturally crave while at the same time calling that sentimentality into question by the artificiality of the contrivance of its framing.

By contrast to this ambiguous portrait of tragic womanhood, Sketch Ninth is a comic piece, a satire of the "progress" and "modernization" that European models of capitalism were alleged to bring to Latin America in the nineteenth century but which historians, such as E. Bradford Burns, have argued benefited the elites while creating mass poverty. In this respect, it should be noted that Melville's narrator's version of Oberlus's self-serving letter to the world, which appears at the end of the tale, claiming himself to be "the most unfortunate ill-treated gentleman that lives" (168), is said to be "full of the strangest satiric effrontery," a detail that Melville goes out of his way to inform us does not appear in the version of the story he found in Porter's Journal (170). Melville borrowed much of the portrait of the Hermit from Porter's *Journal,* but in fashioning his own more outlandish figure, he turned Porter's original from an Irishman named Patrick Watkins into a more broadly representative "European," a "wild white creature" with the single name of Oberlus. Melville's Hermit claims to be an honest farmer who cultivates the land in order to make an honest living and save a modest wealth for "unhappy old age" but who has been sadly mistreated and abused by others (168). He claims as well to be a "patriot . . . exiled by tyranny," but Melville shows him to be ruled by "selfish ambition" and "the love of rule for its own sake." When he does engage with others he does so with "mercantile craftiness" and treachery (164). He "panted" for a chance to prove his potency upon another human, and at the first opportunity, he captures and enslaves a Black sailor, then treats him worse than Crusoe did Friday. Later, when this plan backfires, Oberlus alters his approach and tricks wayward seamen into joining him; but these he soon corrupts, turning them into murderers like himself. In the end he is driven from his island—banished, he says—and escapes in a stolen boat. In his maudlin farewell letter to the world, he claims he was one "long endeavoring by hard labor and much solitary suffering" to support himself, only to be unjustly beaten and robbed by "men professing to be Christians" (168). A deeply dishonest, distorting (and distorted) figure, the Hermit, in Melville's portrait, is the opposite of everything he claims. Caught in suspicious circumstances, concealed "under the hull of a small vessel" about to be launched, with matches in his pocket, he is last observed in a miserable jail in Payta, where prisoners are typically put on public view as an example to others. "And here, for a long time Oberlus was seen; the central figure of a mongrel and assassin band" (169)—hardly an exemplar of the new capitalism or the promise of European progress in Latin America. As Oberlus himself had mockingly warned the world in the exit line to a letter he left behind (along with a rooster), in Hood Island harbor, "don't count your chicks before they are hatched" (168). Clearly, no "chicks" were bound to come from Oberlus's dystopian experiment.

Melville's last sketch brings together a number of nameless "solitaries," mostly sailors, like himself in an earlier point in his career, who have jumped ship—jumped or been banished or abandoned—and then left evidence of their miserable life on the islands. Rather than focusing on a single figure, as he had in the previous sketches, Melville here generalizes, describing various related cases of common sailors on whalers, "or ships bound on dreary and protracted voyages," and far-removed from "the oversight and the memory of human law." As Tarnmoor explains it, they have most likely experienced such discord and unpleasantness on ship or been so badly treated by their commanders that they chose to jump ship onto these deserted islands rather than subject themselves to more tyranny. Lacking any protections on shipboard or recourse to the law on shore, they are desperate, and offered few other opportunities for such a sure chance of escape as these uninhabited isles do. Elsewhere, Melville explains, whether on the islands of Polynesia or in the ports of Peru, the natives have been corrupted by colonialists, to the point where they are "as mercenary and keen of knife and scent, as the retrograde Spaniards," their colonizers, and will return runaway sailors to collect a bounty (170–71). Some sailors end up being abandoned on the islands, either lost or forgotten while tortoise hunting or collecting firewood. Others are cruelly banished there by "inhumane" captains who seek revenge "upon seamen who have given their caprice or pride some singular offence." Most frequently, however, Melville suggests, these sailors jump ship out of desperation, to escape the brutal tyranny of their commanders. Many of them do not survive, of course, or they quickly learn to find their way to more hospitable, inhabited islands elsewhere. The more ingenious ones may manage to endure for a time, if they can find water, food, and the makings of shelter from the equatorial sun. But all that the contemporary traveler will find on the more remote islands are the "relics of hermitages and stone basins" and other signs of "vanishing humanity" left by these fugitives—an occasional stake and bottle, the island equivalent of a post office; or a few gravestones or simple boards—in keeping with the bleak, wasteland features of the islands (171–72). In this final chapter, Melville bears witness to the real and potential tyranny of the ruling class on board ship in the early decades of the nineteenth century and the desperate measures of common sailors, like himself, who were moved to take their chances on a remote, more or less deserted island rather than continue under the command of a real-life tyrant.

When Melville published "The Encantadas" in *Putnam's Monthly* in the spring of 1854, he was publishing in one of the premier journals in the United States at the time, one with a heavy emphasis on travel writing: one issue alone, the previous year, contained articles on Cuba, Siberia, Palestine, Japan, Robinson Crusoe's Island, Popocatepetl, Honolulu, the Polar Seas, the Coral Reefs, and Venice. The three installments of Melville's "Encantadas" must have seemed comfortable in that company; to contemporary readers, they must have looked like travel sketches. But they are that and much more: while focusing on just a handful of figures—sea captains, buccaneers, renegade soldiers, a mixed-race Indian woman—Melville also made them representative figures who tell a larger human story defined by race and gender, class and nation, that together recapitulate much of Latin America's colonial and postcolonial history through nearly the first half of the nineteenth century. What he showed his readers was a fantastic world that was also a miniature of their own, a mixed world where tyranny, colonialism, and the will to power vied continually with the struggle for freedom, self-sufficiency, and hope—a blind sort of hope that is itself a force of nature, ageless and persistent as the Galapagos tortoise.

# 6

## DOCILE MONSTERS AND ENSLAVEMENT IN "THE BELL-TOWER"

"The Bell-Tower" is Melville's most unusual story, one that critics have long regarded as a Hawthornesque exemplum of the artist or an antimachine story with parallels to Melville's "The Tartarus of Maids."[1] There is much to be said for each of these critical viewpoints, and my own reading draws upon both of them, but the moral significance of the story and its relevance to Melville's own time and place, and his *Putnam's Monthly* audience in particular, call for further examination. Unlike "Bartleby," "Benito Cereno," or "The Encantadas," the story conveys little historical specificity, little that is local in a concrete way, and (with one exception) nothing obviously or demonstrably "American." Given the centrality (and ambiguity) of the "monster"[2] or cloaked domino figure in Melville's story, however, and the relative lack of critical and theoretical attention to it, I want to offer a reading informed by monster theory as developed especially by Jeffrey Jerome Cohen, Michel Foucault, and others, with the intention of demonstrating the story's relevance to the early modern period as well as Melville's own cultural moment before the Civil War. Zakiya Hanafi, writing in *The Monster in the Machine*, has observed that "monsters have always been considered highly charged with meaning,"[3] but Cohen takes the idea a step further in suggesting it is possible to read cultures "from the monsters they engender."[4] In his essay "Monster Culture (Seven Theses)," Cohen explores the provocative notion that the monster's body is a "cultural body," a construct, a projection, born at a "metaphoric crossroads" or crisis point as "an embodiment of a certain cultural moment." As such, he argues, the monster "exists only to be read": "Like a letter on the page, the monster signifies something other than itself: it is always a displacement, always inhabits the gap between the time of upheaval that created it and the moment into which it is received, to be born again. These epistemological spaces between the monster's bones are Derrida's familiar chasm of *différance:* a genetic uncertainty principle, the essence of the monster's vitality, the reason it always rises from the dissection table as its secrets are about to be revealed and vanishes into the night."[5] Like Cohen's monster, Bannadonna's creation is defined by a genetic uncertainty principle—is it mechanical or human?—one that grows more uncertain as the story moves from scene to scene and on toward its inevitable conclusion, when the town's mayor and his assistant seize the figure from the tower under cover of night and bury it at sea.

What do we know about the culture that engendered the monster in the bell-tower, Bannadonna's "experimental automaton" (185)? To be sure, Bannadonna is the one who constructs the "domino," and he has aims of his own in doing so, but he can hardly be said to act alone. In fact, he is representative, though his aims are unprecedented. Initially, he is hired by the "state" to create an ambitious monument—"the noblest Bell-Tower in Italy"—as a testament to its civic pride and, by implication, to its prominence and position at a time when other independent city-states also were emerging in Italy and competing with one another for power, trade, and prestige in what became early modern Italy. Melville sets this story "in the south of Europe, nigh a once-frescoed capital," in a quasi-mythic time long before the present time of Melville's narrator, uncertain though that seems to be. In the narrator's present, the broken tower seems ancient and lies prostrate like "some immeasurable pine, fallen, in forgotten days, with Anak and the Titan," the biblical giant and the mythological god respectively (174). While emphasizing the age of this remnant, the narrator stresses even more the extraordinary, superhuman effort required to construct it. He describes the time of the story to be much *like* the time when survivors of the Deluge attempted to build the Tower of Babel— "a high hour of renovated earth, following the second deluge, when the waters of the Dark Ages had dried up, and once more the green appeared"— a time of celebration and self-congratulation. As it was in that Old Testament time, "after so long and deep submersion" in utter darkness, so here:

"the jubilant expectation of the race should, as with Noah's sons, soar into Shinar aspiration" (174), with an ambitious, sky-assaulting plan to build a city with a tower, "its top in the heavens," high enough and sufficiently impressive as to "make a name for ourselves, lest we be scattered abroad upon the face of the whole earth."[6] Considering the celebratory feeling of the time and the suggestion that Italy is awaking from a dark period, it seems clear the time of the story and the building of the bell-tower occurred during the transition between the late medieval period and the early Renaissance in the seventeenth century, at about the same time when what Hanafi calls "sacred monsters" began to disappear and be replaced by "monstrous machines."[7]

As in the biblical story of the Tower of Babel, Melville's bell-tower and the tower's monster were born at what Cohen calls a metaphoric crossroads, a place that leads to other places, as the "embodiment of a certain cultural moment—of a time, a feeling, and a place." Again, it is not Bannadonna who initially aspires to build the bell-tower but the "state" in which he lives. Having already become enriched "through commerce with the Levant," the state voted to erect the noblest tower, and then, because of his repute as an architect, hired Bannadonna to construct it. Bannadonna himself is hugely ambitious (and insecure)—a consequence, presumably, of his status as an "unblest foundling," a cipher who lacks class standing or a family name, like Melville's Ishmael but with Ahab's wounded pride. In the matter of "firm resolve," "no man in Europe at that period went beyond" him (174). Thus, in the end, the dream of the nobles and magistrates who hired him is not exactly his dream. Theirs is formidable, even outsized, but finite; his is greater still, indeed monstrous, as soon becomes clear, and he pursues it not for collective or communal glory but for his own personal "self-esteem" (175), a self-esteem "inspirited" by the dutiful presence of the admiring townspeople who come to watch the tower grow day by day and pay homage to his seemingly superhuman accomplishment. He is an egotist, like the protagonist in Mary Shelley's *Frankenstein; or, The Modern Prometheus* (1818).[8] At the end of every day, after the masons depart, he can be seen standing alone upon the tower's "ever-ascending summit" until late at night, celebrating his accomplishments, yet "wrapped in schemes of other and still loftier piles." And on the holiday declared to acknowledge the occasion when Bannadonna himself is to lay the "climax-stone," he stands at the very top, three hundred feet in the air without a railing, "erect, alone, with folded arms," gazing at the tops of the distant Alps, which served to challenge and inspire him (175), as Melville claimed Mount Greylock, near his home in the Berkshires, inspired him while finishing his own most ambitious narrative, *Moby-Dick*.

Only at the point when it is time to install the tower's bells does he reveal his ambitious, unprecedented plan to unite the bell-tower and the clock-tower in a single structure (a construction, Melville's narrator adds, that would exceed even the famous Campanile and Torre dell'Orologio of St. Mark's in Venice[9]), and put in place a "mammoth" bell of such weight that even some magistrates worried about the danger of such a mass of swaying metal being suspended from the tower. Signaling more than bold ambition or heedlessness in forging ahead with his plan to cast the bell, Bannadonna reveals the immorality of his egotism, when, without a moment's hesitation, he strikes and kills a nervous workman to keep him from accidentally ruining the casting process, an act that leaves a permanent flaw in the bell (176).[10] By this murderous act, Bannadonna reveals his willingness to do *anything* to achieve his goal, and his deeply flawed, "fallen" nature as well. And in their response to this evil deed, particularly their willingness to compromise all moral principles and collude with him in the coverup of his crime, the town authorities show their "fallen" nature, too. Just as he attempts to cover over the resulting "blemish" in the newly cast bell, so too the state, seeking to share in the triumph of the caster's accomplishment, turns a blind eye to his homicide, when the judge "remits" Bannadonna's felony and the priest offers "absolution." Even some commoners, the so-called "charitable" ones, who have little to gain from his achievement, show themselves willing to overlook or forgive his murderous deed, imputing it instead to "sudden transports of esthetic passion": "A kick from an Arabian charger: not sign of vice, but blood" (176). Clearly they, too, wishing to share in the glory of Bannadonna's achievement, are happy to make excuses for him.

Having shown that Bannadonna is not beyond committing murder to realize his plan, Melville suggests he is capable of other dark transgressions as well against both man and nature. From the beginning, he had planned the massive central bell to be "of a singular make" involving a rotary motion, with a mysterious connection to the clockwork. This, however, was publicly revealed only after an extended period of solitude on the part of the mechanician, whom the townspeople knew only to be "engaged upon something for the belfry," something "intended to complete it, and surpass all that had gone before." While most of the townspeople thought the mysterious project must involve a "casting like the bells," others (who "thought they had some further insight") feared there must be some good reason why Bannadonna kept his work concerning this last stage a secret. For all of them, his work took on the mystery of "the forbidden." Only after this suspenseful buildup do we learn that Bannadonna has been surreptitiously creating not simply an "elaborate piece of sculpture, or statue," but a mechanical man, a "pliant" figure capable of stepping into the belfry "almost of itself" (176) and striking the hours precisely at times determined by its creator. Indeed, "a shrewd old blacksmith," a Vulcan figure (like the "man-maker" Perth, in *Moby-Dick*) who might be expected to know something about such things, "ventured the suspicion that it was but a living man" (176–77). Further evidence of the lifelike character of the mysterious figure is seen when the chief magistrate and his associate climb the belfry to inspect the "cloaked object," only to discover that it "seemed now to have changed its attitude." No longer erect or standing, it "seemed now seated upon some sort of frame, or chair," while near the top of the object they noticed the "web of the cloth" wrapped around it had been altered, "so as to form a sort of woven grating," as if intended to permit the figure to breathe, a suggestion made all the more certain when they "thought they discerned a slight sort of fitful, spring-like motion, in the domino," and then spied an earthen cup, "one as might, in mockery, be offered to the lips of some brazen statue, or, perhaps, still worse"—an ominous description that suggests something almost human but monstrous. Such a conclusion seems strengthened by the reaction of the magistrates who gaze at the domino "as at some suspicious incognito—at a Venetian mask" and are stirred by "all sorts of vague apprehensions" (177).

While most critics of this story have assumed the figure in the bell-tower is a mechanical creation, Melville's presentation of the domino, as filtered through the reactions of the two magistrates, suggests real ambiguity as to its true nature.[11] At times it seems mechanical, at others human, and at still others a confusing and unprecedented sort of hybrid. If the last, it would be entirely in keeping with Cohen's idea that the monster is, by definition, "the harbinger of category crisis,"[12] for monsters, Cohen explains, not only refuse "easy categorization," they defy natural law: "they are disturbing hybrids whose externally incoherent bodies resist attempts to include them in any systematic structuration." And for this reason, they are "dangerous, a form suspended between forms that threatens to smash distinctions." Figures of "ontological liminality," monsters appear "at times of crisis as a kind of third term that problematizes the clash of extremes—as 'that which questions binary thinking and introduces a crisis.'"[13] To put the matter succinctly, the "crisis" embodied in Melville's story, the crisis of his time—one that includes slavery while also going beyond it—is the question of whether machines were becoming more human, as they took on more and more of the work historically performed by men and women, while at the same time humans, particularly Africans laboring on plantations in the Western Hemisphere or women working in the mills of New England (as in another of Melville's stories, "The Tartarus of Maids"), were being forced to operate like machines.

How terrible this latter possibility might be is suggested by the figure of the domino, who in human form can be imagined to be a slave, one so abused and broken in spirit, yet so perfectly trained, as to take on the appearance and practical utility of a machine—a version of Michel Foucault's notion of highly trained or disciplined "docile bodies."[14] In *Discipline and Punish,* Foucault focuses on developments in the social and political economy of the late eighteenth century, the so-called classical age, when the body became both "object and target of power" to a degree not seen before, and subject to new methods and techniques. Foucault was especially interested in the sort of "discipline" found in social organizations like the army (or the school, monastery, or hospital) where the soldier becomes "something that can be made": "out of a formless clay, an inapt body, the machine required can be constructed; posture is gradually corrected; a calculated constraint runs slowly through each part of the body, mastering it, making it pliable, ready at all times, turning silently into the automatism of habit." Foucault is less concerned with the brute methods of slavery, which, he says, are based on "a relation of appropriation of bodies," in contrast to the methods of the army or school, which can achieve "effects of utility at least as great" without the cost and violence that characterize slavery.[15] But what he says about the two systems of discipline still serves to illuminate the example of Melville's mechanical man because it can explain what Melville hints at in the hybrid, man-machine character of Bannadonna's creation and how these systems might be seen as relevant for his American audience in *Putnam's Monthly*.

While Melville only glances at the methods Bannadonna must have used to subjugate his man-machine (or enslaved person) to the point of absolute, automatic compliance with his wishes in striking the hours at exactly the right times, we can intuit a good deal about his methods from his creation's abjection and mute compliance with his creator's plan to have him strike the hours, even if it results in the death of Bannadonna himself. Foucault suggests something further about what Bannadonna's methods might have looked like when he observes:

> The historical moment of the disciplines was the moment when an art of the human body was born, which was directed not only at the growth of its skills, or at the intensification of its subjection, but at the formation of a relation that in the mechanism itself makes it more obedient as it becomes more useful, and conversely. What was then being formed was a policy of coercions that act upon the body, a calculated manipulation of its elements, its gestures, its behavior. The human body was entering a machinery of power that explores it, breaks it down, and rearranges it. A "political anatomy," which was also a "mechanics of power," was being born; it defined how one may have a hold over others' bodies, *not only so that they may do what one wishes, but so that they may operate as one wishes*, with the techniques, the speed, and the efficiency that one determines. Thus discipline produces subjected and practiced bodies, "docile bodies." (137–38; my emphasis)

Nothing better explains the irony of Bannadonna's death than the idea that he has achieved such firm control over the domino's body as to lead it to do not simply what its creator wishes but *as he wishes*. In attempting to strike the hour while the "brain" of Bannadonna is in the way, the domino does not do exactly what Bannadonna wishes, but it does perform precisely *as he wishes*—and in spite of the deadly consequences to himself. At this fateful, climactic moment in the narrative, the "mechanics of power" come home to Bannadonna with a vengeance, regardless of the domino's intention. If this is the moment when Bannadonna's body, with its history of evil, is subject to trial by a jury of one, then clearly his creation, like Frankenstein's creature, has judged him to be guilty.

If we read Melville's domino figure not as a machine but as a human being subjugated and beaten down into a form of slavery, we can see more clearly the relevance of the three epigraphs that introduce his story—the first in particular: "Like negroes, these powers own man sullenly; mindful of their high master; while serving, plot revenge."[16] And we can also more confidently appreciate "The Bell-Tower" as an antislavery narrative, one that speaks to the enslaved population's silent hatred of their condition and the inevitability or "automatic" character of their resistance to those who enslave them.[17] Cohen's assertion that "the monster dwells at the gates of difference"[18] becomes especially relevant here, as difference in the form of race enters the story through the epigraph's suggested analogy with African slaves who, "while serving, plot revenge." As Cohen explains, "The monster is difference made flesh, come to dwell among us.... Any kind of alterity can be inscribed across (constructed through) the monstrous body, but for the most part monstrous difference tends to be cultural, political, racial, economic, sexual."[19] In this case, what is truly monstrous is not the "domino" per se but what Bannadonna has done to subjugate it and turn it into a man-machine, all justified in the name of an unspecified difference in appearance or condition that undervalues the standing of the other—poverty, vulnerability, abjection, race, or gender.

A further clue to Melville's method is revealed in the next scene when Bannadonna tries to relieve the two magistrates' "disquietude" (a sign of their moral anxiety but also their lack of courage) about the domino by covering it up with a piece of canvas and then turning their attention instead to the clock-bell and Bannadonna's casting of the "embodied hours"—"twelve figures of gay girls, garlanded, hand-in-hand," who appeared to be dancing in a ring. When the still nervous chief magistrate hears a noise that worries him, Bannadonna dismisses it as nothing but the wind, and then sends the two magistrates away with the promise that he will be "most happy" to receive them again after he has finished the last touches on these figures, and his domino, whom he now refers to as "Haman," has been fixed on "his lofty tree" (178), an image that suggests both crucifixion and human sacrifice. Calling the domino "Haman" is a significant clue to Melville's buried intentions in this tale. While other critics, such as Richard Chase, have identified this name as a reference to "the tyrant in the Book of Esther who ordered Mordecai to be hanged but was later himself hanged on the gallows he had prepared for Mordecai,"[20] the aptness of his name becomes more interesting when it is known that, in the Midrash tradition, Haman had once sold himself into slavery to Mordecai,[21] as Bannadonna seems to hint his domino had sold himself into slavery to him, the architect-mechanician.[22]

Before the two magistrates take leave of Bannadonna, however, they are startled by the "expression of the unchanging face of the Hour Una," which the chief magistrate claims to look "just like that of Deborah, the prophetess, as painted by the Florentine, Del Fonca" (presumably a fictitious painter of the Italian Renaissance), and then the younger "milder magistrate" observes that the smile of Una is different from that of the others and "seems but a fatal one" (179). When Bannadonna tries to explain away the "fatal" difference by reference to what he calls a "law in art" that prevents "the possibility of duplicates," while also pressing them to leave the vicinity of the tower, the magistrates hear something that sounds like "a footfall above." Attempting to mollify his audience, Bannadonna quietly dismisses the sound as nothing more than falling mortar from some unfinished stonework above them. But when the sound continues, one of the magistrates suddenly interrupts to inquire, "Hark!—sure we left no soul above?" to which Bannadonna answers evasively, "no soul, Eccellenza; rest assured, no *soul*.—Again the mortar." It is not until the milder magistrate presses Bannadonna by observing, "But, Una, . . . she seemed intently gazing on you; one would have almost sworn that she picked you out from among us three"—as they have singled out *her* from the other embodied hours—that we can begin to sense Bannadonna's law of art barring duplicates is a charade, meant to cover up the fact that each of the twelve hours is modeled after a different female, possibly all held in captivity somewhere. Such a reading seems subtly confirmed, even indirectly admitted by Bannadonna, when he continues to treat the magistrates as though they are his mental inferiors, saying, "If she did, possibly, it might have been her finer apprehension, Eccellenza" (180). When one of the magistrates replies, "I do not understand you," Bannadonna dismisses him by remarking, "No consequence, no consequence, Eccellenza," before changing the subject in an effort to hurry them from the bell-tower so he can get on with the last of his preparations.[23]

On the final night before the public demonstration of Bannadonna's elaborate clock, some of the town's commoners see and hear signs of activity high in the bell-tower again—not only lights and "strange sounds," but "half-suppressed screams and plainings, such as might have issued from some ghostly engine, overplied" (181), or so they said. These latter sounds suggest the human character of the domino and the violent, coercive means Bannadonna has apparently been employing to force his creature to do his bidding. Immediately after the climactic moment, which we later learn has resulted in the seemingly accidental murder of Bannadonna by his creature as it carries out its programmed action of striking the hour, we are told of other strange happenings that point to the living character of the domino: a curious "spaniel," which followed the magistrates up the tower stairs, "stood shivering as before some unknown monster in a brake: or, rather, as if it snuffed footsteps leading to some other world" (182). Most immediately what they see is Bannadonna's body lying, dead or dying, "prostrate and bleeding at the base of the bell which was adorned by girls and garlands," and "at the feet of the hour Una; his head coinciding, in a vertical line, with her left hand, clasped by the hour Dua." Only at this point do they see the domino looking down over him, "like Jael over nailed Sisera in the tent," but no longer "becloaked." As the now uncovered figure stands before them, the two nobles can see it "had limbs, and seemed clad in a scaly mail, lustrous as a dragon-beetle's." As if to suggest the creature had a will of its own and a history of violent struggle against the mechanician, they also see it was "manacled, and its clubbed arms were uplifted, as if, with its manacles, once more to smite its already smitten victim." Finally, they observe that one foot of the domino was placed under the dead body, "as if in the act of spurning it," the "as if" conveying some uncertainty about what it was they saw and at the same time highlighting their impression of the creature's disdainful, vengeful intention. Did the domino strike with intention or simply mechanically and as programmed by its creator? Is it alive? Does it have consciousness? It's hard to tell for sure, but here and in the concluding pages there are several signs of a hybrid creature or a sui generis man-machine. Adding to the lack of definitiveness, Melville's narrator interjects to say, "Uncertainty falls on what now followed" (182), referring, presumably, to the concluding pages of the story where the narrator attempts to explain the "foundling's fate" (183) and all that transpired after this scene. Almost immediately, however, we are told, "Certain it is, that an arquebuss was called for from below" by the two magistrates. Soon after, a report was heard on the ground below, "followed by a fierce whiz, as of the sudden snapping of a main-spring, with a steely din, as if a stack of sword blades should be dashed upon a pavement"—all implying the destruction of a creature made of metal, rather than flesh, or possibly one made of flesh but sheathed in metal—while "thin wreaths of smoke" were seen from below, "curling" out of the distant belfry's latticework, as if to suggest the creature was expiring (182).

Melville's narrator, however, adds uncertainty to this suggestion by saying some observers "averred that it was the spaniel, gone mad by fear, which was shot," and then, contradicting this claim, he says, "This, others denied. True it was, the spaniel never more was seen; and, probably, for some unknown reason, it shared the burial" of the domino. Was it the domino the two magistrates shot (and "killed"), or was it the spaniel? Only the magistrates know, but not even after the urgency of the moment has passed "would the twain ever disclose the full secrets of the belfry." All we are told is that after "the first instinctive panic" upon witnessing the scene in the belfry, the two magistrates "quickly rehooded the figure in the dropped cloak wherein it had been hoisted. The same night, it was secretly lowered to the ground, smuggled to the beach, pulled far out to sea, and sunk" (182). The two nervous magistrates are the only witnesses to these last events. Only they have any idea about the makeup of the domino, whether human or mechanical, living or dead, and only they are in a position to examine the creature closely before it is buried at sea.

But evidently they make no effort to discover its true character and quietly vow to remain silent about what they know.[24] The fate of the domino, therefore, perfectly exemplifies Cohen's assertion that "the monster always escapes." "We see the damage that the monster wreaks, the material remains (the footprints of the yeti across Tibetan snow, the bones of the giant stranded on a rocky cliff), but the monster itself turns immaterial and vanishes, to reappear someplace else," often in some other form.[25] Why does the monster always manage to escape? It escapes because its "body is both corporal and incorporeal; its threat is its propensity to shift," as Melville's domino shifts from one form to another—from what looks like a machine to a living creature and then back again to a machine (or possibly a living creature enclosed in an elaborate metal restraint or "mail"). Moreover, the monster is never observed except in fragments or snatches (a hood torn open to create breathing holes; limbs that are manacled; a foot inserted beneath a dead body; the sounds of "screams and plainings" in the tower heard from the ground) or obscurely, subjectively, through the eyes and ears of limited or unreliable witnesses, like the two nervous magistrates and the fearful townspeople.

The monster always escapes, but it is also, as Cohen argues, "revenant." Like a vampire, it returns "in slightly different clothing, each time to be read against contemporary social movements or a specific, determining event: *la décadence* and its new possibilities, homophobia and its hateful imperatives, the acceptance of new subjectivities unfixed by binary gender, a fin de siècle social activism paternalistic in its embrace."[26] Melville's monster is similarly "revenant"; after being dumped into the sea, it, too, returns, or is prophesied to return, not in the same form but in the forms hinted at in the three epigraphs to the story, explicitly and most relevantly, for Melville's original audience, the first one: "Like negroes, these powers own man sullenly; mindful of their higher master; while serving, plot revenge." Writing in 1853, less than a decade before the Civil War, Melville recognized the suffering and injustice of slavery and could anticipate that people held in servitude in the South and elsewhere would resist, if given the opportunity, and turn against their masters—as the captives on the slave ship *San Dominick* in "Benito Cereno" had done.[27]

At the same time, by focusing on the dangers of the sort of hybridity or blending that had been going on since the Renaissance, when machines began to take on more and more of the work, *and character or complexity,* of human beings, and African captives of the slave trade had begun to be treated like machines, "The Bell-Tower" warns against those who would confuse the categories of man and machine on an even larger scale. In Melville's view, *the monster is not the machine but the human drive to dominate the world,* as in the ancient time of Babel after the first Deluge (referred to in the opening paragraphs of the story), whether by developing ever more sophisticated machines or pressing more and more humans into servitude to do the work of others. This seems confirmed in the concluding pages of Melville's story where the narrator attempts to explain "the entire motive and mode, with their origin, of the secret design of Bannadonna"—first by dismissing what it is not and then by asserting what it is—as a necessary first step toward explaining the mystery of "the foundling's fate" (183). Although Bannadonna is said to have lived and worked in a time when others, like Albertus Magnus (an early interpreter of Aristotle and proponent of science) and Cornelius Agrippa (a later German who wrote on magic and the occult), were "hopelessly infected with the craziest chimeras of his age," and though he aspired to create something "apparently transcending not alone the bounds of human invention, but those of divine creation," the means he proposed to employ were "alleged to have been confined within the sober forms of sober reason." Unlike the visionaries, natural philosophers, alchemists, and theosophists of this transitional period before the Renaissance who sought to find "some germ of correspondence" between "the finer mechanic forces and the ruder animal vitality," or discover in nature other forms of hidden, rarified, or transcendent knowledge, Bannadonna was a "practical materialist" who attempted to achieve his goal, "not by logic, not by crucible, not by conjuration, not by altars; but by plain vice-bench and hammer": "In short, to solve nature, to steal into her, to intrigue beyond her, to procure some one else to bind her to his hand;—these, one and all, had not been his objects; but, asking no favors from any element or any being, of himself, to rival her, outstrip her, and rule her. He stooped to conquer. With him, common sense was theurgy; machinery, miracle; Prometheus, the heroic name for machinist; man, the true God" (184).

To be sure, the explanation of events the narrator offers at the end of his tale is not authoritative but conjectural, deriving as it does from "some few" of the "less unscientific minds" of the town—less unscientific than those of the populace at large, at any rate, who view the foundling's fate as the product of "supernatural agency." Still, even these "less unscientific minds" make a huge leap in assuming they can see as well into Bannadonna's "soul" as into the event of his death at the hands of his domino. As already observed, none of them had ever seen the domino at close range, and regardless of its true makeup, it was buried at sea by the two magistrates shortly after Bannadonna was killed. Their theory begins with the hunch that the foundling "derived the first suggestion of his scheme"—namely, to "devise some metallic agent, which should strike the hour with its mechanic hand, with even greater precision than the vital one"—from observing examples of actual bell-ringing watchmen whose "intelligent features" are obscured when viewed from a distance below. Conjecturing further, they take the position that Bannadonna was no ordinary "projector," but an unusually enterprising and ambitious one, whose original scheme, "by insensible gradations, proceeding from comparatively pigmy aims to Titanic ones," had reached "an unheard of degree of daring" (183):

> He still bent his efforts upon the locomotive figure for the belfry, but only as a partial type of an ulterior creature, a sort of elephantine Helot, adapted to further, in a degree scarcely to be imagined, the universal conveniences and glories of humanity; supplying nothing less than a supplement to the Six Days' Work; stocking the earth with a new serf, more useful than the ox, swifter than the dolphin, stronger than the lion, more cunning than the ape, for industry an ant, more fiery than serpents, and yet, in patience, another ass. All excellences of all God-made creatures, which served man, were here to receive advancement, and then to be combined in one. Talus was to have been the all-accomplished Helot's name. Talus, iron slave to Bannadonna, and, through him, to man. (183–84)

Having emphasized first the mechanical nature of the domino in the early pages and then its human character in the middle ones, Melville's narrator returns to his earlier practice of highlighting its mechanical character in the final pages, but now its makeup is presented on the authority of the commoners of the town, not the more knowing magistrates. The result serves as evidence of Melville's intention to create a true hybrid in the figure of the domino—a mechanical man or "monster." With this, even the "less unscientific minded" among the townspeople seem to agree, for in the end they believe Bannadonna allowed his "fancy some little play" (or was it his "utilitarian ambition collaterally extended"?): "In figure, the creature for the belfry should not be likened after the human pattern, nor any animal one, nor after the ideals, however wild, of ancient fable, but equally in aspect as in organism be *an original production; the more terrible to behold, the better*" (185; my emphasis).[28] Still, to an uncertain degree, the "monster" of the final paragraphs of Melville's story is more the creation of these "less unscientific" townspeople than it is the creation of Bannadonna himself. His creation has been seen close at hand by just two other people in the community, and they were so fearful of what they saw as to try to banish it from existence forever by burying it at sea.

Cohen argues that the creature's function is to instill precisely this kind of fearful response to the unknown or forbidden. Its job, in other words, is to "police the borders of the possible"[29] and warn against transgressing them. Because the monster, by definition, stands in a position "at the limits of knowing," it serves to warn against "exploration of its uncertain demesnes": "The giants of Patagonia, the dragons of the Orient, and the dinosaurs of Jurassic Park together declare that curiosity is more often punished than rewarded, that one is better off safely contained within one's own domestic sphere than abroad, away from the watchful eyes of the state. The monster prevents mobility (intellectual, geographic, or sexual), delimiting the social spaces through which private bodies may move. To step outside this official geography is to risk attack by some monstrous border patrol or (worse) to become monstrous oneself."[30]

Certainly the domino in Melville's story, and the domino's action of killing its creator, serves to warn against the sort of unbridled ambition and defiance of natural and moral law evidenced by Bannadonna, who would do anything, from committing murder to creating a monstrous figure by whatever means possible, including, evidently, brutal enslavement and ruthless, dehumanizing training, to achieve his goal. Returning again to the three epigraphs at the start of the story, we can see they all speak to the borders or limits that the monster in the bell-tower in effect "patrols" and warns against:

"Like negroes, these powers own man sullenly; mindful of their higher master; while serving, plot revenge."

"The world is apoplectic with high-living of ambition; and apoplexy has its fall."

"Seeking to conquer a larger liberty, man but extends the empire of necessity."

But while the latter two epigraphs speak only to generalized cultural conditions without regard to social markers of difference such as race, ethnicity, nationality, or gender, the first expressly addresses the racial difference between Africans and whites, slaves and masters, and the country's national debate, in the 1840s and 1850s, over slavery. Given the explicit terms of the first epigraph, the domino in the bell-tower does not need to be an enslaved African for the reader to recognize that it symbolically stands for one, just as Bannadonna himself does not have to be a white slave owner for us to see that he exemplifies such a figure, in one or more of his various cultural embodiments.

That first epigraph thus also provides a clear instance of the relevance of Cohen's observation that "the monster dwells at the gates of difference": "The monster is difference made flesh, come to dwell among us. In its function as dialectical Other or third-term supplement, the monster is an incorporation of the Outside, the Beyond—of all those loci that are rhetorically placed as distant and distinct but originate Within. Any kind of alterity can be inscribed across... the monstrous body, but for the most part monstrous difference tends to be cultural, political, racial, economic, sexual."[31] Insofar as this equivalence can be seen to operate in the figure of the monster in "The Bell-Tower," where a machine is made to work (and look) like a man, but compelled or programmed to do so with the perfect precision and regularity of a machine, the reader is likely to develop a sense of sympathy for this abject creature or to experience a degree of fellow feeling that a contemporary, particularly one who holds racist views about the inferiority of Africans, might not naturally share regarding a racial other like an enslaved African. Perhaps this also provides a clue as to why Melville chose to write an antislavery story in the oblique form of a moral exemplum. We know that, in other instances, he felt it necessary to treat his subject matter indirectly, as when in his essay-review, "Hawthorne and His Mosses," he spoke of the need for an author, particularly a "profound" one such as Hawthorne or Shakespeare, to work indirectly or hold back when seeking to tell the Truth: "For in this world of lies," he explains, "Truth is forced to fly like a scared white doe in the woodlands; and only by cunning glimpses will she reveal herself, as in Shakespeare and other masters of the great Art of Telling the Truth,—even though it be covertly, and by snatches."[32]

Cohen's Thesis VI, his penultimate one, has it that "Fear of the Monster Is Really a Kind of Desire." At the very least, fear of the monster can coexist with desire. Thus, "The monster is continually linked to forbidden practices, in order to normalize and to enforce," as Bannadonna's domino enforces the laws against murder, pride, and heightened ambition or overreaching as embodied in his master, as well as the moral laws against racism and slavery. For, Cohen goes on to observe: "The monster also attracts. The same creatures who terrify and interdict can evoke potent escapist fantasies; the linking of monstrosity with the forbidden makes the monster all the more appealing as a temporary egress from constraint. This simultaneous repulsion and attraction at the core of the monster's composition accounts greatly for its continued cultural popularity.... We distrust and loathe the monster at the same time we envy its freedom, and perhaps its sublime despair."[33]

Thus, the reader can take some pleasure in the monster's turning against his creator, even to the point of killing him, something he can do because as a mechanical man the domino (ostensibly) lacks conscience, but also because the man he kills, Bannadonna, has committed murder and other crimes against humanity, and fails to live by any moral code beyond that of his own will or desire. As a creature without a conscience, Bannadonna is another kind of monster, but not so different from ourselves, perhaps, or from the readers of Melville's own time.

Cohen's final thesis, "The Monster Stands at the Threshold . . . of Becoming," suggests this is all but inevitably so:

> Monsters are our children. They can be pushed to the farthest margins of geography and discourse, hidden away at the edges of the world and in the forbidden recesses of our mind, but they always return. And when they

come back, they bring not just a fuller knowledge of our place in history and the history of knowing our place, but they bear self-knowledge, *human knowledge*.... They ask us to reevaluate our cultural assumptions about race, gender, sexuality, our perception of difference, our tolerance toward its expression. They ask us why we have created them.[34]

In Melville's story, it is not exactly true that the monster "always returns," but it is the case that the *conditions* for the return of the monster remain, and as a consequence, readers can imagine the monster's return in another form, in another time and place. Melville more than hints at such a suggestion, making it all but explicit, in the first of his three epigraphs, concerning the "negroes" who will inevitably rebel against their "master." In the end, however, the town's people have learned nothing. Bannadonna—despite his "unhappy end," his crime, his pride, his ambition—remains a "rare genius" in the eyes of the republic, and so they "decreed him a stately funeral" after his death. The "great bell," too—despite its "defect, deceptively minute, in the casting," which carried the telltale mark of Bannadonna's earlier crime—also continued to be regarded as a thing of "glory," until "on the first anniversary of the tower's completion" an earthquake felled it (186).

# CONCLUSION

Melville came to the writing of short fiction reluctantly, and only after the commercial and critical failures of *Moby-Dick* and *Pierre*. He had rejected an earlier invitation from Evert Duyckinck to write something for *Holden's Dollar Magazine,* and at the same time made it clear he had no interest in writing for the popular press.[1] Even after the poor reception of *Moby-Dick* and the more hostile one of *Pierre,* he continued to want to work up long narratives, particularly a version of "the story of Agatha" he had heard about while visiting Nantucket, a story he tried to convince Hawthorne to take on before deciding to give it a try himself (if this manuscript ever existed, he probably destroyed it[2]); or "another book—300 pages, say," as he wrote his publisher, Harper & Brothers, in November of 1853, "—partly of nautical adventure, and partly—or, rather, chiefly, of Tortoise Hunting Adventure," and rather disingenuously claimed to "have now in hand, and pretty well on towards completion."[3] No such lengthy manuscript is known ever to have existed; he was probably making inflated claims about work he may have begun on what became Sketch Second, "Two Sides to a Tortoise," in "The Encantadas." In any case, by the early summer of 1853, he had apparently switched gears and decided to try to write short fiction for American magazines after all, for his mother-in-law, Hope Savage Shaw, reported in a letter to her nephew in July of that year that he had been "admirably paid" by *Harper's New Monthly Magazine* for "Cock-A-Doodle-Doo!," the first of seven stories for which he received payment in advance of their appearance there.[4] Moreover, before the end of that same year he had also begun to do business with *Harper's* new competitor, *Putnam's*

*Monthly*, where he arranged to publish "Bartleby, the Scrivener," in two installments, the first of seven stories to be published there over the next two years. By the time *The Piazza Tales* was published in 1856, Melville had written fifteen stories and published all but one, namely, "The Two Temples." "The Piazza," his sixteenth story, was published for the first time as the introductory narrative for his collection; it never appeared separately in either *Harper's* or *Putnam's Monthly*.

Considering the virtuosity of the stories Melville proposed to include in his collection, *The Piazza Tales* can be said to represent both a turning point and a culmination in Melville's career as a writer. After devoting three years and more to writing short stories, he pulled together five of the seven stories he had published in *Putnam's Monthly*, rather quickly composed a new sixth, "The Piazza," as an introduction, and offered them as a separate collection to Dix & Edwards, the new owner of *Putnam's Monthly*. Six perfectly constructed stories; six experiments in embodiment, confinement, personal trial, and point of view; six visions of the world that American readers of the time were likely to know little about—each distinct, and each cast in the form of a different genre: a quasi-fantasy or daydream of an invalided author obsessed with a mountain he can look out on from the new piazza of his farmhouse; the confession of a Wall Street lawyer trying to deal with the recalcitrance of his newest employee; the eyewitness report of an American sea captain's encounter with a slave ship off the coast of Chile; a performance piece about a lightning-rod peddler's sales call during a thunderstorm; a series of sketches by a pseudonymous author, Salvator R. Tarnmoor, about a wild assortment of characters struggling to survive on the Galapagos Islands; and a parable about an ambitious architect and the man-machine he creates to toll the hours in the early days of the modern age. In a collection to be published by the new owner of *Putnam's Monthly*, it would have been hardly possible for Melville to have included any of the seven stories he had previously published in *Harper's*, all but one of which ("The Tartarus of Maids") were relatively light, satiric, and comic in tone. There were two additional tales published in *Putnam's Monthly* that might have been included in *The Piazza Tales*—"I and My Chimney" and "The Apple-Tree Table" (and, in theory, there was a third, "The Two Temples," which *Putnam's* had earlier rejected on the grounds that "some of our church readers" might have found it disturbing)[5]—engaging, entertaining pieces, but they presumably showed too much geniality for Melville to want to feature them in his new collection; and, too, they might have been viewed as hinting at conflicts in Melville's own domestic life that would prove hurtful to his wife and daughters, or seem out of place in a collection devoted to more serious social issues like the economic exploitation of women; urban alienation and anomie; slavery and the slave trade; colonialism; and the technological equivalent of what is known today as the posthuman.

Each of the stories in *The Piazza Tales* is a kind of puzzle, requiring the reader's careful attention and engagement to sort through the evidence and make sense of it or complete it. Not all of the stories Melville wrote during this period are puzzles, but these six are. The author has mostly removed himself from all but the first of the ones he chose for inclusion, leaving readers to make sense of confusing situations and ambiguous characters on their own, with only a minimum of authorial assistance or intrusion. Even in the quasi-autobiographical "The Piazza," the voice of the narrator is so distinctive and strange at times—so wistful, so preoccupied with escaping his illness in fantasies and "reading the Midsummer Night's Dream, and all about Titania"—as not to permit readers to confuse this character with Melville himself. "Bartleby" is narrated by the scrivener's lawyer-employer, who struggles to make sense of his employee even as the reader must struggle to make sense of him and the lawyer as well, for although the lawyer is sometimes quite eager to provide information about himself, readers are left to make their own judgments about what he chooses to reveal. "Benito Cereno" is told from the point of view of a conventionally minded American captain, who has hardly a clue about the true state of affairs on the slave ship, so the reader has no choice but to struggle along with him. "The Lightning-Rod Man" is a lighter tale, but it too presents challenges for the reader since both of the central characters, the salesman and the narrator who is his target, appear to be trying to deceive the other, a fact that early reviewers and later critics, too, seem to have missed. "The Encantadas," as mentioned earlier, is narrated by a worldly pseudonymous figure, Salvator R. Tarnmoor, who is clearly not to be equated with Melville himself. However, in this case, authorial interventions or warnings are provided by a series of epigraphs, borrowed from Spenser's *The Faerie Queen* and other early English writers, that raise doubts about the surface claims of the narrator. Finally, "The Bell-Tower" is narrated by an anonymous, ahistorical figure who speaks in the erudite, Olympian voice of one who is knowledgeable about many things—the Old Testament, ancient myths, and early modern history, for example—and starts his narrative with three enigmatic epigraphs, identified as "From a Private MS.," that urge the reader to consider the story as a parable about slavery, ambition, and necessity respectively. Here, however, we are offered at least some authorial direction in the first epigraph concerning vengeful "negroes," but are still left to work out any connections between the themes of this epigraph and Melville's story on our own.

At the same time, Melville's stories seem to have been originally designed, but also chosen for inclusion in *The Piazza Tales*, with an eye toward surprising readers, and altering or deepening their perspective on characters and conditions outside the normal range of their experience, while building up sympathy for characters who suffer because of their status as other. Except for "The Lightning-Rod Man," the stories in *The Piazza Tales* move inexorably toward a revelation of human suffering—male, female, Black, white, but almost always poor; these stories are designed to develop in the reader a feeling of recognition and appreciation for the suffering of minority bodies as well as a sense of social conscience, though typically without providing more than hints about how that suffering might be mitigated or ameliorated. Each tale tells a story about a different sort of bodily suffering: sickness and the misery of menial work for the poor seamstress Marianna ("The Piazza"); the pain of alienation, poverty, and meaningless work for a depressed young scrivener ("Bartleby"); the trauma of slavery and the slave trade for Babo and his fellow Africans ("Benito Cereno"); the misery of exploitation or abuse for characters who seek refuge on a deserted archipelago ("The Encantadas"); the horrific experience of slave-breaking and bondage to man and machine ("The Bell-Tower"). All of these stories tell of exploitation or oppression of the weak or vulnerable by the strong or by unnamed forces in the culture at large. (Some of the tales published in *Harper's Monthly* also portray characters who suffer, from poverty particularly: "The Happy Failure," "The Fiddler,"

"Poor Man's Pudding and Rich Man's Crumbs," "The Tartarus of Maids," and "Jimmy Rose," but with the exception of the "The Tartarus of Maids," with its grotesque allegory of female reproduction, these are mostly wry, satiric, sentimental pieces, not meant to stir the reader's conscience, unlike the stories in *The Piazza Tales*.) Among the stories in *The Piazza Tales*, only "The Lightning-Rod Man" takes on the subject of social and economic corruption in a market economy, where money and goods are expected to change hands honestly, but some form of deceit, distrust, or loss of faith hangs over every transaction. Only "The Lightning-Rod Man" presents characters that use scare tactics and practice deception and dishonesty in the name of profit and public service. In this, it can be seen to look ahead to *The Confidence-Man: His Masquerade* (1857), the novel Melville chose to set on April Fools' Day on a Mississippi steamboat named *Fidèle*, where the avatars of the title character appear in an array of disguises while engaging in transactions with other passengers that seem designed to make off with their money, while testing—and undermining—their faith in humankind.

Thus, *The Piazza Tales* can be said to represent a turning point in Melville's career in a second way, too—not simply as a move from long fiction to short but from short fiction back to long again, though with a new set of themes and a newly experimental, satiric format. I suspect that "The Lightning-Rod Man" was the primary catalyst for this second turn, both in the portrayal of the lightning-rod salesman, who seems to be an early incarnation of the salesmen who engage in confidence schemes in *The Confidence-Man*, and in the portrayal of the lightning-rod peddler's potential customer, who turns out to be something of a con man himself, only slyer, faster thinking, and more commanding, like an early avatar of the Cosmopolitan, the ultimate "man charmer" and a dominant figure in *The Confidence-Man*. To be sure, Melville portrayed other performance artists in *The Piazza Tales*, including the ingenious Babo and the other leaders of the rebellious Africans in "Benito Cereno" who hide their intentions behind a façade of abjectness and docility; and possibly Hunilla in Sketch Eighth of "The Encantadas" as well. But "The Lightning-Rod Man" seems to me to mark the origin or source of Melville's turn to *The Confidence-Man* in another sense as well, for as I have argued above, the narrator of that tale seems patterned after the sly, silver-tongued Benjamin Franklin, the American inventor of the lightning rod, whose life and writings Melville had researched extensively in preparation for composing the "Lightning-Rod" story and the separate role he would play in *Israel Potter, His Fifty Years of Exile*, published serially in *Putnam's Monthly* just months after he had completed "The Lightning-Rod Man." As portrayed in *Israel Potter*, Franklin was a particularly winning, sagelike example of a confidence man, whose personality Israel captures when he observes downheartedly, "Every time he comes in [to Israel's Paris hiding place] he robs me, . . . with an air all the time, too, as if he were making me presents."[6] In the personality of Franklin, the man who, in Melville's description, "Having carefully weighed the world . . . could act any part in it," Melville seems to have discovered a rich and promising, "original," home-grown character,[7] an American performance artist who inspired and carried Melville through his writing of "The Lightning-Rod Man" and much of *Israel Potter*, too, before finally giving it his complete attention in *The Confidence-Man*. There every scene is an experiment in the art of performance, and raises questions about the truth or honesty, deception or falsity of the performers and the state of trust between players in the public sphere. On the *Fidèle*, every salesmen and every customer is a performing body, and all are on trial.

# NOTES

## Introduction

1. Interestingly, Melville employs another disability as a plot device in his first book, *Typee* (1846), where he portrays himself as suffering a leg wound while making his way into Typee Valley, an injury that provides a reason for him to stay and learn about the natives' culture while he heals.
2. Comprehensive studies of Melville's magazine stories, not limited to *The Piazza Tales*, include Richard Harter Fogle's *Melville's Shorter Tales;* Warner Berthoff's "Introduction" to *Great Short Works of Herman Melville;* R. Bruce Bickley Jr.'s *The Method of Melville's Short Fiction;* Marvin Fisher's *Going Under: Melville's Short Fiction and the American 1850s;* William B. Dillingham's *Melville's Shorter Fiction, 1853–1856;* and Graham Thompson's *Herman Melville: Among the Magazines.*
3. See Sealts, "Historical Note," *Piazza Tales,* 498.
4. My calculations are based on entries included in Leyda's *Melville Log,* 2:481ff., and largely confirmed in Sealts, "Historical Note," *Piazza Tales,* 493. See also Sealts, "Chronology," in *Pursuing Melville,* 221–31.
5. Parker, *Herman Melville,* 2:271–72.
6. Greenspan, *George Palmer Putnam,* 285–322; see esp. 287–89.
7. Greenspan, *George Palmer Putnam,* 287–88. For a fuller discussion of *Putnam's* effort to appeal to a more educated, intellectual, analytical audience than the audience for *Harper's,* which tended to attract relatively conventionally minded readers with a preference for sentimental writing, see Post-Lauria, "Canonical Texts," 196–205.
8. Greenspan, *George Palmer Putnam,* 292.
9. Sealts, "Historical Note," *Piazza Tales,* 499.
10. Higgins and Parker, *Contemporary Reviews,* 471.
11. Hetherington, *Melville's Reviewers,* 251. Here the reviewer echoes lines from Poe's "Dream-Land."
12. Hetherington, *Melville's Reviewers,* 252.
13. Higgins and Parker, *Contemporary Reviews,* 481–82.
14. Hetherington, *Melville's Reviewers,* 252.

15. Hetherington, *Melville's Reviewers*, 254.
16. Hetherington, *Melville's Reviewers*, 91.
17. Hetherington, *Melville's Reviewers*, 250.
18. Henry James, "The Art of Fiction" (1884).
19. "Hawthorne and His Mosses," in *Piazza Tales*, 244.
20. "Hawthorne and His Mosses," in *Piazza Tales*, 251.
21. Sealts, "Historical Note," *Piazza Tales*, 602–4.
22. Sealts, *Melville's Reading*, 91–92. (See also Leyda's Papers in MS Box 1, folder 29, Melville Society Archive at the New Bedford Whaling Museum Library.)
23. See Bergmann, who in "'Bartleby' and *The Lawyer's Story*," 432–36, argues that Melville likely knew about this novel from advertisements published in the *New York Times* and *New York Tribune* on February 18, 1853, and appropriated the "narrative structure" and opening lines that served to set up the story. See Sealts, "Historical Note," *Piazza Tales*, 576.
24. See my "Bartleby the Transcendentalist," 30–44. Sealts observes that "contemporary comment suggested" the lawyer "and his forlorn clerk may have been patterned after living models." See *Melville's Reading*, 89–90.
25. See Sealts, "Historical Note," *Piazza Tales*, 618.
26. Chapter 32, "Cetology," *Moby-Dick*, 136. For another measure of the extensiveness of Melville's reading throughout his life, see Sealts, *Melville's Reading*.
27. Reported by Charles F. Briggs, the editor of *Putnam's*, in a letter to Melville dated May 12, 1854; see Sealts, "Historical Note," *Piazza Tales*, 605–6.

## 1. "The Piazza" and Melville's Sickroom

1. See Waggoner, "Hawthorne and Melville," 420–24; Fisher, "Fallen World," in *Going Under*, 13–28; Dillingham, "One Spot of Radiance," in *Melville's Short Fiction*, 319–40.
2. Breinig, "Destruction of Fairyland," 282.
3. *Piazza Tales*, 4. Future references to "The Piazza" are to the Northwestern/Newberry edition and appear parenthetically in my text.
4. Chapter 12, "Biographical," in *Moby-Dick*, 55.
5. Quoted from *Piazza Tales*, 360. See also Parker, *Herman Melville*, 2:152.
6. Quoted in Parker, *Herman Melville*, 2:286, 281.
7. Martineau, *Life in the Sickroom*, 132.
8. The meaning of "hebenon" is uncertain and controversial. See, for example, Bradley, "Cursed Hebenon," 85–87.
9. Ironically, Melville himself was in some financial difficulty at this time and, though not exactly poor, was carrying a large personal debt to the former owner for financing the improvements to his new farmhouse. See Parker, *Herman Melville*, 2:209.
10. Quoted in Frawley, "Prisoner to the Couch," 174–88, esp. 182, 173, 176. There is no hard evidence to suggest Melville was familiar with Martineau's *Life in the Sickroom*, but he did own a copy of her *The Hour and the Man: A Historical Romance*, 3 vols. (London: Moxon, 1841), a gift from Mrs. J. R. Morewood and, according to Sealts, "acknowledged in Melville's letter of 12? Sep 1851: 'The "Hour & the Man" is exceedingly acceptable to me.'" See *Melville's Reading*, 197. Martineau was well known in

the United States, having visited there in 1834 and then published *Society in America* (1837), an early sociological study. Others, too, have written about the links between heightened consciousness and confinement, going back to the cloistered nun Teresa de Cartagena, whose growing deafness forced her further and further into isolation, as described in *Arboleda de los Enfermos* (Grove of the infirm; ca. 1475), and up to the time of another of Melville's contemporaries, Margaret Fuller, who tells the story in *Summer on the Lakes, in 1843* about the invalided Seeress of Prevorst of Bavaria. See Hsy, "Disability," in *Cambridge Companion*, 24–40, where he observes that "Teresa's narrative invites readers to approach deafness not as a crisis or impairment but as a transformation in sensory orientation that affords new kinds of experiences" (30).
11. Martineau, *Life in the Sickroom*, 139.
12. Frawley, "Prisoner to the Couch," 184.
13. See Parker, *Herman Melville*, 2:152.
14. Martineau, *Life in the Sickroom*, 163. See also chapter 8, "The Power of Ideas in the Sick-Room."
15. One memorable example of impoverished, suffering womanhood from earlier in Melville's writing is captured in "What Redburn Saw in Launcelott's-Hey," chapter 37 of *Redburn* (1849), where the title character is shocked to hear wailing near the docks of Liverpool, where his ship was moored, and catches a glimpse of "the figure of what had been a woman," her arms folding to her "livid bosom two shrunken things like children," deep in a cellar (180).
16. Martineau, *Life in the Sickroom*, 60.
17. Martineau, *Life in the Sickroom*, 44–45.
18. Martineau, *Life in the Sickroom*, 59.
19. Reynolds, in *Beneath the American Renaissance*, argues that "Before 1855 the only jobs that were generally available to the mass of American women were the onerous, low-paying ones of sewing, factory work, teaching, and storekeeping.... Particularly wretched were seamstresses, who in the two decades after the Panic of 1837 often lived in squalid, crowded tenements and worked long hours for bare subsistence pay." See chapter 12, "Types of American Womanhood," 337–67, esp. 352–54. Significantly, Melville wrote about the suffering and exploitation of women in factories, too, during this period in "The Tartarus of Maids," published in *Harper's Monthly* in 1855, a year before *The Piazza Tales*.

## 2. "Bartleby, the Scrivener"

1. "Bartleby, the Scrivener," in *Piazza Tales*, 29. Future references to "Bartleby" are to the Northwestern/Newberry edition and appear parenthetically in my text.
2. Melville had earlier entertained a similar split in "The Journey and the Pamphlet," Book XIV of *Pierre; or, The Ambiguities* (1852), where the "young Enthusiast Pierre" happens upon a copy of the fictitious Plotinus Plinlimmon's Lecture First on "Chronometricals and Horologicals," an ironic work that also appears to be informed by Emerson's writings. Here, Melville's Plinlimmon writes, there are two orders of time, two ways of thinking and being, one earthly and one transcendent: for example, "Bacon's brains were mere watch maker's brains; but Christ was a chronometer; and the most

exquisitely adjusted and exact one, and the least affected by all terrestrial jarrings, of any that have ever come to us." Quoted in *Pierre*, 210–11.

3. There is no record that Melville owned any of Emerson's prose works until 1862. See Sealts, *Melville's Reading*, 175–76.
4. Melville to Evert A. Duyckinck, March 3, 1849, in *Correspondence*, 121. Leyda, in *Melville Log*, 1:287, speculates that Melville heard Emerson speak on "Mind & Manners in the Nineteenth Century" on February 5.
5. "Sophia Hawthorne to her sister Elizabeth, Oct?" (Leyda, *Melville Log*, 2:924–25). Melville probably read these "essays" on September 5 or 6, 1850.
6. It seems likely Melville's attention would have been drawn to a recent publication of Emerson's, and we know Hawthorne owned this 1849 collection. It is also possible that Melville borrowed a copy of this collection from another source (such as the well-stocked shelves of his friend Evert Duyckinck, before their estrangement in February 1852). *Nature, Addresses, and Lectures* was reviewed on November 3, 1849 in *The Literary World* (374–76), which Duyckinck coedited with his brother George L. According to Sealts, Melville "was probably a regular subscriber—at least during the period of Evert Duyckinck's editorship [October 1848–December 1853]—until he canceled his subscription in a letter of 14 Feb 1852" (see *Melville's Reading*, 193).
7. "The Transcendentalist," *Emerson's Prose and Poetry*, 101. References are to this edition and appear parenthetically in the text.
8. For a fuller discussion of parallels between "Bartleby" and Emerson's essay, see my "Bartleby the Transcendentalist," 30–44. Colin Dayan, in "Bartleby's Screen," also explores material and immaterial or spiritual representations of the scrivener, but specifically in relation to changing concepts of property and the law in the nineteenth century.
9. In his portrayals of the lawyer and the scrivener, Melville might have been influenced also by Emerson's "The Conservative," which was published in *The Dial* (October 1842) and in *Nature, Addresses, and Lectures*. The Conservative and the Reformer of this essay are, generally speaking, philosophically in agreement with Emerson's Materialist and Transcendentalist respectively (see *Complete Works*, 1:295–326).
10. Post-Lauria, in "Canonical Texts," 196–205, argues that this is the type of intellectual, socially conscious audience *Putnam's Monthly* was trying to cultivate when it started publication in 1853, unlike its more popular, large-market competitor, *Harper's New Monthly Magazine*.
11. I take this idea from Mitchell and Snyder in *Narrative Prosthesis*, where they make the case that disability is a major example of the "deviance" that drives the reader's engagement with narrative while also providing the "interruptive force" that questions and confronts "cultural truisms" and "normalizing prescriptive ideals" (48, 51). See esp. chapter 2, 47–64.
12. Quoted in Foley, "From Wall Street to Astor Place," 93.
13. There are several helpful, illuminating discussions of "Bartleby" in the context of Wall Street culture at mid century, starting with Louise K. Barnett's early Marxist reading, "Bartleby as Alienated Worker," 379–85; followed by Michael T. Gilmore's "'Bartleby the Scrivener' and the Transformation of the Economy," 132–45; David Kuebrich's "Melville's Doctrine of Assumptions," 381–405; Naomi C. Reed's "Specter of Wall

Street," 248–73; and Lori Duin Kelly's "Office Setting as Organizational Structure," 1–8. Relevant here, too, is Alex Benson's "'Bartleby' on Speed," 120–37, on Melville's "representations of work" and "related questions of temporal plurality."
14. Scarry, *Body in Pain*, 47–48. For a contrary reading, see chapter 5 in *Passive Constitutions*, 83–108, where Branka Arsić offers as one of several poststructuralist interpretations the view that Bartleby is a "painless being" whose body feels no pain while his soul secretly suffers. Other chapters regard him as a melancholic, a "junkie," a bachelor, and a witness, among other categories.
15. In "Loomings," the opening chapter of *Moby-Dick*, Ishmael speaks of the captive office workers of Manhattan, "all landsmen," who, "of week days pent up in lath and plaster—tied to counters, nailed to benches, clinched to desks," long to escape to sea.
16. By contrast, the work environment in "The Tartarus of Maids" is described as "a spacious place, intolerably lighted by long rows of windows, focusing inward the snowy scene without" (*Piazza Tales*, 328), but in this case the frozen landscape outside is a constant reminder to the "girls" how cold and forbidding it is there in contrast to the warmth inside the factory that allows them to work without stopping.
17. Gilmore, in "'Bartleby the Scrivener' and the Transformation of the Economy," 132–45, was the first to demonstrate that the lawyer's expectations of his employees are often in keeping with practices that were becoming standard in New York offices of the 1840s and 1850s, but he also sees the lawyer as continuing to embody "both the decencies and the limitations of the older ['household'] economic order" (135). Later efforts to historicize the lawyer's office practices include Kuebrich, "Melville's Doctrine of Assumptions," 381–405, and Foley, "From Wall Street to Astor Place," 87–116.
18. See Kuebrich, "Melville's Doctrine of Assumptions," 381–405, esp. 403; and Goldfarb, "Charity as Purchase," 233–61, esp. 242. Other critics who have examined the lawyer's moral sense according to varying standards (legal, Ciceronian, and self-interested) include Matteson, "A New Race Has Sprung Up," 25–49; Miskolcze, "Lawyer's Trouble with Cicero," 43–53; and Kari Nixon, "If You Don't Know Me," n.p.
19. Delbanco, *Melville: His World and Work*, 221.
20. Supporting this view of the lawyer's efforts, Dan McCall, in *Silence of Bartleby*, writes that "Critics . . . read the passage [i.e., the lawyer's statement beginning, 'I might give alms to his body'] as a rather too fond farewell, as if 'his soul I could not reach' means that the Lawyer quits. But the man immediately contradicts by his action what he has just concluded. He reaches for that soul. And he does a very smart thing: saying to himself that he may not be able to do it, that he may lack what he needs to reach an adequate understanding, he resolves to suggest to Bartleby that he return to his native place, wherever that might be." "You must go 'home,'" he advises him, "and I will help pay for your trip" (56).
21. For example, Hillman and Maude, "Introduction," in *Cambridge Companion to the Body*, 1–9, assert that "Neurologically-oriented cognitive philosophers such as Antonio Damasio have . . . persuasively argued that thinking and feeling are intrinsically embodied processes," and quote Damasio in illustration: "The soul breathes through the body, and suffering, whether it starts in the skin or in a mental image, happens in the flesh" (7).

22. Scarry, *Body in Pain*, 4.
23. Scarry, *Body in Pain*, 5.
24. Scarry, *Body in Pain*, 6, 9.
25. Scarry, *Body in Pain*, 11.
26. See note 13 above.
27. For another reading of Melville's efforts to minimize the potential sentimentality of the lawyer and scrivener's relationship, one based on an idea that the editors of *Putnam's Monthly* rejected the sentimental style of its competitor *Harper's New Monthly Magazine* and instead preferred to publish fiction that stressed social analysis over emotions, see Post-Lauria's "Canonical Texts," 196–205.
28. Several critics have attempted to diagnose what ails Bartleby in terms of illness or disability. See Bollas, "Melville's Lost Self," 401–11; Sullivan, "Bartleby and Infantile Autism," 43–60; Beja, "Bartleby and Schizophrenia," 555–68; Brown, "Empire of Agoraphobia," 139–50; Desmarais, "Anorexia," 82–93; and Savarese, "Nervous Wrecks and Ginger-nuts," on patent medicines, 19–49. See also Deleuze, "Bartleby; or, The Formula," 68–90, on psychosis and schizophrenia, though Deleuze ends by arguing that "even in his catatonic or anorexic state, Bartleby is not the patient, but the doctor of a sick America." Finally, Arsić, in *Passive Constitutions*, makes several conditional diagnoses of the scrivener—as a melancholic, an idiot, a junkie, and so on—that tend to cancel each other out, leaving a passive indeterminate figure at the story's center.
29. The idea of betrayal is perhaps relevant in that the lawyer can be regarded as attempting to buy off his conscience with the payment of silver coins rather than doing something more meaningful to care for the scrivener, but any suggestion of a parallel with the story of Judas Iscariot, who betrayed Jesus in exchange for thirty pieces of silver, seems strained, since, unlike Judas, the lawyer is not paid for his actions but instead pays for preferential treatment for Bartleby.
30. The lawyer here echoes Job 3:14, "with kings and counselors of the earth who rebuilt ruins for themselves," a line that elevates the lawyer's feeling for Bartleby and suggests genuine respect while also acknowledging the futility of the sympathy he has come to feel for him.

## 3. "Casting a Shadow"

1. Quoted in "Notes" on "Benito Cereno," in *Piazza Tales*, 581. Future references to "Benito Cereno" are to the Northwestern/Newberry edition and appear parenthetically in my text.
2. Karcher, in *Shadow Over the Promised Land*, was the first critic to make the case that Melville's "portrayal of Babo as an almost disembodied brain—'his slight frame, inadequate to that which it held'—reverses the conventional racist stereotype of the Negro as all brawn and no brain" (130). White Americans' belief in Africans' inferior intelligence was widespread in the nineteenth century, thanks in part to the popularity of the pseudo-scientific craniological studies of Samuel George Morton, particularly *Crania Americana* (1839) and *Crania Ægyptiaca* (1844), and the ethnological writings of Josiah Nott and George Gliddon, especially *Types of Mankind* (1854). For a fuller discussion, see Otter, *Melville's Anatomies*, 101–26.

3. Several critics have pointed to Melville's repeated use of the "bachelor" trope to suggest inexperience or innocence, as seen also in the title of Melville's "Paradise of Bachelors" and, in *Moby-Dick,* in the *Pequod*'s encounter with the *Bachelor,* whose captain claims not to believe in Moby-Dick "at all." However, H. Bruce Franklin has also argued, in connection with "Benito Cereno," that Melville surely knew that "one of the most famous of all pirate vessels" was called the *Bachelor's Delight* and that, among other associations with piracy, Melville's Captain Delano is alleged by Benito Cereno to be a pirate when Delano claims ownership of the *San Dominick* after he and his men rescue Cereno and retake the slave ship. See "Past, Present, and Future," 230–46, esp. 237.
4. Sundquist develops these connections at length in his informative study, *To Wake the Nations,* 139–54.
5. Delano, *A Narrative of Voyages and Travels* (1817), as reproduced in *Piazza Tales,* 809–47.
6. This phrase derives from Melville's review, "Hawthorne and His Mosses," reprinted in *Piazza Tales,* 249, where Melville writes that "genius, all over the world, stands hand in hand, and one shock of recognition runs the whole circle round," but I use the phrase here in its everyday sense.
7. In Freudian terms, this "double-plot" experience is known as *Nachträglichkeit* or "afterwardness."
8. I am indebted to Greg Forter, "Freud, Faulkner, Caruth," 259–85, for his discussion of traumatic reversal in narrative as it applies to Faulkner. The phrase "double plot" derives from Forter's discussion but has its origin in John Cawelti's "Faulkner and the Detective Story's Double Plot," 1–15.
9. For an illuminating discussion of the legal complexities of Delano's Samaritan impulses, which appear both early and late in Melville's story, see Downes, "Melville's 'Benito Cereno' and the Politics of Humanitarian Intervention," 465–88. For a very different political assessment of Delano's attempt to lead the retaking of the *San Dominick* after he and Cereno have escaped the rebellion on the slave ship, see "'Benito Cereno' and Manifest Destiny," 48–68, where Emery explores evidence of Melville's concern about "mid-century arguments for American intervention in Latin America," particularly in Cuba.
10. In technical terms, this can happen also because, as the American Psychiatric Association's *Diagnostic and Statistical Manual* explains in defining trauma, specifically Post Traumatic Stress Disorder, "Negative alterations in cognition or mood associated with the event begin or worsen after exposure to the event. These negative alterations can take various forms, including an inability to remember an important aspect of a traumatic event; such amnesia is typically due to dissociative amnesia and is not due to head injury, alcohol, or drugs (Criterion D1)"; see 275.
11. Forter's explanation of this process in connection with the parallel case of Faulkner's *Absalom, Absalom!* is further instructive here: Faulkner's technique "asks us to 'ingest' details that remain at first cognitively indigestible, until such time as a second set of details retrodetermines their significance. The strategies thus seek collectively to induce a kind of signification trauma in the reader. They work to 'say' through the novel's form that the story it tells is itself a trauma that must be transmitted and known as trauma. They work, in other words, to transmit a form of psychic

disequilibrium 'directly' to the reader, rather than offering a merely cognitive knowledge of the traumas the book explores" (279).

12. For a careful discussion of the question whether the rebellious slaves on the *San Dominick* have not only flayed the body of Aranda but cannibalized it, see "Walking Shadows," in *Sign of the Cannibal*, 171–200, esp. 184, where Geoffrey Sanborn argues that Cereno's deposition makes it clear that "Babo's decision to macerate and exhibit Aranda's body is the product of a strategy" to "keep the [Spanish] seamen in subjection" and "to prepare a warning of what road [the Spaniards] should be made to take did they or any of them oppose him."

13. According to Melville's fictional version of the deposition, Babo was also the one who ordered the skeleton of Don Alexandro to be "prepared" so it could be substituted for the *San Dominick*'s figurehead; Babo who "traced the inscription below it"; Babo who was "the plotter from first to last" and "ordered every murder, and was the helm and keel of the revolt" (111–12).

14. Quoted in *A Narrative of Voyages and Travels*, in *Piazza Tales*, 831.

15. For a fuller discussion of the trope of black minstrelsy in "Benito Cereno," see Sundquist, *To Wake the Nations*, 152–54. Sundquist points out that an essay on "Negro Minstrelsy—Ancient and Modern" appeared in *Putnam's Monthly* in January 1855, during "the time at which he [Melville] was composing his title" for his story.

16. Later described as a "scabbard" that was "artificially stiffened" and "empty" (116).

17. For another reading of Don Benito's wardrobe, and what it reveals about Delano's class consciousness in contrast to his inability to read or judge the relative nakedness of the slave bodies on the *San Dominick*, see Nicola Nixon's "Men and Coats," 85–94.

18. See Herman, *Trauma and Recovery*, 85–94. See also Blum, "Concept of the Reconstruction of Trauma," where Blum explores the distinction between "shock trauma" and "strain trauma," and quotes Freud as offering an expanded view of trauma that goes "beyond external stimulation": "The essence of a traumatic situation is an experience of helplessness on the part of the ego in the face of accumulation of excitation, whether of external or internal origin" (9). Though Blum warns that the term "strain trauma" may be misleading, on the grounds that all trauma, "by its very definition," always has "the immediate effect of helplessness" (12–13), the idea, when linked to Herman's studies, helps to explain how captivity—such as that experienced by the enslaved Africans and then by Benito Cereno—can have a traumatizing effect. More generally, without mentioning trauma, Sanborn, "Walking Shadows," 198, argues that "For a contemporary audience, it would have been abundantly clear that the brokenness of his [Cereno's] body is a consequence of the brokenness of his mind," but Sanborn then goes on to assert, with limited supporting evidence, that the "disease that kills him is quite obviously tuberculosis," since we are told early on "that he has a 'tendency to some pulmonary complaint' . . . and that he repeatedly experiences 'febrile and transient' fits of 'hectic animation' that die away into 'indifference and apathy'" (58, 91). These are symptoms that also appear in victims of trauma.

19. Sharks were often found trailing after sailing ships of all kinds in the nineteenth century, in anticipation of the chance to feed on discarded refuse, offal, and even human bodies (dead or alive), but they were especially known to follow after slave ships in Middle Passage, since the mortality rate among slaves was so high and their bodies

had to be disposed of quickly. As Rediker, in *Slave Ship*, 38–39, also reports, captains of slave ships often used the threat of throwing rebellious slaves, or even their own recalcitrant sailors, to the sharks as a way to "terrorize" them into docility.
20. See chapter 4, "Captivity," in Herman, *Trauma and Recovery*, 74–95. Also see Rediker, *Slave Ship;* and Hartman, *Scenes of Subjection.*
21. This is in contrast to Melville's brief description, in *Redburn* (57), of the treatment of Africans in "the middle passage, where the slaves were stowed, heel and point, like logs, and the suffocated and dead were unmanacled, and weeded out from the living every morning, before washing down the decks."
22. See Grandin, *Empire of Necessity*, 173.
23. These include Matthiessen, *American Renaissance*, 508; Williams, "Follow Your Leader," 61–76; Feltenstein, "Melville's 'Benito Cereno,'" 245–55; Fogle, "Monk and Bachelor," 155–78; Kaplan, "American National Sin," 12–27; Yellin, "Black Masks," 678–89; among others.
24. Blum, in "Concept of the Reconstruction of Trauma," 24, argues that trauma, by definition, has always been associated "not only with automatic anxiety but with enormous anger, with rage."
25. See Rediker, *Slave Ship*, 7–10 and chapter 8, "Sailor's Vast Machine," 222–62, esp. 239–44. A well-known early example of eyewitness testimony about sexual abuse of enslaved females can be found in Olaudah Equiano's *Interesting Narrative*, 93–94.
26. See Alexander, *Trauma: A Social Theory.*

## 4. Playing Smart, Playing Dumb

1. Hershel Parker, with an assist from Harrison Hayford, was the first to recognize Melville's story as an example of a standard kind of tale, in "Salesman Story," 154–58. For support of the idea that Melville engaged with the British and American theater of the 1850s in relation to his short-story writing from this period, particularly in "Two Temples" and "Fiddler," see Collins, *Drama of the American Short Story.*
2. "The Lightning-Rod Man," in *Piazza Tales*. Future references to "The Lightning-Rod Man" are to the Northwestern/Newberry edition and appear parenthetically in my text.
3. In "Salesman Story," Parker argues that it was more popular than most of Melville's other tales when it appeared for the first time in *Putnam's Monthly*, but in its review of *The Piazza Tales*, the *Southern Literary Messenger* 22 (June 1856): 480, called it "a very flat recital which we would never have suspected Melville of producing," adding it was rarely singled out for praise in any of the reviews of *The Piazza Tales*. See Higgins and Parker, eds., *Contemporary Reviews*, 472–73. Even more recent assessments of the story usually fail to recognize the subtle humor of this tale. One exception, Dillingham, in *Melville's Shorter Fiction*, 168–82, asserts that the situation of the story, particularly the narrator's forceful ejection of the Yankee peddler, is "not without its humor" (168–69), but he has little more to say about the subject.
4. Goffman, "On Face-Work," 5.
5. This term, which Leyda was the first to track down, may derive from Melville's reading of Cotton Mather's *Magnalia Christi Americana,* chapter II, book VI, "Ceraunius,

Relating Remarkables Done by Thunder," a copy of which Melville's local Pittsfield library had acquired in 1853, about the time Melville wrote this tale. See Leyda, "Introduction," xxvi–xxvii.

6. Quoted in Cohen, ed., *Franklin's Experiments*, 391–92. See also "Melville on Science," 559, where Emery quotes Lucius Lyon, Franklin's well-known successor in the study of lightning, as concluding, "Whatever situation is chosen, the greatest care should be taken to avoid going near the fire-place, since the chimneys are most likely to attract the electrical fluid"; see Lyon's *A Treatise on Lightning Conductors* (New York: G. P. Putnam, 1853), 170–71, published a year before Melville's story by Melville's own publisher. Emery provides a detailed discussion of Melville's apparent borrowings from Franklin and, to a lesser extent, from Lyon.
7. See *Frame Analysis*, 24, where, speaking of "Role Theory," Goffman "analyzes human activity in terms of its enactment of socially determined roles."
8. Leyda, "Introduction," xxvi. Also, according to the *Oshkosh Daily Northwestern* (April 25, 1891), the sale of lightning rods in France, where Franklin was lionized, was nonetheless thought to go against God's rule, or perhaps their salesmen simply proved so annoying that "they who would sell Franklin rods were arrested."
9. See Dray, *Stealing God's Thunder*, 213–14 and 111.
10. Quoted in Dray, *Stealing God's Thunder*, 111.
11. For a detailed discussion of Melville's apparent borrowings from Franklin and Lyon, see Emery's "Melville on Science," 555–68.
12. Concerning the latter, compare Franklin's claim: "If the clothes are wet, if a flash in its way to the ground should strike your head, it may run in the water over the surface of your body; whereas, if your clothes were dry, it would go through the body, because the blood and other humors, containing so much water, are more ready conductors." See his *Letters and Papers on Electricity*, 220.
13. Fisher is one critic who identifies the setting with the Berkshires and believes Melville renamed them the "Acroceaunian" [i.e., Acroceraunian] hills.
14. Dray, in *Stealing God's Thunder*, 56, points out that, while in Philadelphia and in the early stages of his study of lightning, Franklin "read dispatches from other colonies of the damage to houses, churches, trees, and human beings" and later, while experimenting with lightning rods, published notices of the dangers of lightning strikes in his *Gazette*. For example, "We hear from Susquehanna, that on Sunday . . . a Man was struck dead by the Lightning; that another Man was so stunned that it was some time before he recovr'd; and that a child, who sat betwixt the legs of one of them, rece'vd no damage" (quoted in *Stealing God's Thunder*, 87). Moreover, as Matthews has shown, in "Peddlers of the Rod," marketers of lightning rods in the nineteenth century continued the practice of exploiting fears about electrical storms in periodicals such as *The Cultivator* by citing stories of sensational accidents resulting in injury or death while at the same time repeating Franklin's own safety instructions from the 1750s.
15. The reference to Criggan may have a personal connection to Franklin, who spent fifteen years in England as a diplomat during two London missions (1757–62 and 1765–75), periods that included extensive travel in England (and Scotland), so he had good reason to be familiar with the town's name and notable happenings there,

particularly incidents of lightning strikes, which he habitually collected and published in his *Pennsylvania Gazette*.
16. Goffman, "On Face-Work," 8.
17. Dray also observes that the members of Franklin's Junto Club discussed the matter and raised still another inconsistency concerning lightning's putative "presumption," namely, its questionable aim in wasting itself on trees and other inanimate objects (*Stealing God's Thunder*, 100). Krider, in "Benjamin Franklin and Lightning Rods," also quotes Franklin as being similarly relieved by what was implied in the discovery "that it is not Lightning from the Clouds that strikes the Earth, but Lightning from the Earth that Strikes the Clouds," for it suggested mankind was not being "presumptuous" or interfering with the will of God in seeking the protection afforded by a lightning rod (45). Krider quotes *The Papers of Benjamin Franklin*, edited by L. W. Labaree et al. (New Haven: Yale University Press, 1959–), 4:463.
18. See Kimpel, "Two Notes," 30. Later assessments that interpreted Melville's story as an allegorical treatment of evangelical Christianity in conflict with skepticism or doubt, include Bickley, *Method of Melville's Short Fiction*, 67–70; Fisher, *Going Under*, 118–24; and Silver, "Temporality of Allegory," 1–33. Critics who question this dominant reading include Emery, who, in "Melville on Science," argues that the lightning-rod man represents "not fire-and-brimstone Christianity, but science, as 'preached' by Lyon, Franklin, and their meteorological pals" (559); and Matthews who, in "Peddlers of the Rod," 55–70, views the story as satirizing instead two secular "American types—the rural democrat and the door-to-door salesman" (57).
19. A variation of this basic conflict can be found in "Who Is the Lightning-Rod Man?" 273–79, where Verdier views the title character as a figure of Satan, who tempts the narrator with science, but is ultimately defeated in a scenario suggesting Man's "ultimate victory" over temptation "through faith."
20. See, for example, Fisher, *Going Under*, 118–24.
21. Matthews, "Peddlers of the Rod," 57.
22. Emery, in "Melville on Science," quotes Franklin, in *Letters and Papers on Electricity*, 189–202.
23. For an early discussion of the source of this inscription, see Cornish, "Latin Verse on Franklin," 17. Cornish argues that the phrase should be attributed to the comte de Mirabeau, not the marquis de Condorcet. However, according to both Dray (*Stealing God's Thunder*, xvi) and Krider ("Benjamin Franklin and Lightning Rods," 48), the epigram was composed by Anne-Robert Jacques Turgot, an economist and one-time comptroller-general of France, in June 1776.

## 5. "The Encantadas, or Enchanted Isles"

1. Howard, *Herman Melville*, 209–10.
2. See Dillingham, *Melville's Shorter Fiction*, 75–103; Fisher, *Going Under*, 28–50; Albrecht, "Thematic Unity," 463–77. More recent efforts at describing the unity of these sketches include Beecher, "Variations on a Dystopian Theme," 88–95; Tanyol, "Alternative Taxonomies," 242–79, comparing Melville's "purposeful inexactness" in describing the Galapagos islands with Darwin's precision and authoritative classifications; Freeburg,

"Embodying the 'Assaults of Time,'" 132–63, regarding the sketches as embodying a "ubiquitous black geography" together with themes of "unrealized colonial possibility"; and Chura, "Demon est deus inversus," 47–76, concerning Melville's postmodern dissent from Emerson's worldview.

3. The pseudonym was not included in "The Encantadas" when the work was collected later in *The Piazza Tales*, the result, perhaps, of a printer's oversight or, more likely, a product of the fact that Melville's own name appeared on the title page as the author of all the stories in the collection. On the editors' decision to retain the pseudonym in the Northwestern-Newberry edition of *The Piazza Tales*, see "Notes" on "The Encantadas," in *Piazza Tales*, 606–7. Specq's insightful reading of the narrator, in "Prophecy," 153–80, as a picturesque painter in the tradition of Salvator Rosa seems especially apt when applied to the serialized version of the sketches that appeared anonymously in the *Putnam's Monthly* version of the story, but it becomes problematic when applied to the version published in the first edition of *The Piazza Tales*, where the reference to the pseudonym of Salvator R. Tarnmoor—the key to a Rosa-esque reading of "The Encantadas"—has been removed. I follow the Northwestern-Newberry editors who view the omission of Tarnmoor's name in the first edition of *The Piazza Tales* as probably being "editorial or compositorial" (606). I also maintain the fiction of the Tarnmoor pseudonym in my discussion of the "author" of "The Encantadas," but I continue to regard Melville as the original, implied author who silently supplies the epigraphs from Spenser et al., for the sketches. Those poetic epigraphs not only set a mood for each piece but also provide a potentially ironic frame that comments on Tarnmoor's versions of the stories in the sketches.

4. "The Encantadas, or Enchanted Isles," in *Piazza Tales*, 143. Future references to "The Encantadas" are to the Northwestern-Newberry edition and appear parenthetically in my text.

5. For a useful parallel reading of the fragmented character of "The Encantadas," one emphasizing the loose structure of the archipelago as an organizing principle in Melville's writing, see Jonik's "Isles of Absentees," 165–85. Jonik writes, "The archipelago evokes a type of writing that leaves its elements uncemented yet formally held together. In this sense, it is not a 'form' per se but the constant unmaking of form, a deformation in both fragmentation and extension" (167). Jonik's essay appeared after my earlier published discussion of fragmentation in "The Encantadas": "'Facts Picked Up in the Pacific': Fragmentation, Deformation, and the (Cultural) Uses of Enchantment," in *"Whole Oceans Away": Melville and the Pacific*, edited by Jill Barnum, Wyn Kelley, and Christopher Sten (Kent, OH: Kent State University Press, 2007), 213–23.

6. Harter, *Bodies in Pieces*, 10. See also Barthes, *S/Z*, 67–68.

7. Harter, *Bodies in Pieces*, 12–14.

8. See, for example, Howarth's "Darwin and Melville," 95–113. In fact, Howarth tends to read both Darwin's and Melville's accounts as biographical reports that reveal the author's own personal psychology (in Melville's case, defined by "violent self-loathing, barely subliminated") and life circumstance, and to ignore the fact that much of "The Encantadas" is fiction.

9. Melville demonstrated a continuing interest in towers, and wrote informally about the special vantage point they provided onto surrounding landscapes as well as the

excitement that came with panoramic views from an elevated vantage point. On his 1856 trip to Europe and the Middle East, for example, when touring Constantinople, he commented enthusiastically in his journal on the view from the Serasker Tower, a nineteenth-century watch tower "in the Saracenic style": "From the top, my God, what a view! Surpasses everything. The Propontis, the Bosphorous, the Golden Horn, the domes, the minarets, the bridges, the men of war, the cypresses.—Indescribable." See "Journal 1856–57," in *Journals*, 60.

10. H. Bruce Franklin, in "Island Worlds of Darwin and Melville," 353–70, claims that Melville seems to have implicitly questioned or parodied many of Darwin's observations in *Voyage*, including his claim that he was able to find "only eleven kinds" of waders and waterbirds and only one kind of gull, whereas Melville (or his narrator) says he had seen "unnumbered seafowl" and "gulls of all varieties" (364). More recently, Wertheimer, in "Mutations: Melville, Representation, and South American History," 133–59, sees Melville as dissenting, "politically and aesthetically, from a key aspect of Darwin's earliest theory of historical representation" according to which Darwin thought it was not possible "to describe or paint the difference of savage & civilized man" if viewed from sufficient distance, whereas Melville recognized the difference but regarded it as "an emblem of the effects of colonization rather than as a natural given." Similarly to what I contend here, Wertheimer argues that "Melville's 'fictional' stories of conflict were the very contingent products of a critical New World milieu: the post-colonial South American waters where history had a richly hybrid pedigree" (134).

11. See Parker's volume 1 of *Herman Melville*; also Sealts, *Melville's Reading*, 171. Of the several discussions comparing Melville's and Darwin's responses to the Galapagos Islands, the most illuminating and instructive, in my view, are Franklin's and Tanyol's. Franklin was the first to point out what may be a silent dismissal of Darwin in Melville's omission of the biologist from his list of "three eye-witness authorities worth mentioning touching the Enchanted Isles."

12. See Hanke and Rausch, eds., *People and Issues in Latin American History*, 27.

13. Similarly, Jonik, in "Melville's 'Permanent Riotocracy,'" 229–58, borrowing a term from Gilles Deleuze, sees the human figures in the late sketches as "so many 'outlandish individuals,' such as Queequeg," or "outlandish strangers," who come together with the "outlandish beings" or animals of the Galapagos, in forming "an outlandish collective, an 'incomputable host of fiends.'" Certainly I agree with this estimation and with Jonik's follow-up conclusion as well: "Put differently, in Melville's Galapagos, the archipelago serves as the topology of a non-identitarian community. It evokes a politics of relation—an 'outlandish politics'—that draws together solitaries in their differences, yet is open-ended and not governed by a unifying (territorial) identity or wholeness," (230), though I regard Melville's buccaneers as something of an exception.

14. Curiously, this is an act of censorship that contradicts the narrator's earlier argument that it is futile to ban (or in this case censor) books, when "events" (which are harder to "censor") can be much more harmful than books.

15. Albrecht, in "Thematic Unity," 463–77, coined the useful term "heretics of a commercial culture" for the buccaneers, a term that is especially relevant to his reading of the sketches in relation to the circles of Hell in Dante's *Inferno*.

16. Fernandez-Armesto, *The Americas*, 126–27.
17. Here Melville closely followed one of his sources, James Colnett's *A Voyage to the South Atlantic* (1798).
18. See *New Columbia Encyclopedia*, 2154–55.
19. See "Ends of Enchantment," 207–29, especially 212–17, where Lazo explains that the "Creole adventurer from Cuba" seems to be based not only on José de Villamil but also on Narciso Lopez, "the filibustering Creole who worked with John L. O'Sullivan and exiled Cuban writers to build support for the filibustering expeditions to Cuba. Well-known in the mid-nineteenth century, Lopez shared some biographical similarities with Villamil."
20. In a richly detailed, historical discussion of this sketch, "Tracking Melville's 'Dog-King,'" 71–93, Spengler argues that Tarnmoor, Melville's persona, "curiously expresses sympathy for this 'unfortunate Creole' who uses vicious dogs to police" his little colony, "until his subjects revolt and force him into exile." Such sympathy, Spengler goes on to argue persuasively, reflects "not only the ambivalence of the antebellum United States regarding Spanish America but also its investment in maintaining white creole authority in the face of black and indigenous resistance" (71).
21. See Anderson, *Imagined Communities*, 53.
22. Sattelmeyer and Barbour, "Sources and Genesis," 398–417.
23. Charles F. Briggs, the editor of *Putnam's*, wrote to Melville after "The Encantadas" was published to apologize for making "a slight alteration" at the end of the Chola widow sketch by omitting "a few words," but then added that he received "good evidence" he did not "mutilate the touching figure you introduced" when James Russell Lowell wrote him to say that "the figure of the cross in the ass' neck, brought tears into his eyes, and he thought it the finest touch of genius he had seen in prose" (quoted in "Notes," on "The Encantadas" in *Piazza Tales*, 605–6).
24. Moses, in "Hunilla and Oberlus," 339–42, credits Leon Howard, in "Melville and Spenser—A Note on Criticism," *Modern Language Notes* 46 (1931): 291–92, and Russell Thomas, in "Melville's Use of Some Sources in 'The Encantadas,'" *American Literature* 3 (1932): 432–56, as having identified the epigraphs to "The Encantadas," but adds that neither of them "commented on the ostensible incongruity of the Spenserian epigraph when applied to the Chola widow" (340n7).
25. It is relevant to mention here that in the case of the real-life Agatha Robertson, the husband who abandoned her did not die but finally returned to her after seventeen years. At least the theoretical possibility of a "dead" husband who is not in fact dead had presented itself to Melville, both in the original Agatha story and in the last two epitaphs, from Chatterton and Collins, for Sketch Ninth. See Melville's "Agatha letters" to Nathaniel Hawthorne, dating from late 1852, in Melville, *Correspondence*, 231–42, esp. 234.

## 6. Docile Monsters and Enslavement in "The Bell-Tower"

1. Concerning the story's indebtedness to Hawthorne, see Sweeney, "Melville's Hawthornian Bell-Tower," 279–86; and Bickley, *Method of Melville's Short Fiction*, 95–100, among others. For the view that the story offers a critical assessment of technology

and technological progress, see, for example, Fenton, "Melville and Technology," 219–32; and Bach, "Melville's Theatrical Mask," 43–56.
2. "The Bell-Tower," in *Piazza Tales*, 182. Future references to "The Bell-Tower" are to the Northwestern-Newberry edition and appear parenthetically in my text.
3. Hanafi, *Monster in the Machine*, 2.
4. Jeffrey Jerome Cohen, "Monster Culture (Seven Theses)," 3–25.
5. Cohen, "Monster Culture (Seven Theses)," 4.
6. Genesis 11:1–4.
7. Hanafi, *Monster in the Machine*, 4. See also: "From the earliest written records to present day, a necessary condition of defining a sacred monster is that which is inanimate yet moves of its own accord" (54).
8. Melville purchased a copy of Shelley's novel in London, in 1849. See Sealts, *Melville's Reading*, 214.
9. Melville later visited St. Mark's Cathedral during his trip to Europe in 1857, but mentioned only cryptically, "Up Bell Tower" in his Journal entry for "Wednesday April 1st." See *Journals*, 118.
10. Hurh, "Dread: Space, Time, and Automata," 203–44, offers an illuminating post-Hegelian reading of this moment and of the story more generally, one based on "the turn to fear in metaphysical philosophy," according to which Bannadonna's lashing out at the workman is not motivated by egotism or pride but "a more general and second-order dread, a fear of fright" (232–33).
11. Fisher, in *Going Under*, 100–101, also sees ambiguity or "uncertainty" as to whether the domino is "a machine with human attributes, or a human viewed in a mechanistic, subhuman way," and goes on to draw parallels with "the perfect slave," emphasizing the significance of Bannadonna's claim that his creature has no "soul," as apologists for slavery such as John C. Calhoun had asserted about later generations of Africans under slavery.
12. This is Cohen's Thesis III.
13. Cohen, "Monster Culture (Seven Theses)," 6. Concerning the subject of "category crisis," Cohen refers to Marjorie Garber's *Vested Interests: Cross-Dressing and Cultural Anxiety* (New York: Routledge, 1992); see 11. Hanafi, in *Monster in the Machine*, 2, also writes about the sense of crisis prompted by the "hybrid character" of early "sacred monsters" who create "confusion and horror because they appear to combine animal elements with human ones."
14. In theory, as Melville would later make explicit in the colloquy between the Missouri Bachelor and the Philosophical Intelligence Officer, in chapter 21 of *The Confidence-Man*, the best servants are little more than "machines"—lacking independence, agency, or a will of their own.
15. Foucault, "Docile Bodies," 135–69, esp. 135.
16. This first epigraph, along with the others, appeared in the *Putnam's Monthly* version of the story but not in the first edition of *Piazza Tales*. As in the case of the omission of Tarnmoor's name from the original collected *Piazza Tales* version of "The Encantadas," I regard this omission as a major oversight, comparable to the printer's omission of "The Epilogue" from the British edition of *Moby-Dick*, for without the three epigraphs, it is hardly possible to read Melville's "The Bell-Tower" as a parable

implying heavy social commentary. Here, too, I follow the Northwestern-Newberry editors, who argue that these omissions may have been (1) Melville's "own excisions"; (2) "wounds" or "erasures" by an editor; or (3) "printing-house errors" (619). While the editors of the Northwestern-Newberry edition of *Piazza Tales* assert that all three epigraphs "are evidently by Melville himself, and therefore no external source exists with which to compare their texts," it seems clear the first one echoes John Milton's *Paradise Lost* (II.332-40), a work Melville knew intimately: ". . . for what peace will be given / To us enslav'd, but custody severe, / And stripes, and arbitrary punishment / Inflicted? and what peace can we return, / But to our power hostility and hate, / Untamed reluctance, and revenge though slow, / Yet ever plotting how the conquerour least / May reap his conquest, and may least rejoice / In doing what we most in suffering feel?"

17. Other critics, notably Karcher, in *Shadow Over the Promised Land*, 143-59, have read "The Bell-Tower" as an antislavery story, but Karcher concentrates on parallels with Melville's "Benito Cereno" in her discussion. See also Fisher, *Going Under*, 95-104; and Castronovo, "Radical Configurations," 523-47.

18. This is Cohen's Thesis IV.

19. Cohen, "Monster Culture (Seven Theses)," 7.

20. Chapter 3, "The Ruined Tower," in *Herman Melville*, 123, where Chase also makes the point that "Taken naively, the name suggests 'half man'—and, of course, Herman."

21. See "Haman" in *Wikipedia*.

22. Wilson, in "No Soul Above," 32, offers another suggestion about the significance of the name "Haman," pointing out that it is a near homonym for "human," thus accentuating uncertainty about "whether the cloaked figure is human."

23. This whole scene appears to me to be indebted to the archly ironic exchanges between Montresor and Fortunato in Poe's "The Cask of Amontillado" (1846).

24. Though significantly different in some details, the monster's burial at sea in "The Bell-Tower" may have its origin in Mary Shelley's *Frankenstein*, where, after the "monster" has murdered Victor's wife near the end of the narrative, he eludes his creator and "running with the swiftness of lightning, plunged into the lake," only to reappear again with Viktor in pursuit, until finally, Viktor dies and the monster, as explained by Viktor's friend Walton, jumped from Viktor's ship onto his own ice-raft and "was soon borne away by the waves" (quoted in Mary Shelley's *Frankenstein*, ed. Johanna M. Smith [Boston: Bedford/St. Martin's, 2000], 168, 188). Melville obtained a copy of *Frankenstein* (London: Bentley, 1849) from his British publisher at the time, Richard Bentley, "in London, 1849 . . . probably on 19 Dec'"; see Sealts, *Melville's Reading*, 214.

25. Cohen, "Monster Culture (Seven Theses)," 4.

26. Cohen, "Monster Culture (Seven Theses)," 5.

27. For a Hegelian reading of slavery and the Revolution in Haiti/San Domingo, one predicated on the idea that "Those who once acquiesced to slavery demonstrate their humanity when they are willing to risk death rather than remain subjugated," see Buck-Morss, "Hegel and Haiti," 821-65, esp. 848. Melville's "Benito Cereno" is set against the historical backdrop of the rebellion in San Domingo, as evidenced by his decision to change the name of the slave ship, in his fictional version of the story, to the *San Dominick*.

28. In *The Confidence-Man,* Melville created another sort of monster, the shape-shifting "man-charmer" called the Cosmopolitan.
29. This, in brief, is Cohen's Thesis V.
30. Cohen, "Monster Culture (Seven Theses)," 12.
31. This is Cohen's Thesis IV. Cohen, "Monster Culture (Seven Theses)," 7.
32. "Hawthorne and His Mosses," in *Piazza Tales,* 244.
33. Cohen, "Monster Culture (Seven Theses)," 16–17.
34. Cohen, "Monster Culture (Seven Theses)," 20.

## Conclusion

1. See Leyda, *Melville Log,* 1:404–5.
2. See Sealts, "Historical Note," in *Piazza Tales,* 482–83.
3. Sealts, "Historical Note," *Piazza Tales,* 487.
4. Sealts, "Historical Note," *Piazza Tales,* 484.
5. Sealts, "Historical Note," *Piazza Tales,* 491.
6. *Israel Potter, His Fifty Years of Exile,* 53, 48.
7. The term "original" here derives from chapters 43–44 of *The Confidence-Man,* where the Cosmopolitan, Frank Goodman, the final avatar of the title character, who becomes the central figure in the second half of the novel, as Christ is the central figure in the second division or New Testament portion of the Christian Bible, is described as "quite an original."

BIBLIOGRAPHY

Albrecht, Robert C. "The Thematic Unity of Melville's 'The Encantadas.'" *Texas Studies in Literature and Language* 14 (1972): 463–77.
Alexander, Jeffrey C. *Trauma: A Social Theory*. Malden, MA: Polity, 2012.
Anderson, Benedict. *Imagined Communities: Reflections on the Origin and Spread of Nationalism*. 1983. Rev. ed. New York: Verso, 1991.
Arsić, Branka. *Passive Constitutions, or, 7½ Times Bartleby*. Stanford, CA: Stanford University Press, 2007.
Bach, Bert C. "Melville's Theatrical Mask: The Role of Narrative Perspective in His Short Fiction." *Studies in the Literary Imagination* 2.1 (April 1969): 43–56.
Barnett, Louise K. "Bartleby as Alienated Worker." *Studies in Short Fiction* 11.4 (Fall 1974): 379–85.
Barthes, Roland. *S/Z*. Translated by Richard Miller. New York: Noonday Press, 1974.
Beecher, Jonathan. "Variations on a Dystopian Theme: Melville's 'Encantadas.'" *Utopian Studies* 11.2 (2000): 88–95.
Beja, Morris. "Bartleby and Schizophrenia." *Massachusetts Review* 19 (1978): 555–68.
Benson, Alex. "'Bartleby' on Speed." *Leviathan* 21.1 (March 2019): 120–37.
Bergmann, Hans. "'Bartleby' and the Lawyer's Story." *American Literature* 47 (November 1975): 432–36.
Berthoff, Warner. "Introduction." In *Great Short Works of Herman Melville*, edited by Warner Berthoff, 9–18. New York: HarperCollins, 1969.
Bickley, R. Bruce, Jr. *The Method of Melville's Short Fiction*. Durham, NC: Duke University Press, 1975.
Blum, Harold P. "The Concept of the Reconstruction of Trauma." In *The Reconstruction of Trauma: Its Significance in Clinical Work*, edited by Arnold Rothstein, M.D., 7–27. Madison, CT: International Universities Press, 1986.
Bollas, Christopher. "Melville's Lost Self: Bartleby." *American Imago* 31.4 (Winter 1974): 401–11.
Bradley, Henry. "'Cursed Hebenon' (or 'Hebona')." *Modern Language Review* 15.1 (1920): 85–87.
Breinig, Helmbrecht. "The Destruction of Fairyland: Melville's 'Piazza' in the Tradition of the American Imagination." *ELH* 35.2 (June 1968): 254–83.

Brown, Gillian. "The Empire of Agoraphobia." In *Herman Melville: A Collection of Critical Essays*, edited by Myra Jehlen, 139–50. Englewood Cliffs, NJ: Prentice Hall, 1994.

Buck-Morss, Susan. "Hegel and Haiti." *Critical Inquiry* 26.4 (Summer 2000): 821–65.

Castronovo, Russ. "Radical Configurations of History in the Era of American Slavery." *American Literature* 65.3 (1993): 523–47.

Cawelti, John. "Faulkner and the Detective Story's Double Plot." *Clues: A Journal of Detection* 12.2 (1991): 1–15.

Chase, Richard Volney. *Herman Melville: A Critical Study*. New York: Macmillan, 1949.

Chura, Patrick. "Demon est deus inversus: Literary Cartography in Melville's 'The Encantadas.'" *49th Parallel* 5 (2015): 47–76.

Cohen, I. Bernard, ed. *Benjamin Franklin's Experiments: A New Edition of Franklin's Experiments and Observations on Electricity*. Cambridge, MA: Harvard University Press, 1941.

Cohen, Jeffrey Jerome. "Monster Culture (Seven Theses)." In *Monster Theory: Reading Culture*, edited by Jeffrey Jerome Cohen, 3–25. Minneapolis: University of Minnesota Press, 1996.

Collins, Michael J. *The Drama of the American Short Story, 1800–1865*. Ann Arbor: University of Michigan Press, 2016.

Cornish, James. "Latin Verse on Franklin." *Notes & Queries* 5 (January 3, 1852): 17.

Dayan, Colin. "Bartleby's Screen." *Leviathan* 17.2 (June 2015): 1–17.

Delano, Amasa. *A Narrative of Voyages and Travels, in the Northern and Southern Hemispheres: Comprising Three Voyages Round the World; Together with a Voyage of Survey and Discovery in the Pacific Ocean and Oriental Islands*. Boston, 1817. Rpt. as "Melville's Source for 'Benito Cereno'" in the Northwestern-Newberry edition of *The Piazza Tales*, 809–47.

Delbanco, Andrew. *Melville: His World and Work*. New York: Alfred A. Knopf, 2005.

Deleuze, Gilles. "Bartleby; or, The Formula." In *Essays Critical and Clinical*, translated by Daniel W. Smith and Michael A. Greco, 68–90. Minneapolis: University of Minnesota Press, 1997.

Desmarais, Jane. "Anorexia and Passive Resistance: A Literary Case Study." *Soundings: A Journal of Politics and Culture* 18 (2001): 82–93.

*Diagnostic and Statistical Manual* (DSM 5-R). Washington, DC: American Psychiatric Publishing, 2013.

Dillingham, William B. *Melville's Shorter Fiction, 1853–1856*. Athens: University of Georgia Press, 1977.

Downes, Paul. "Melville's 'Benito Cereno' and the Politics of Humanitarian Intervention." *South Atlantic Quarterly* 103.2–3 (2004): 465–88.

Dray, Philip. *Stealing God's Thunder: Benjamin Franklin's Lightning Rod and the Invention of America*. New York: Random House, 2005.

Emerson, Ralph Waldo. *The Complete Works of Ralph Waldo Emerson*. Edited by Edward Waldo Emerson. 12 vols. Boston: Houghton, Mifflin, 1903.

———. "The Transcendentalist." In *Emerson's Prose and Poetry*, edited by Joel Porte and Saundra Morris, 93–104. New York: Norton Critical Edition, 2001.

Emery, Allan Moore. "'Benito Cereno' and Manifest Destiny." *Nineteenth-Century Fiction* 39 (June 1984): 48–68.

———. "Melville on Science: 'The Lightning-Rod Man.'" *New England Quarterly* 56.4 (December 1983): 555–68.

Equiano, Olaudah. *The Interesting Narrative of the Life of Olaudah Equiano, Written by Himself.* Edited by Robert J. Allison. 1789. Rpt. Boston: Bedford Books, 1995.

Feltenstein, Rosalie. "Melville's 'Benito Cereno.'" *American Literature* 19 (1947): 245–55.

Fenton, Charles A. "'The Bell-Tower': Melville and Technology." *American Literature* 23 (May 1951): 219–32.

Fernandez-Armesto, Felipe. *The Americas: A Hemispheric History.* New York: Modern Library, 2003.

Fisher, Marvin. *Going Under: Melville's Short Fiction and the American 1850s.* Baton Rouge: Louisiana State University Press, 1977.

Fogle, Richard Harter. *Melville's Shorter Tales.* Norman: University of Oklahoma Press, 1960.

———. "The Monk and the Bachelor: Melville's *Benito Cereno.*" *Tulane Studies in English* 3 (1952): 155–78.

Foley, Barbara. "From Wall Street to Astor Place: Historicizing Melville's 'Bartleby.'" *American Literature* 72.1 (March 2000): 87–116.

Forter, Greg. "Freud, Faulkner, Caruth: Trauma and the Politics of Literary Form." *Narrative* 15.3 (October 2007): 259–85.

Foucault, Michel. "Docile Bodies." In *Discipline and Punish: The Birth of the Prison,* translated by Alan Sheridan, 135–69. New York: Pantheon Books, 1975.

Franklin, Benjamin. *Letters and Papers on Electricity,* vol. 5, *The Works of Benjamin Franklin.* Edited by Jared Sparks. 10 vols. Boston: Hilliard, Gray, and Co., 1836–40.

Franklin, H. Bruce. "The Island Worlds of Darwin and Melville." *Centennial Review* 3 (Summer 1967): 353–70.

———. "Past, Present, and Future Seemed One." In *Critical Essays on Herman Melville's "Benito Cereno,"* edited by Robert E. Burkholder, 230–46. New York: G. K. Hall, 1992.

Frawley, Maria. "'A Prisoner to the Couch': Harriet Martineau, Invalidism, and Self-Representation." In *The Body and Physical Difference: Discourses of Disability,* edited by David T. Mitchell and Sharon L. Snyder, 174–88. Ann Arbor: University of Michigan Press, 1997.

Freeburg, Christopher. "Embodying the 'Assaults of Time': 'The Encantadas.'" In *Melville and the Idea of Blackness: Race and Imperialism in Nineteenth-Century America,* 132–63. New York: Cambridge University Press, 2012.

Gilmore, Michael T. "'Bartleby the Scrivener' and the Transformation of the Economy." In *American Romanticism and the Marketplace,* 132–45. Chicago: University of Chicago Press, 1985.

Goffman, Erving. *Frame Analysis: An Essay on the Organization of Experience.* Harmondsworth, UK: Penguin, 1974.

———. "On Face-Work: An Analysis of Ritual Elements in Social Interaction." In *Interaction Ritual: Essays on Face-to-Face Behavior,* 5–45. Garden City, NY: Doubleday & Co., 1967.

Goldfarb, Nancy D. "Charity as Purchase: Buying Self-Approval in Melville's 'Bartleby, the Scrivener.'" *Nineteenth-Century Literature* 69.2 (September 2014): 233–61.

Grandin, Greg. *Empire of Necessity: Slavery, Freedom, and Deception in the New World.* New York: Metropolitan Books, 2014.

Greenspan, Ezra. "*Putnam's Monthly* and 'the Putnam Public.'" In *George Palmer Putnam, Representative American Publisher,* 285–322. University Park: Penn State University Press, 2000.

Hanafi, Zakiya. *The Monster in the Machine: Magic, Medicine, and the Marvelous in the Time of the Scientific Revolution.* Durham, NC: Duke University Press, 2000.

Hanke, Lewis, and Jane M. Rausch, eds. *People and Issues in Latin American History: The Colonial Experience.* New York: Markus Wiener Publishing, 1993.

Harter, Deborah. *Bodies in Pieces: Fantastic Narrative and the Poetics of the Fragment.* Stanford, CA: Stanford University Press, 1996.

Hartman, Saidiya. *Scenes of Subjection: Terror, Slavery, and Self-Making in Nineteenth-Century America.* New York: Oxford University Press, 1997.

Herman, Judith. *Trauma and Recovery: The Aftermath of Violence—From Domestic Abuse to Political Terror.* New York: Basic Books, 1992.

Hetherington, Hugh W. *Melville's Reviewers, British and American, 1846–1891.* Chapel Hill: University of North Carolina Press, 1961.

Higgins, Brian, and Hershel Parker, eds. *Herman Melville: The Contemporary Reviews.* New York: Cambridge University Press, 1995.

Hillman, David, and Ulrika Maude. "Introduction." In *The Cambridge Companion to the Body in Literature,* edited by David Hillman and Ulrika Maude, 1–9. New York: Cambridge University Press, 2015.

Howard, Leon. *Herman Melville: A Biography.* Berkeley: University of California Press, 1951.

Howarth, William. "Darwin and Melville in the Galapagos." *Iowa Review* 30.3 (Winter 2000–2001): 95–113.

Hsy, Jonathan. "Disability." In *The Cambridge Companion to the Body in Literature,* edited by David Hillman and Ulrika Maude, 24–40. New York: Cambridge University Press, 2015.

Hurh, Paul. "Dread: Space, Time, and Automata in *The Piazza Tales.*" In *American Terror: The Feeling of Thinking in Edwards, Poe, and Melville,* 203–44. Stanford, CA: Stanford University Press, 2015.

Jonik, Michael. "'Isles of Absenteees': The Form of the Archipelago in Melville's Writing." In *Melville as Poet: The Art of "Pulsed Life,"* edited by Sanford E. Marovitz, 165–85. Kent, OH: Kent State University Press, 2013.

———. "Melville's 'Permanent Riotocracy.'" In *A Political Companion to Herman Melville,* edited by Jason Frank, 229–58. Lexington: University Press of Kentucky, 2013.

Kaplan, Sydney. "Herman Melville and the American National Sin: The Meaning of 'Benito Cereno.'" *Journal of Negro History* 57 (1957): 12–27.

Karcher, Carolyn L. *Shadow Over the Promised Land: Slavery, Race, and Violence in Melville's America.* Baton Rouge: Louisiana State University Press, 1980.

Kelly, Lori Duin. "Office Setting as Organizational Structure in 'Bartleby the Scrivener.'" *Sage* (January–March 2017): 1–8.

Kimpel, Ben D. "Two Notes on Melville." *American Literature* 16 (1944): 29–32.

Krider, E. Philip. "Benjamin Franklin and Lightning Rods." *Physics Today* 59.1 (January 2006): 42–48.

Kuebrich, David. "Melville's Doctrine of Assumptions: The Hidden Ideology of Capitalist Production in 'Bartleby.'" *New England Quarterly* 69.3 (September 1996): 381–405.

Lazo, Rodrigo. "The Ends of Enchantment: Douglass, Melville, and U.S. Expansionism in the Americas." In *Frederick Douglass and Herman Melville: Essays in Relation,* edited by Robert S. Levine and Samuel Otter, 207–29. Chapel Hill: University of North Carolina Press, 2008.

Leyda, Jay. "Introduction." In *The Complete Stories of Herman Melville*, edited by Jay Leyda, xxvi–xxvii. New York: Random House, 1949.

———. *The Melville Log: A Documentary Life of Herman Melville, 1819–1891*. 2 vols. 1951. Rpt. with a new supplement. New York: Gordian Press, 1969.

Martineau, Harriet. *Life in the Sickroom: Essays by an Invalid*. 2nd ed. London: Edward Moxon, 1844.

Matteson, John. "'A New Race Has Sprung Up': Prudence, Social Consensus, and the Law in 'Bartleby the Scrivener.'" *Leviathan* 10.1 (2008): 25–49.

Matthews, Joshua. "Peddlers of the Rod: Melville's 'The Lightning-Rod Man' and the Antebellum Periodical Market." *Leviathan* 12.3 (October 2010): 55–70.

Matthiessen, F. O. *American Renaissance: Art and Expression in the Age of Emerson and Whitman*. New York: Oxford University Press, 1941.

McCall, Dan. *The Silence of Bartleby*. Ithaca, NY: Cornell University Press, 1989.

Melville, Herman. *The Confidence-Man: His Masquerade*. 1857. Vol. 10 of *The Writings of Herman Melville*, edited by Harrison Hayford, Hershel Parker, and G. Thomas Tanselle. Evanston and Chicago: Northwestern University Press and the Newberry Library, 1984.

———. *Correspondence*. Vol. 14 of *The Writings of Herman Melville*, edited by Lynn Horth. Evanston and Chicago: Northwestern University Press and the Newberry Library, 1993.

———. *Israel Potter, His Fifty Years of Exile*. 1855. Vol. 8 of *The Writings of Herman Melville*, edited by Harrison Hayford, Hershel Parker, and G. Thomas Tanselle. Evanston and Chicago: Northwestern University Press and the Newberry Library, 1982.

———. *Journals*. Vol. 15 of *The Writings of Herman Melville*, edited by Howard C. Horsford with Lynn Horth. Evanston and Chicago: Northwestern University Press and the Newberry Library, 1989.

———. *Moby-Dick; or, The Whale*. 1851. Vol. 6 of *The Writings of Herman Melville*, edited by Harrison Hayford, Hershel Parker, and G. Thomas Tanselle. Evanston and Chicago: Northwestern University Press and the Newberry Library, 1988.

———. *The Piazza Tales and Other Prose Pieces, 1839–1860*. Vol. 9 of *The Writings of Herman Melville*, edited by Harrison Hayford, Alma A. MacDougall, and G. Thomas Tanselle. Evanston and Chicago: Northwestern University Press and the Newberry Library, 1987.

———. *Pierre; or, The Ambiguities*. 1852. Vol. 7 of *The Writings of Herman Melville*, edited by Harrison Hayford, Hershel Parker, and G. Thomas Tanselle. Evanston and Chicago: Northwestern University Press and the Newberry Library, 1971.

———. *Redburn, His First Voyage*. 1849. Vol. 4 of *The Writings of Herman Melville*, edited by Harrison Hayford, Hershel Parker, and G. Thomas Tanselle. Evanston and Chicago: Northwestern University Press and the Newberry Library, 1969.

Miskolcze, Robin. "The Lawyer's Trouble with Cicero in Herman Melville's 'Bartleby, the Scrivener.'" *Leviathan* 15.2 (June 2013): 43–53.

Mitchell, David I., and Sharon L. Snyder. *Narrative Prosthesis: Disability and the Dependencies of Discourse*. Ann Arbor: University of Michigan Press, 2000.

———, eds. *The Body and Physical Difference: Discourses of Disability*. Ann Arbor: University of Michigan Press, 1997.

Moses, Carole. "Hunilla and Oberlus: Ambiguous Companions." *Studies in Short Fiction* 22.3 (Summer 1985): 339–42.

*New Columbia Encyclopedia.* Edited by William H. Harris and Judith Levey. New York: Columbia University Press, 1975.

Nixon, Kari. "If You Don't Know Me by Now: The Failure of Care in 'Bartleby the Scrivener.'" *Disability Studies Quarterly* 34.4 (December 2014): 15 pages (online journal).

Nixon, Nicola. "Men and Coats; or, the Politics of the Dandiacal Body in Melville's 'Benito Cereno.'" *PMLA* 114 (May 1999): 359–72.

Otter, Samuel. *Melville's Anatomies.* Berkeley: University of California Press, 1999.

Parker, Hershel. *Herman Melville: A Biography, 1851–1891.* 2 vols. Baltimore: Johns Hopkins University Press, 1988, 2002.

———. "Melville's Salesman Story." *Studies in Short Fiction* 1.2 (1964): 154–58.

Post-Lauria, Sheila. "Canonical Texts and Context: The Example of Herman Melville's 'Bartleby, the Scrivener: A Story of Wall Street.'" *College Literature* 20.2 (June 1993): 196–205.

Rediker, Marcus. *The Slave Ship: A Human History.* New York: Penguin, 2007.

Reed, Naomi. "The Specter of Wall Street: 'Bartleby, the Scrivener' and the Language of Commodities." *American Literature* 76.2 (2004): 248–73.

Reynolds, David S. *Beneath the American Renaissance: The Subversive Imagination in the Age of Emerson and Melville.* New York: Alfred A. Knopf, 1988.

Sanborn, Geoffrey. "Walking Shadows: 'Benito Cereno' and the Colonial Stage." In *The Sign of the Cannibal: Melville and the Making of the Postcolonial Reader*, 171–200. Durham, NC: Duke University Press, 1998.

Sattelmeyer, Robert, and James Barbour. "The Sources and Genesis of Melville's 'Norfolk Isle and the Chola Widow.'" *American Literature* 50.3 (November 1978): 398–417.

Savarese, Ralph James. "Nervous Wrecks and Ginger-nuts: Bartleby at a Standstill." *Leviathan* 5.2 (October 2003): 19–49.

Scarry, Elaine. *The Body in Pain: The Making and Unmaking of the World.* New York: Oxford University Press, 1985.

Sealts, Merton M., Jr. "The Chronology of Melville's Short Fiction, 1853–1856." In *Pursuing Melville, 1940–1980: Chapters and Essays*, 221–31. Madison: University of Wisconsin Press, 1982.

———. "Historical Note." In *The Piazza Tales and Other Prose Pieces, 1839–1860*, by Herman Melville, 457–533. Evanston: Northwestern University Press and the Newberry Library, 1987.

———. *Melville's Reading: Revised and Enlarged.* Columbia: University of South Carolina Press, 1988.

Shelley, Mary. *Frankenstein; or, The Modern Prometheus.* 1818. Rpt. Boston: Bedford/St. Martin's, 2000, edited by Johanna M. Smith.

Silver, Sean R. "The Temporality of Allegory: Melville's 'The Lightning-Rod Man.'" *Arizona Quarterly* 62.1 (Spring 2006): 1–33.

Specq, François. "Prophecy and the Grotesque in Melville's 'Encantadas.'" In *Transcendence: Seekers and Seers in the Age of Thoreau*, 153–80. Higganum, CT: Higganum Hill Books, 2006.

Spanglar, Nicholas. "Tracking Melville's 'Dog King': Creole Sympathies and Canine Warfare in the Americas." *Leviathan* 21.3 (October 2019): 71–93.

Sten, Christopher. "Bartleby the Transcendentalist: Melville's 'Dead Letter' to Emerson." *Modern Language Quarterly* 35 (March 1974): 30–44.

Sullivan, William P. "Bartleby and Infantile Autism: A Naturalistic Explanation." *Bulletin of the West Virginia Association of College English Teachers* 3.2 (Fall 1976): 43–60.
Sundquist, Eric J. *To Wake the Nations: Race in the Making of American Literature*. Cambridge, MA: Belknap Press, 1993.
Sweeney, Gerard M. "Melville's Hawthornian Bell-Tower: A Fairy-Tale Source." *American Literature* 45.2 (May 1973): 279–85.
Tanyol, Denise. "The Alternative Taxonomies of Melville's 'The Encantadas.'" *New England Quarterly* 80.2 (June 2007): 242–79.
Thompson, Graham. *Herman Melville: Among the Magazines*. Amherst: University of Massachusetts Press, 2018.
Verdier, Douglas L. "Who Is the Lightning-Rod Man?" *Studies in Short Fiction* 18 (1981): 273–79.
Waggoner, Hyatt H. "Hawthorne and Melville Acquaint the Reader with Their Abodes." *Studies in the Novel* 2 (Winter 1970): 420–24.
Wertheimer, Eric. "Mutations: Melville, Representation, and South American History." In *Imagined Empires: Incas, Aztecs, and the New World of American Literature, 1771–1876*, 133–59. New York: Cambridge University Press, 1999.
Williams, Stanley T. "'Follow Your Leader': Melville's 'Benito Cereno.'" *Virginia Quarterly Review* 23 (1947): 61–76.
Wilson, Ivy G. "'No Soul Above': Labor and the 'Law in Art' in Melville's 'The Bell-Tower.'" *Arizona Quarterly* 63.1 (Spring 2007): 27–47.
Yellin, Jean Fagan. "Black Masks: Melville's 'Benito Cereno.'" *American Quarterly* (Fall 1970): 678–89.

# INDEX

Adams, John, 88
aesthetic theory, 13–14, 21
"Agatha" project (unpublished), 8, 9, 115, 141
Agrippa, Cornelius, 135
Albertus Magnus, 135
Albrecht, Robert C., 159n15
Alexander, Jeffrey C., 79
alienation and loneliness: in "Bartleby," 6, 58, 144; in "The Encantadas," 3, 104, 110, 113, 116; in "The Piazza," 6, 28, 29, 32, 34, 36–38; urban, 143
allegory: in "The Bell-Tower," 7, 8; in "The Encantadas," 107; in "The Lightning-Rod Man," 95, 157n18; in *Mardi*, 23; persona of Melville in *The Piazza Tales* reading, 23; in "The Piazza," 29, 34; in "The Tartarus of Maids," 145. *See also* parable
alterity. *See* other, the
ambiguity: in "The Bell-Tower," 123, 124, 127–28, 133–34, 137, 161n11; as common denominator in *The Piazza Tales*, 13, 143; in *The Confidence-Man*, 92; in "The Encantadas," 105, 108, 117, 119; in "The Lightning-Rod Man," 7; in "The Piazza," 25. *See also* duplicity and deception
Anderson, Benedict, *Imagined Communities*, 114

anonymous publications or narrators, 8, 9, 117, 144, 158n3
"Apple-Tree Table, The," 142
Arrowhead home in Berkshires: addition of piazza to, 9, 21, 26; change in Melville's perspective after move to, 30; debt of Melville for purchase and remodeling, 9, 148n9; Greylock view from, 21–28, 126; publications written at, 22
Arsić, Branka, 151n14, 152n28
Astor, John Jacob, 43
autobiographical material used by Melville, 5–6, 8, 10, 15, 21–22, 37, 143, 158n8

*Bachelor's Delight* (pirate vessel), 153n3
bachelor trope, 153n3
Barbour, James, "The Sources and Genesis of Melville's 'Norfolk Isle and the Chola Widow'" (with Sattelmeyer), 115
Barnett, Louise K., "Bartleby as Alienated Worker," 56, 150n13
Barthes, Roland, *S/Z*, 102
"Bartleby, the Scrivener," 39–61; alienation and loneliness in, 6, 58, 144; anonymous publication of, 9; anticapitalist sentiments of, 6, 11, 43–44; Astor as lawyer's impressive client, 43; biblical allusions in,

{173}

"Bartleby, the Scrivener" (*continued*)
60; body vs. soul in, 39, 43, 58; change and growth of lawyer-narrator in, 15, 42, 51–61; comic elements in, 42, 50, 58; compared to "The Bell-Tower," 123; compared to "The Encantadas," 108; compared to "The Piazza," 37, 41, 50, 58; compared to "The Tartarus of Maids," 45, 151n16; confession of lawyer in, 39, 57–59; critical reception of, 11, 52–53, 151n20; dead letter motif in, 43, 57, 60; Emerson and, 4, 16, 39–45, 55, 61, 150nn8–9; enigma of Bartleby to lawyer, 44, 46, 50, 54, 61, 142; as fragmented tale, 42; indifference of lawyer to harmful conditions suffered by his clerks, 44, 46–47, 50; innocence of lawyer-narrator in, 14, 42–43; landlord's removal of Bartleby to Tombs, 41, 54–55, 57, 59–60; lawyer-narrator's motive to become witness/reporter in, 13, 43, 55–57, 143; Maitland's "The Lawyer's Story" as basis of, 16, 148n23; moral sense of lawyer-narrator in, 52–53, 151n18; Nippers (copyist) in, 47–49, 51, 59; office becoming residence of Bartleby, 46, 50, 58–59; office confinement in, 49–50; power of sympathy in, 53, 82; property ownership as materialist principle in, 46; resistance and refusal of Bartleby to work and later to lawyer's help, 3, 44–46, 50–51, 53–55, 58–61; sentimentality underplayed in, 42, 53, 57, 152n27; speechlessness and impassivity of Bartleby in, 44–45, 54; suffering and misery of Bartleby and clerks from their work, 1, 3, 4, 8, 18, 39, 40–41, 45, 47–50, 52–54, 144, 152n28; sympathy and empathy of lawyer in, 6, 41, 47, 51–57, 60–61, 82; as tragedy, 53; transcendentalist vs. materialist conflict in, 39–45; trial or testing in, 45–46, 48, 50–51; Turkey (copyist) in, 47–48; Wall Street setting of, 1, 18, 41, 44, 49, 150n13, 151n16

Beaumont, Francis, 16
Beecher, Jonathan, 157n2
Bellis, Peter J., *No Mysteries Out of Ourselves: Identity and Textual Form in the Novels of Herman Melville*, 5
"Bell-Tower, The," 123–40; antislavery sentiments of, 11, 18, 130, 134–39, 162n17; Bannadonna's egotism, 125–26, 136, 161n10; biblical references in, 16–17, 124–25, 131, 135; compared to "Bartleby," 123; compared to "Benito Cereno," 123; compared to "The Encantadas," 123; compared to *Moby-Dick*, 125, 127; compared to "The Tartarus of Maids," 123, 128; critical reception of, 12; duplicates prevented by "law in art," 131; epigraphs in, 130, 134, 137, 140, 144, 161n16; Italian town as setting of, 1, 124–25; at metaphoric crossroads, 123, 125; murder of workman by Bannadonna, 126–27, 161n10; mythological references in, 17, 124; narrator in, 15, 144; as parable or Hawthornesque exemplum, 7, 123, 138, 142, 160n1, 161–62n16; town authorities' role in, 124–26, 130, 133–34. *See also* man-machine in "The Bell-Tower"
"Benito Cereno," 62–82; antislavery sentiments of Melville and, 6–7, 11, 18, 72, 162n17; appearance of whites and blacks as hints on *San Dominick*, 68–71, 73, 76, 154n17; Aranda's murder and dismemberment in, 65, 66, 71, 75–78, 154n12; Babo (rebel leader) in, 18, 63–64, 66, 68, 70–75, 78–81, 145, 152n2, 154nn12–13; black minstrelsy, trope of, 73, 154n15; bodily trials and traumas of

slavery in, 1–2, 4, 7, 8, 18, 62, 66, 68, 75, 77–80, 144; captain-narrator's failure to recognize true state of affairs on *San Dominick*, 14–15, 63–64, 67–68, 71–72, 74, 81–82, 143; Cereno's escape to Delano's boat, 64, 66, 78–79; Cereno's mental and physical state in, 3, 65–66, 71, 74–78, 80, 154n18; change of perception/point of view in, 12–13, 64–65, 74, 81; commedia dell'arte and, 73; compared to "The Bell-Tower," 123; critical reception of, 11, 62; Delano's *Narrative* as source for, 15, 62–65, 80; depositions and trial of rebels, 18, 62, 63, 66, 75–76, 80; double plot in, 66; figurehead of ship, 68, 71, 154n13; humanity and intelligence of African slaves in, 63, 65–67, 71–72, 74, 80–82, 152n2; performance of rebels in, 17–18, 68, 71–74, 145; power of sympathy and empathy in, 81–82; punishment of slave rebels, 64, 80–81; racism in, 14, 18, 63, 71, 74, 81; reader's shadow trauma in, 67–68, 80, 153–54n11; revenge as motive of slave rebels, 78–79, 134; San Domingo slave revolt and, 162n27; sharks following slave ships, 77, 154–55n19; shaving scene in, 70–71, 73–75; slave treatment by Aranda, 77–78, 80; surprise/shock at end in, 62–63, 65–68, 71–72, 74; *Tryal* slave ship as basis for, 7, 64; violence of rebellion on slave ship, 2–4, 6–7, 66–71, 75, 77–79, 130, 134
Benson, Alex, 151n13
Bergmann, Hans, 148n23
Berlanga, Tomas de, 102
biblical references, 16–17, 23, 60, 69, 104, 124–25, 131, 135, 152nn29–30
bigotry of main characters, 14–15. *See also* class; racism
*Billy Budd, Sailor*, 62

Blum, Harold P., 154n18, 155n24
bodily pain and bodily trials: in "Bartleby, the Scrivener," 1, 3, 4, 8, 18, 39, 40–41, 45, 47–50, 52–54, 144, 152n28; collective dimension to trauma, 79; as common denominator in *The Piazza Tales*, 1–2; emotional vs. physical pain, 54, 151n21; identity and, 5, 19; inexpressibility of, 54–55; of Melville, 22, 25–26, 28; *The Piazza Tales* presenting in various settings and genres, 7–8, 142; shock vs. strain trauma, 154n18; trauma in *Diagnostic and Statistical Manual*, 153n10; trauma theory, 4; in *Typee*, 147n1; unshareability of, 54–55. *See also* invalidism and sickroom confinement; slavery and slave trade
Breinig, Helmbrecht, 21–22
Briggs, Charles Frederick, 10, 160n23
buccaneers. *See* piracy and pirates
Burney, James, *A Chronological History of the Discoveries in the South Sea or Pacific Ocean*, 16
Burns, E. Bradford, 119

Calhoun, John C., 161n11
Cameron, Sharon, *The Corporeal Self: Allegories of the Body in Melville and Hawthorne*, 5
capitalism, 8, 11, 43, 46, 119, 120
captivity. *See* confinement, captivity, entrapment; slavery and slave trade
Cawelti, John, 153n8
censorship, 101, 159n14
Cervantes, Miguel de, *Don Quixote*, 17, 23
Channing, William Ellery, Jr., 13
"Charlemagne," Greylock viewed in terms of, 23, 24, 31, 38
Chase, Richard, 131, 162n20
Chatterton, Thomas, 117, 160n25

Chorley, Henry, 12
Chura, Patrick, 158n2
class: in "Benito Cereno," 73, 154n17; of central characters in *The Piazza Tales*, 14; in "The Encantadas," 104, 121; marker as "other," 2, 130; Melville's earlier treatment of, 18; modern progress and, 119; in "The Piazza," 6, 18, 21, 30, 35, 37–38; "povertiresque" persons, depiction of, 37; in *Redburn*, 149n15
clerical workers, in *Moby-Dick*, 151n15. *See also* "Bartleby, the Scrivener"
"Cock-A-Doodle-Doo!," 8, 141
Cohen, Jeffrey J., "Monster Culture (Seven Theses)," 4, 123–25, 128, 130, 134, 137–40, 161n13
Collins, William, 117, 160n25
Colnett, James, *A Voyage to the South Atlantic and Round Cape Horn into the Pacific Ocean*, 15, 100, 110, 160n17
colonialism and imperialism, 2, 18, 69, 103–4, 109, 112–14, 120–22, 143, 157–58n2
comic and humorous writing, 8, 11, 15, 24, 42, 50, 58, 142. *See also* "Lightning-Rod Man, The"
confidence man (con man), 84, 90, 146
*Confidence-Man, The: His Masquerade*: Cosmopolitan as monster in, 163n28; "The Lightning-Rod Man" anticipating duplicity in, 7, 12, 84, 92, 94, 98, 145; Melville's penchant for fragments in, 99; "original" central figure in second half of, 163n7; performance in, 145–46; servants as machines in, 161n14
confinement, captivity, entrapment, 2, 142; in "Bartleby, the Scrivener" lawyer's office, 49–50; in "The Encantadas," 104, 110–11, 119–21; fear of death by entrapment in "The Lightning-Rod Man," 84, 98. *See also* invalidism and sickroom confinement
Cornelius Agrippa, 135
Cornish, James, 157n23
Cowley, William, 100, 109, 110, 113; *Voyage Round the Globe*, 15
creation myth, 104
Creole communities, 114, 160n19
creolization of eighteenth century, 112
Cuba, 104, 113–15, 153n9
cultural body, monster as, 123
cultural institutions or social organizations: discipline of, 128–29; granting power or privilege, 2
cultural mediation of experience, 104, 111
Curtis, George William, 10, 62

Damasio, Antonio, 151n21
Dante, *Inferno*, 99, 159n15
Darwin, Charles, *The Voyage of the Beagle*, 16, 103, 104, 107, 110, 157n2, 159nn10–11
Davis, Clark, *After the Whale: Melville in the Wake of Moby-Dick*, 5
Dayan, Colin, 150n8
deception and disguise. *See* duplicity and deception
Delano, Amasa, *A Narrative of Voyages and Travels, in the Northern and Southern Hemispheres*, 15, 62, 70
Delbanco, Andrew, 53
Deleuze, Gilles, 152n28, 159n13
Derrida, Jacques, 124
desolation. *See* alienation and loneliness
*différance*, 124
Dillingham, William B., 99, 155n3
disability. *See* bodily pain and bodily trials; invalidism and sickroom confinement
Dix & Edwards, 9–12, 142
docile bodies, 4, 71, 74, 78, 128–29
double plot, 66, 99, 153nn7–8

Downes, Paul, 153n9
Dray, Philip, *Stealing God's Thunder: Benjamin Franklin's Lightning Rod and the Invention of America,* 88, 93–94, 156n14, 157n17, 157n23
dream. *See* imagined journey or dream vision
duplicity and deception: in "The Bell-Tower," 131; in "Benito Cereno" performance of rebels, 17–18, 68, 71–74, 145; as common denominator in *The Piazza Tales,* 17–18; in *The Confidence-Man,* 7, 146; duplicates prevented by "law in art" as charade, 131; in "The Lightning-Rod Man," 7, 84–88, 96–97, 143, 145; runaway sailors presenting themselves as shipwrecked, 117; in "The Encantadas," 107, 109, 117–20
Duyckinck, Evert, 40, 141, 150n6

Edwards, Jonathan, 95
embodiment, 1–3, 5, 39, 142; of cultural moment, 123, 125, 138. *See also* bodily pain and bodily trials
Emerson, Ralph Waldo: "The Conservative," 150n9; *Essays, First Series* and *Essays, Second Series,* 40; Melville and, 4, 16, 39–41, 55, 61, 149n2, 150nn3–9, 158n2; *Nature, Addresses, and Lectures,* 40, 150n5; "The Transcendentalist," 4, 16, 39–46
Emery, Allan Moore, 153n9, 156n6, 156n11, 157n18
empathy. *See* sympathy and empathy
"Encantadas, The, or Enchanted Isles," 99–122; bodily trial (exploitation or abuse) of surviving on wasteland in, 2, 7, 110–11, 144; comedic nature of sketches in, 19, 104, 107, 119; compared to "Bartleby," 108; compared to "The Bell-Tower," 123; confinement in, 104, 110–11, 119–21; consisting of ten sketches, 7; critical reception of, 11; earlier voyagers as sources for, 15–16, 100, 109–10, 159n11; enchantment in, 100–103, 105–7, 110–11; epigraphs in, 3, 16–17, 105–6, 111–12, 117–18, 144, 158n3, 160nn24–25; fragmented structure of, 7, 99–101, 106, 111, 116, 158n5; Galapagos setting of, 1, 7, 101–2; hierarchies of power, discovery of, 103; Hunilla ("Chola widow") in, 3, 19, 37, 82, 101, 110–11, 115–18, 145; meaning of "enchantment" and, 107; Melville's personal observations of Galapagos Islands as basis for, 7, 15, 99, 103; narrator (Tarnmoor) as reliable witness/reporter in, 13, 15, 100–101, 109; power of sympathy in, 82; pseudonymously published by Tarnmoor, 9, 100, 143, 158n3, 161n16; published in *Putnam's,* 121, 158n3; Rock Rodondo sketches, 100, 103, 107–9; superstition in, 110; transformation and deformation in, 102–3, 106–7, 110–11, 118, 158n5; underlying unity in pieces of, 99, 157n2; von Hagen's epilogue to, 113–14; worldview constructed by sketches, 99–100; Sketch First: "The Isles at Large," 103, 104–5, 106; Sketch Second: "Two Sides to a Tortoise," 103, 105–7, 141; Sketch Third: "Rock Rodondo," 100, 103, 104, 107–8; Sketch Fourth: "A Pisgah View from the Rock," 15, 100, 104, 107–9; Sketch Fifth: "The Frigate, and Ship Flyaway," 104, 109–10; Sketch Sixth: "Barrington Isle and the Buccaneers," 104, 111–13; Sketch Seventh: "Charles' Isle and the Dog-King," 104, 110, 112, 113–15, 117; Sketch Eighth: "Norfolk Isle and the Chola Widow," 3, 19, 37, 82, 101, 104, 110–11, 112, 115–18,

178 INDEX

"Encantadas, The, or Enchanted Isles" (*continued*)
145, 160n23; Sketch Ninth: "Hood's Isle and the Hermit Oberlus," 100, 104, 110, 112, 119–21; Sketch Tenth: "Runaways, Castaways, Solitaries, Grave-Stones, Etc.," 104, 112, 120–21

enchantment: "The Piazza" enchanted landscape, 33. *See also* "Encantadas, The, or Enchanted Isles"; fantasy

entrapment. *See* confinement, captivity, entrapment

epigraphs: in "The Bell-Tower," 130, 134, 137, 140, 144, 161n16; in "The Encantadas," 3, 16–17, 105–6, 111–12, 117–18, 144, 158n3, 160nn24–25

Equiano, Olaudah, 79, 155n25

European revolutions of 1848, 23

evangelical Christian faith, 95–96, 157n18

exploitation, 2, 7

factory workers laboring like machines, 128

fantasy, 6, 23, 25, 29–30, 32, 142; method of writing, 102–3

fatalism, 96–97

Faulkner, William, 153n8, 153n11

Fernandez-Armesto, Felipe, 112

"Fiddler, The," 8, 144, 155n1

filibustering expeditions, 114, 160n19

Fisher, Marvin, 156n13, 161n11

Fletcher, John, 16

Foley, Barbara, 151n17

Forter, Greg, 4, 153n8, 153n11

Foucault, Michel, 2, 123; *Discipline and Punish: The Birth of the Prison*, 4, 128–29

fragmentation and fragmented world: in "Bartleby," 42; in "The Encantadas," 7, 99–101, 106, 111, 116, 158n5; enchantment accompanying, 106; island group as fragments of whole, 101–2,

104, 158n5; *Mardi*'s structure and, 102; in *Moby-Dick*, 99; monster appearing only in fragments or snatches, 134; of South America, 115; writing method of constructing through fragments, 102

"Fragments from a Writing Desk," 6, 99

framing. *See* performance and framing

Frankenstein, 7, 125, 130, 162n24

Franklin, Benjamin: as American original, 146; American Revolutionary War role, 97; *Autobiography*, 4; Criggan's lightning strikes and, 156–57n15; *Experiments and Observations on Electricity*, 87; "The Lightning-Rod Man" and, 4, 16, 85, 87–89, 91, 98, 146, 156n6, 156n11; Melville's fascination with, 98; origins of and dangers posed by lightning, 87–89, 93, 96, 156n12, 156n14, 157n17; rationalist tradition of, 95, 157n18

Franklin, H. Bruce, 153n3, 159nn10–11

fraud. *See* duplicity and deception

Frawley, Maria, 28

Freeburg, Christopher, 157–58n2

freedom: desire for home rule and nationhood, 112, 114–15; desire of slaves to be free, 64, 66, 130; lawlessness as form of, 114; in mixed world, 122; of monster, 139; runaway sailors and, 114–15, 117, 120–21

Freud, Sigmund, 153n7, 154n18

Fuller, Margaret, 149n10

Galapagos Islands, 3, 7, 14, 99–100, 102–10, 142, 157n2, 159nn10–11

Garber, Marjorie, 161n13

"'Gees, The,'" 8

gender: abandonment and, 115–16, 118; of central characters in *The Piazza Tales*, 14; employment and economic exploitation of American women, 6, 18, 21–22, 29–30, 35–38, 128, 149n19; in "The Encantadas,"

104; long-suffering women, respect for, 116; marker as "other," 2, 130; in *Redburn,* 149n15; revenge sought by female slaves in "Benito Cereno," 79; sentimental tradition associated with, 19, 116; sexual abuse of women slaves, 79, 155n25; social oppression of, 111; in "The Tartarus of Maids," 149n19

genetic uncertainty principle, 124

Gilmore, Michael T., 150n13, 151n17

Gliddon, George, 152n2

Godwin, Parke, 10

Goffman, Erving, 4, 84–85, 87, 156n7

Goldfarb, Nancy D., "Charity as Purchase: Buying Self-Approval in Melville's 'Bartleby, the Scrivener,'" 52

G. P. Putnam & Co., 8

Grandin, Greg, 78

Haitian (San Domingo) slave revolt (1791), 64, 162n27

Hanafi, Zakiya, *The Monster in the Machine,* 123, 125, 161n13

"Happy Failure, The," 8, 144

Harper & Brothers, 8–9, 141

*Harper's Monthly Magazine / Harper's New Monthly Magazine,* 8–10, 11, 141–42, 144–45, 152n27

Harter, Deborah, *Bodies in Pieces: Fantastic Narrative and the Poetics of the Fragment,* 4, 102, 106

Hawthorne, Nathaniel: Melville correspondence with, 8, 115, 141; Melville's review of *Mosses from an Old Manse,* 13, 139, 153n6; Melville's "The Bell-Tower" as Hawthornesque exemplum, 7, 123, 138, 142, 160n1, 161–62n16; Melville visiting home of, 40, 150nn5–6; "The Old Manse," 21

Hawthorne, Sophia, 40

"Hawthorne and His Mosses," 13, 139, 153n6

Hayford, Harrison, 155n1

Hegel, Georg Wilhelm Friedrich, 161n10, 162n27

heightened perception. *See* visionary powers/heightened sensitivity

Herman, Judith, 4, 75, 154n18

Hillman, David, 151n21

*Holden's Dollar Magazine,* 141

Holy Stones, use of, 24

Howard, Leon, 99, 160n24

Howarth, William, 158n8

humor. *See* comic and humorous writing

Hurh, Paul, 161n10

"I and My Chimney," 10, 142

Idealists (Transcendentalists), 16, 39–46, 55, 61

identity issues: in "The Encantadas," 159n13; of lawyer in "Bartleby," 44; in Melville's writings, 5; in "The Piazza," 25, 35

imagined journey or dream vision: in "The Encantadas," 107; in *Moby-Dick,* 32; in "The Piazza," 3, 6, 8, 21–25, 28–30, 32–37, 142

intelligence: of African slaves, 63, 65–67, 71–72, 74, 80–82, 152n2; in "The Bell-Tower," 132, 136; game of intelligence in "The Lightning Rod," 97

invalidism and sickroom confinement: of "Benito Cereno" captain, 74–75; heightened perception of, 8, 27–28; leisure time of invalid, 23–24, 28–29; Melville's own experiences, 6, 25–26; omniscience of, 28; in "The Piazza," 1, 6, 22–24, 142; reader's reaction to disability, 150n11; view from window in sickroom, 27–28, 31–32

## 180 INDEX

*Israel Potter*: Franklin's caricature in, 4, 16, 85, 91, 97, 146; publication in *Putnam's Monthly*, 91; written at Arrowhead, 22

James, Henry, 13, 103
"Jimmy Rose," 8, 145
Jonik, Michael, 158n5, 159n13

Karcher, Carolyn L., 152n2, 162n17
Kelly, Lori Duin, 151n3
Kimpel, Ben D., 95
Krider, E. Philip, 157n17, 157n23
Kuebrich, David, "Melville's Doctrine of Assumptions: The Hidden Ideology of Capitalist Production in 'Bartleby,'" 52, 150n13, 151n16

Latin America. *See* South American colonies and revolutions
Lazo, Rodrigo, 113–14, 160n19
*Leviathan: A Journal of the Melville Society*, 5
Leyda, Jay, 87–88, 155n5
"Lightning-Rod Man, The," 83–98; anticipating *The Confidence-Man*, 7, 12, 84, 92, 94, 98, 145; Berkshire mountain cottage as setting of, 1, 87–89, 156n13; as comic set piece ("salesman story"), 83–85, 142, 155n1, 155n3; Criggan cited as town struck by lightning, 89–90, 92–93, 156–57n15; critical reception of, 12, 143, 155n3; dangers posed by storms, 83, 87, 89, 90, 91, 156n12, 156n14; as dual performance/competition of traveling salesman and customer-narrator, 4, 7, 83–90, 92–93, 96–97, 143, 145–46; duplicity and deception in, 7, 84–88, 96–97, 143, 145; Franklin and, 4, 16, 85, 87–89, 91, 98, 146, 156n6, 156n11; Melville's personal encounter with salesman as basis for, 7, 16, 97; missteps of narrator-host as performance aimed to deceive in, 85, 86–89; pride as part of customer-narrator's act, 91–92; publication in *Putnam's Monthly*, 91, 155n3; religion, paganism, or science in, 88–92, 95, 156n8, 157nn18–19; salesman's pitch and scare tactics, 7, 83–84, 93–94, 97–98, 145; triumph of customer-narrator in, 2, 3, 84, 94–95, 97–98; "in wrong face," 85–86, 90, 93, 98

lightning science and electrical science, 16, 83, 88, 90, 93, 97, 156n6, 157n17. *See also* Franklin, Benjamin
locations chosen as distant, out-of-the-way places, 1, 7–8, 14, 89, 101–3
loneliness. *See* alienation and loneliness
Lopez, Narciso, 160n19
Lowell, James Russell, 19, 160n23
Lyon, Lucius, *Treatise on Lightning Conductors*, 89, 156n6, 156n11, 157n18

Magnus, Albertus, 135
Maitland, James A., "The Lawyer's Story," 16, 148n23
man-machine in "The Bell-Tower": ambiguity as to true nature of, 123, 124, 127–28, 133–34, 137, 161n11; Bannadonna's creation of, 124–25, 127, 129–30; burial at sea, 124, 133, 137, 162n24; evidence of hybrid creature, 133, 136–37; genetic uncertainty principle and, 18, 124; Haman as name of "domino," 131, 162n22; Hour Una's appearance, 131–32; killing its creator in its trial run, 2, 3, 7, 18, 129–30, 132, 137; slave bondage of, 18, 128–31, 134–39, 144; violent struggle between Bannadonna and domino, 132–33. *See also* monster in monster theory
*Mardi: and a Voyage Thither*, 23, 102
Martineau, Harriet: *The Hour and the Man*, 148n10; *Life in the Sickroom*, 4, 26, 27–28,

31, 148n10; "Power of Ideas in the Sick-Room," 29; *Society in America,* 149n10
materialists, 2, 16, 39–44, 150n9
Mather, Cotton, 155–56n5
Matthews, Joshua, 95–96, 156n14, 157n18
Maude, Ulrika, 151n21
McCall, Dan, 151n20
mechanical man. *See* man-machine in "The Bell-Tower"
Melville, Maria (mother), 25, 28
Milton, John, *Paradise Lost,* 17, 162n16
Mitchell, David T.: *Leviathan: A Journal of the Melville Society* (special issue, ed.), 5; *Narrative Prosthesis* (with Snyder), 4, 150n11; "'Too Much of a Cripple': Ahab, Dire Bodies, and the Language of Prosthesis in *Moby-Dick,*" 5
*Moby-Dick:* antislavery sentiments of Melville in, 6; bachelor trope in, 153n3; cetology chapters of, 106–7; compared to "The Bell-Tower," 125, 127; compared to "The Piazza," 35; compared to Rock Rodondo sketches in "The Encantadas," 107; critical failure of, 8, 9, 141; "The Gilder," 35; identity and bodily issues in, 5; "Loomings," 151n15; Melville's literary background mentioned in, 17, 148n26; Melville's penchant for fragments in, 99; "Queen of the Fairies" ("Queen Mab") in, 32; Queequeg's island home as imagined or transcendent truth in, 25; race and class in, 18; spell cast by sunlight in, 35; "The Try-Works," 2; whaling terminology of, 2; written at Arrowhead, 22, 126
monster in monster theory: attraction of monster as part of forbidden practices, 139; "category crisis" prompted by hybrid character, 161n13; as cultural body, 123; escape of, 134; as figure of "ontological liminality," 128; at "gates of difference," 130, 138; genetic uncertainty principle and, 124; hybrid character of "sacred monsters," 161n13; "revenant," 134, 140; standing "at threshold of becoming," 139–40; warning against transgressing borders of possible, 137. *See also* man-machine in "The Bell-Tower"
moral sense and law: in "The Bell-Tower," 123, 126, 130, 137, 139; in "The Encantadas," 103; of lawyer-narrator in "Bartleby, the Scrivener," 52–53, 151n18
Morrell, Benjamin, *Narrative of Four Voyages to the South Seas,* 16
Morton, Samuel George, 152n2
Moses, Carole, "Hunilla and Oberlus: Ambiguous Companions," 117, 160n24
Mount Greylock (Berkshires), 21–28, 31–32, 38, 89, 126
mystery and suspense: in "Bartleby," 47, 51, 55; in "Benito Cereno," 11, 62–63, 65–68, 71–72, 74, 75, 80; as common denominator in *The Piazza Tales,* 6, 13–14, 17; in "The Bell-Tower," 127; in "The Encantadas," 1, 3. *See also* ambiguity; duplicity and deception
mythological references, 17, 91–92, 95, 124, 144

narrative reality: deposition use in "Benito Cereno," 62–63; method and challenges of writing, 102; "The Piazza" changing from romance to, 37
nature: anamorphism (process of change), 106; customer-narrator as enthusiast in "The Lightning-Rod Man," 84–86; devotees, 24; natural law and order, 74, 103, 106, 108, 128; as source of illness and unhealthiness, 26–27
Nott, Josiah, 152n2

O'Brien, Fitz-James, "Our Authors and Authorship," 12
*Omoo*, 12
other, the: Bartleby as enigma to lawyer, 44, 46, 50, 54, 61, 142; encounters with in "The Encantadas," 108; encounters with in *The Piazza Tales*, 1; Marianna representing in "The Piazza," 22, 37, 38; markers of, 2; monster as "difference made flesh," 130, 138
Otter, Samuel: *Leviathan: A Journal of the Melville Society* (special issue, ed.), 5; *Melville's Anatomies*, 5

painterly perspective, 30
parable, 12, 142, 144, 161–62n16
"Paradise of Bachelors, The, and the Tartarus of Maids," 8; bachelor trope in, 153n3; compared to "Bartleby," 45, 151n16; compared to "The Bell-Tower," 123, 128; compared to "The Piazza," 22, 37; as diptych, 99; "The Encantadas" recalling, 107; gender in, 145, 149n29; published in *Harper's*, 142
Parker, Hershel, 155n1, 155n3
peddler's pitch. *See* "Lightning-Rod Man, The"
performance and framing: in "Benito Cereno," 17–18, 68, 70–74, 145; dishonesty of Hunilla's presentation as, 119, 145; epigraphs used as frames, 158n3; of traveling salesman and customer in "The Lightning-Rod," 4, 7, 83–90, 92–93, 96–97, 145–46
performance theory, 4
persona: of customer-narrator in "The Lightning-Rod Man," 84, 87; of Melville in *The Piazza Tales* narrator, 23. *See also* Tarnmoor, Salvator R.
perspective and point of view: "Bartleby" lawyer-narrator, 15, 42, 51–61; "Benito Cereno" told from captain-narrator's point of view, 12–15, 63–64, 67–68, 71–72, 74, 81–82, 143; binary view of the world, 105–6; change in Melville's after move to Berkshires, 30; differences among stories in *The Piazza Tales*, 5–8, 14; in "The Encantadas," 105–6; "The Lightning-Rod Man" narrator, 83, 142–43; painterly perspective, 29–30; in "The Piazza," 21–22, 27, 29–30, 34–35, 37; shifting within story, 12; Tarnmoor as voyager-narrator in "The Encantadas," 14–15, 105–6, 109–10, 117, 120, 142, 143, 158n3, 160n20
"Piazza, The," 21–38; Berkshire setting of, 1, 21, 22, 23–24; compared to "Bartleby," 37, 41, 50, 58; compared to "The Encantadas," 37; compared to *Mardi: and a Voyage Thither*, 23; compared to *Moby-Dick* chapter "The Gilder," 35; compared to "The Paradise of Bachelors and the Tartarus of Maids," 22, 37; contact with nature as cause of illness in, 26–27; critical reception of, 12; daydream or fantasy in, 3, 6, 8, 21–25, 28–30, 32–37, 142; as discourse on sickness and disability, 4, 6, 22–23, 26–27; *Don Quixote* references in, 17, 23; enhanced vision of narrator in, 28–29; fairyland metaphor in, 21–22, 25, 27, 32–34; humor of narrator in, 15, 24; imaginary realm as source of higher truth in, 22, 32; infestation of worms, appearance of, 27, 32; leisure time of invalid in, 23–24, 28–29; Milton references in, 17; Mount Greylock in, 28–29, 38; narrator's bodily trial of illness/invalidism in, 1, 3, 8, 21, 26, 31 32, power of sympathy in, 82; previously unpublished, 10, 142; as quasi-autobiographical tale, 5–6, 8, 10, 15, 21–25, 37, 143; seamstress Marianna

engaged in tedious toil in, 6, 18, 22, 29–30, 35–37; Shakespeare references in, 17, 23, 26, 31–32, 34; Spenser's *Faerie Queene* in, 33–35; as two-part tale, 22, 25, 28; views from windows and piazza, description of, 27–28, 31–36

*Piazza Tales, The:* classic literary or intertextual nature of stories in, 16–17, 23; common denominators among stories in, 1–4, 13–19, 143–44; critical reception of, 11–12, 13, 15, 155n3; embodiment themes in, 1–3, 5, 142; human suffering as revealed in, 144; immediacy of story openings in, 13; mysteries and puzzles presented within, 13–14, 143, 144; omniscient narrator lacking in stories in, 17; order of stories in, 6–7, 10; possible additional tales not included, 142–43; proposal and original title of, 10; pseudonym "Tarnmoor" omitted from original publication of, 158n3, 161n16; sentimental tradition and, 19; social critique in, 18–19, 24, 143; sources for stories in, 15–16; trial, testing, or trying-out theme in, 3–4, 17–18; variety of types of stories in, 3, 5, 142; weak sales of, 11; written at Arrowhead, 22

Pierce, Franklin, 10

*Pierre,* 5, 8, 9, 22, 26, 37, 141, 149n2

piracy and pirates, 111–13, 153n3, 159n15

Plato's Cave, 36

Poe, Edgar Allan, 12, 66, 147n11, 162n23

point of view. *See* perspective and point of view

"Poor Man's Pudding and Rich Man's Crumbs," 8, 37, 99, 145

Porter, David, 100–101, 109–10; *Journal of a Cruise Made to the Pacific Ocean,* 15, 119

post-human world, 8, 143

Post-Lauria, Sheila, 53, 150n10

poverty. *See* class

power or privilege: cultural institutions' role in granting, 2; hierarchies of, 103, 108; mechanics of power over others' bodies, 129–30; Renaissance views of, 4. *See also* colonialism and imperialism

property ownership, 46, 150n8

Putnam, George Palmer, 9–10

*Putnam's Monthly / Putnam's New Monthly Magazine:* antislavery stance of, 10; audience of, 10–11, 14, 18, 123, 129, 143, 147n7, 150n10; "The Bell-Tower" epigraphs and, 161n16; "The Encantadas" published in, 121, 158n3; on filibustering expeditions, 114; *Israel Potter* published in, 146; "The Lightning-Rod Man" published in, 91, 155n3; Melville contributing to, 8, 141–42; Melville's use of pseudonym in, 100; mission of social consciousness, 152n27; "Negro Minstrelsy" essay in, 154n15; sold to Dix & Edwards, 9–10, 12, 142; stories from *The Piazza Tales* published in, 5, 9, 10, 142

race: black minstrelsy, trope of, 73, 154n15; body's marker as difference of, 2, 130, 138; collective dimension to trauma against, 79; in "The Encantadas," 104; Melville's earlier treatment of, 18

racism: assumption of white racial superiority, 72, 81–82, 152n2; in "Benito Cereno," 14, 18, 62, 72, 74, 80; persistent racism and unconscious guilt, 82; of readers of "The Bell-Tower," 138; removal of constraints of law and custom leading to oppression of, 111. *See also* intelligence; slavery and slave trade

*Redburn,* 18, 149n15, 155n21

Rediker, Marcus, *The Slave Ship,* 79, 155n19

Reed, Naomi C., 150n13

religion, 88, 91–92, 95–97, 143, 156n8
Renaissance, 4, 134; transitional period proceeding, 125, 135
resistance and rebellion: of Bartleby, 3, 44–46, 50–51, 53–55, 58–61; against Creole King in "The Encantadas," 114, 160n20. *See also* "Benito Cereno"; slave rebellion
Reynolds, David S., 149n19
riotocracy, 114, 159n13
Robertson, Agatha, 115, 160n25
romance: persona of Melville getting relief from reading, 32; persona of Melville in *The Piazza Tales* telling, 23; "The Piazza" changing to reality from, 37
Rosa, Salvator, 9, 100, 158n3

Sanborn, Geoffrey, 154n12, 154n18
Sattelmeyer, Robert, "The Sources and Genesis of Melville's 'Norfolk Isle and the Chola Widow'" (with Barbour), 115
Scarry, Elaine, *The Body in Pain: The Making and Unmaking of the World*, 4, 48, 54–56
science, 95–96. *See also* lightning science and electrical science
Sealts, Merton M., Jr., 148n10, 148n24, 150n6
self-indulgence, 24, 125–26
sentimental stories, 19, 116, 119
Shakespeare, William: *Hamlet*, 17, 23, 26; *King Lear*, 23; *Macbeth*, 17, 23; *A Midsummer's Night's Dream*, 15, 17, 23, 31–32, 143; storytelling of, 13–14; truth and, 139
sharks following slave ships, 77, 154–55n19
Shaw, Hope Savage (mother-in-law), 141
Shaw, Lemuel (father-in-law), 9, 26
Shelley, Mary, *Frankenstein; or, The Modern Prometheus*, 125, 161n8, 162n24
short story writing by Melville, 8–11, 141–42. *See also* storytelling ability of Melville
slave rebellion: in Cuba, 115; in Haiti, 64, 162n27; on *San Dominick* in "Benito Cereno," 2–4, 6–7, 66–71, 75, 77–79, 130, 134
slavery and slave trade: antislavery sentiments of Melville, 6–7, 11, 72, 130, 134, 138, 162n17; apologists on Black slaves' having no "soul," 161n11; "The Bell-Tower" domino figure as slave, 18, 128–31, 134–39, 144; bodily traumas and dehumanizing pain of, 1–2, 8, 62, 66, 75, 81, 144, 154n18; in "The Encantadas," 119–20; Foucault and, 128–29; Haman as biblical slave, 131; pre-Civil War debate over, 65, 128, 134, 138; *Putnam's* antislavery stance, 10. *See also* "Benito Cereno"
Snyder, Sharon L., *Narrative Prosthesis* (with Mitchell), 4, 150n11
social consciousness, 2, 6–7, 18–19, 21, 143–45, 150n10
social interaction theory, 4, 85, 156n7
South American colonies and revolutions, 114–15, 119, 121–22, 153n9, 159n10
Spanish ships: pirate attacks on treasure ships of, 113; slave ship (*see* "Benito Cereno")
Specq, François, 158n3
Spengler, Nicholas, 160n20
Spenser, Edmund: *Faerie Queene*, 16–17, 23, 33–35, 105–6, 117, 144, 158n3, 160n24; *Mother Hubberd's Tale*, 111–12
storytelling ability of Melville, 1, 2, 12–13, 42; use of epigraphs (*see* epigraphs)
Sundquist, Eric J., 153n4
surprise and suspense. *See* mystery and suspense
Sweeney, Gerard M., 160n1
sympathy and empathy: in "The Bell-Tower" for monster, 138, 139; in "Benito Cereno," 81–82; in "The Encantadas," 82; lawyer in "Bartleby" and, 6, 41, 47, 51–57,

60–61, 82; for oppressed and marginalized people, 18–19, 144; in "The Piazza," 37–38, 82; power of sympathy, 18–19, 53, 82, 144; of sick person for those who lack access to saving power of great ideas, 29; testing of, in *The Piazza Tales*, 15

Tanyol, Denise, 157n2, 159n11
Tarnmoor, Salvator R.: deception in enhancing Hunilla's story, 118–19; as Melville's pseudonym, 9, 100; as voyager-narrator in "The Encantadas," 14–15, 105–6, 109–10, 117, 120, 142, 143, 158n3, 160n20
"Tartarus of Maids, The." *See* "Paradise of Bachelors, The, and the Tartarus of Maids"
technological progress, 160–61n1
tedious work: in "Bartleby," 1, 4, 8, 18, 40–41, 47–49, 144; in "The Piazza," 30, 36–38, 144
Teresa de Cartagena, 149n10
test/testing. *See* trial, testing, or trying-out theme
Tetzel, Johann, 95
Thomas, Russell, 160n24
"Tortoises or Tortoise-Hunting" (unfinished), 99
towers, 107–8, 124–25, 158–59n9. *See also* "Bell-Tower, The"
tragedy: "Bartleby" as, 6, 50, 53; in "The Encantadas," 19, 111, 115, 118–19; persona of Melville in *The Piazza Tales* reading, 23
Transcendentalists (Idealists), 16, 39–46, 55, 61, 150n9
trauma. *See* bodily pain and bodily trials
travels of Melville: to Constantinople, 159n9; to exotic places, 24–25; to Galapagos Islands, 7, 15, 99, 103; to Polynesia, 34; to St. Mark's Cathedral, 161n9

travel writing, 8, 14, 31, 107, 121
trial, testing, or trying-out theme: in "Bartleby," 17, 45–46, 48, 50–51; "bodies on trial" in "The Encantadas," 104, 105; as common denominator in *The Piazza Tales*, 2–4, 17–18; in *The Confidence-Man*, 145; Galapagos Islands as "test case" within a larger world, 103; in "The Lightning-Rod Man," 17, 86, 93. *See also* bodily pain and bodily trials
truth: authors telling indirectly, 139; Hunilla's story and, 101, 118; imaginary realm as source of higher truth in "The Piazza," 22, 32, 38; Queequeg's island home as imagined or transcendent truth in *Moby-Dick*, 25; of suffering and vulnerability of others, 38. *See also* duplicity and deception
Turgot, Anne-Robert Jacques, 157n23
"Two Temples, The," 95, 142–43, 155n1
*Typee*, 5, 12, 18, 147n1

Verdier, Douglas L., 157n19
Villamil, José, 114, 160n19
visionary powers/heightened sensitivity: from illness in "The Piazza," 4, 8, 27–28; other writers referring to confinement's link to, 149n10; of seamstress in "The Piazza," 36
von Hagen, Victor Wolfgang, 113–14

War of 1812, 104, 109–10
wars among colonial powers and wars for independence, 112, 113
Wertheimer, Eric, 159n10
*White-Jacket*, 5
Williams, Raymond, 2
willing suspension of disbelief, 25, 33
Wilson, Ivy G., 162n22
women. *See* gender

PECULIAR BODIES:
*Stories and Histories*

*Lame Captains and Left-Handed Admirals: Amputee Officers in Nelson's Navy*
Teresa Michals

*Beyond the Moulin Rouge: The Life and Legacy of La Goulue*
Will Visconti

*Sapphic Crossings: Cross-Dressing Women in Eighteenth-Century British Literature*
Ula Lukszo Klein

*Sight Correction: Vision and Blindness in Eighteenth-Century Britain*
Chris Mounsey

www.ingramcontent.com/pod-product-compliance
Lightning Source LLC
Chambersburg PA
CBHW020934230426
43666CB00008B/1678

**LITERARY STUDIES**

"Ingenious and persuasive. A truly original study on a topic of considerable importance to the field of nineteenth-century American literature."—BRIAN YOTHERS, University of Texas at El Paso, author of *Melville's Mirrors: Literary Criticism and America's Most Elusive Author*

"Christopher Sten's excellent book contributes significantly to our understanding of the career, literary techniques, and entwined aesthetic and political concerns of this major American author." —SAMUEL OTTER, University of California, Berkeley, author of *Melville's Anatomies*

"A critical gem characteristic of Sten's lucidity, the beauty and craft of his prose style, and the clarity of his argument, this book speaks to urgent concerns in a post-pandemic world. It resonates deeply with a number of immediate crises, while connecting gracefully with deep critical traditions. It will be read as illuminating much more than Melville's short stories."—WYN KELLEY, MIT School of Humanities, Arts, and Social Sciences, author of *An Introduction to Herman Melville*

*Melville's Other Lives* is the first book-length study on *The Piazza Tales*—the only authorized collection of Herman Melville's short fiction—and the first book to explore the rich and varied subject of embodiment in any published collection of Melville's stories. Christopher Sten provides fresh critical readings of the six stories in Melville's book based on issues of invalidism or disability, pain, trauma, enslavement, performance, and monstrosity in relation to systems of cultural value defined by race, class, and gender.

**CHRISTOPHER STEN** is Professor Emeritus of English and American Literature at George Washington University and coeditor of *"This Mighty Convulsion": Whitman and Melville Write the Civil War*.

**PECULIAR BODIES: STORIES AND HISTORIES**

**UNIVERSITY of VIRGINIA PRESS**

Charlottesville and London
www.upress.virginia.edu

COVER ART: From *The Encantadas Concluded and Bartleby the Scrivener,* Matt Kish, 2019 (used by permission of the artist); iStock/gaff

COVER DESIGN: Cecilia Sorochin